LinkedIn®

FOR

DUMMIES®

LinkedIn® For Dummies®

Cheat Sheet

Tips for Job Searching Using LinkedIn

While Chapter 12 talks extensively about how to use LinkedIn to find a job, here are some tips that can help you out.

1. Make sure your profile is up-to-date, accurate, and matches whatever you provide to a hiring manager or recruiter.

2. Stay on top of your Network Updates so you know if someone in your network has been promoted or moved to a company where you would like to work.

3. Use Advanced People Search to find 2nd or 3rd degree network connections that work at a desired target company. Request an Introduction to that person and ask for advice or an informational interview.

4. Advertise your skills and knowledge by answering questions posted in LinkedIn Answers.

5. Connect with everyone you have worked with, since these people know your professional capabilities well and could potentially recommend you on LinkedIn.

6. Make sure your profile highlights measurable accomplishments that you did at your jobs. For example, instead of saying that you "managed the sales force," it would be better if you stated that "I managed a 37% growth in revenue in the last four quarters."

7. Do a search and connect with as many recruiters as you can to find jobs in your target industry or job focus.

8. Use LinkedIn Company Profiles to see which of your network connections works at a particular company, and specific information about the company that you need for your cover letter and interview.

9. Don't forget to use LinkedIn's job board. Currently, there are over 5 million postings available when you search the Web on LinkedIn's job board.

10. If you find and apply for a job using LinkedIn's job board, see if the job poster is someone in your extended network. If so, ask for a referral or Introduction to that person so you can connect with him or her and make a great impression!

Building Your Network Top Ten Checklist

Here's a smattering of things you should do when you want to develop and grow your LinkedIn network. *Remember:* The more you do, the more contacts you could have in your network!

10. Fill out your LinkedIn profile (see Chapter 3).

9. Check for former colleagues and classmates who are on LinkedIn by using specific LinkedIn search tools (see Chapter 6).

8. Import your Outlook contacts (see Chapter 10).

7. Import your Webmail contacts (see Chapter 10).

6. Check for people who share a group or affiliation with you (see Chapter 14).

5. Go through your business cards for potential contacts and search for them on LinkedIn. Send them an Invite or Request to Join (see Chapter 6).

4. Search through your 1st degree network connections (see Chapter 6).

3. Advertise yourself through LinkedIn Answers (see Chapter 7).

2. Use the People You May Already Know feature (see Chapter 9).

1. Meet people on LinkedIn (through LinkedIn Answers, Groups, Jobs, and People Search) and then invite them to your network (see Chapters 4, 7, 12, and 14).

LinkedIn® For Dummies®

Cheat Sheet

Quick Tips to Enhance Your Profile

Log into your LinkedIn account and click Edit My Profile from the left navigation menu, then follow these tips to enhance your profile:

- Create a customized URL. For example, you can set up your LinkedIn profile to be found at `www.linkedin.com/in/joelelad` instead of the default, which could be `www.linkedin.com/in/4JPA678`.

- Add as many past employers as you have had so the largest amount of former co-workers can find you.

- Make sure your professional headline emphasizes any keywords you want to use to promote yourself.

- Make your profile public and set it to Full View so your LinkedIn profile will show up in Web search results.

- Add links from your LinkedIn profile to Web sites you are trying to promote, like your blog, e-commerce store, or company Web site.

- For Web site links that you add to your profile, select Other and rename each link to include meaningful keywords, so instead of it saying "My Blog" it would say "Joel's E-Commerce Product Blog."

- Include all of your main e-mail addresses in your profile so people can connect with you. LinkedIn does not display your e-mail addresses to the public; they simply keep your e-mail addresses on file for when someone tries to connect with you.

- Fill out the summary field of your profile with all of your critical skills and important career-related keywords.

- Add a professional photo to your profile (something classy).

- Add a link to your LinkedIn profile in your e-mail signature file.

General LinkedIn Tips

- Always keep your left navigation menu expanded so you can see every option for easy access.

- Start leaving recommendations for 1st degree network connections that you feel have earned a great one.

- Invest a good amount of time up front to create a great detailed profile.

- Spend a bit of time, on a consistent basis, to update and maintain your LinkedIn network.

- Use lots of search terms in Advanced Search to find the right person. If you get no results, remove one or two words and try again.

- Research someone on LinkedIn before meeting him or her in a job interview or business meeting.

- Do a reference check on any potential job hires using LinkedIn before you make an offer to candidates.

- Get some free market research by posting a question on LinkedIn Answers.

- Scan through your Network Updates to stay aware of what your network is doing.

- Use the LinkedIn status function (What am I working on?) to keep your network apprised of your business.

For Dummies: Bestselling Book Series for Beginners

LinkedIn®
FOR
DUMMIES®

by Joel Elad

WILEY

Wiley Publishing, Inc.

LinkedIn® For Dummies®

Published by
Wiley Publishing, Inc.
111 River Street
Hoboken, NJ 07030-5774

www.wiley.com

Copyright © 2008 by Wiley Publishing, Inc., Indianapolis, Indiana

Published by Wiley Publishing, Inc., Indianapolis, Indiana

Published simultaneously in Canada

For general information on our other products and services, please contact our Customer Care Department within the U.S. at 800-762-2974, outside the U.S. at 317-572-3993, or fax 317-572-4002.

For technical support, please visit www.wiley.com/techsupport.

Wiley also publishes its books in a variety of electronic formats. Some content that appears in print may not be available in electronic books.

Library of Congress Control Number: 2008935818

ISBN: 978-0-470-28135-2

Manufactured in the United States of America

10 9 8 7 6 5 4 3 2 1

WILEY

About the Author

Joel Elad is the head of Real Method Consulting, a company dedicated to educating people through training seminars, DVDs, books, and other media. He holds a master's degree in Business from UC Irvine, and he has a bachelor's degree in Computer Science and Engineering from UCLA. He also operates several online businesses, including NewComix.Com, and is launching a new blog.

Joel has written five books about various online topics, including *Starting an Online Business All-In-One Desk Reference For Dummies*, *Web Stores Do-It-Yourself For Dummies,* and *Wiley Pathways: E-business.* He has contributed to *Entrepreneur* magazine and Smartbiz.com, and has taught at institutions such as the University of California, Irvine. He is an Educational Specialist trained by eBay and a former Internet instructor for the Learning Annex in New York City, Los Angeles, San Diego, and San Francisco.

Joel lives in San Diego, California. In his spare time, he hones his skills in creative writing, Texas Hold 'Em poker, and finance. He is an avid traveler who enjoys seeing the sights both near and far, whether it's the Las Vegas Strip or the ruins of Macchu Picchu. He spends his weekends scouring eBay and local conventions for the best deals, catching the latest movies with friends or family, and enjoying a lazy Sunday.

Dedication

To my best friend Magda, who faces life and adversity as strongly as she values our friendship. You amaze and inspire me, and I hope you never give up on anything! Friends Forever. — Joel

Author's Acknowledgments

First and foremost, I have to give the BIGGEST thanks to the great team at Wiley who made this book project possible. Thanks to Bob Woerner for pushing this project forward and having the confidence to put me in place. An absolute, huge, bear-hug thanks to Mark Enochs for putting up with my fast and furious submissions; he definitely kept me on track to make this book happen. And where would I be without a copy editor like Virginia Sanders; she made me sound so clear and grammatically correct!

Secondly, I want to acknowledge the absolutely terrific folks at LinkedIn for being open, eager, and absolute quality professionals to work with on this project. The big shoutout goes to CS, you know who you are! Adam Nash, Kay Luo, Mario Sundar, and Jay Thomas, thank you so much for your time, advice, stories, and access. You definitely made this book a better read because of your help.

I have to give a special thanks to Scott Allen, who was instrumental in getting this book project started, and I appreciate your help and support, as well as your infinite knowledge on the subject.

Thanks, as always, goes out to my friends and new LinkedIn contacts who provided me with stories, examples, and endless amounts of encouragement. I especially want to thank Cynthia Beale, Michael Bellomo, Janine Bielski, Hal Burg, Eric Butow, Anthony Choi, Joan Curtis, Lynn Dralle, Steve Hayes, Chuck Hester, Rob Keller, Kyle Looper, Carol Mendolsohn, David Nakayama, Kristie Spilios, Jan Utstein, and Michael Wellman. As crazy as it sounds, I have to thank the associates and managers at several San Diego Kinko's locations for helping me as I holed up there for months to get this done, especially the Oceanside location on Vista Way (I LOVE THIS KINKO'S) and the Hazard Center Mission Valley location. Lastly, thanks to my family for putting up with my late-late-night writing sessions and frequent seclusion to get this book ready for publication. Your support is always invaluable.

Publisher's Acknowledgments

We're proud of this book; please send us your comments through our online registration form located at www.dummies.com/register/.

Some of the people who helped bring this book to market include the following:

Acquisitions and Editorial

Senior Project Editor: Mark Enochs

Executive Editor: Bob Woerner

Copy Editor: Virginia Sanders

Editorial Manager: Leah Cameron

Editorial Assistant: Amanda Foxworth

Sr. Editorial Assistant: Cherie Case

Cartoons: Rich Tennant
(www.the5thwave.com)

Composition Services

Project Coordinator: Katie Key

Layout and Graphics: Ana Carrillo,
Reuben W. Davis, Christin Swinford

Proofreaders: John Greenough,
Sossity R. Smith, Amanda Steiner

Indexer: Valerie Haynes Perry

Publishing and Editorial for Technology Dummies

> **Richard Swadley,** Vice President and Executive Group Publisher

> **Andy Cummings,** Vice President and Publisher

> **Mary Bednarek,** Executive Acquisitions Director

> **Mary C. Corder,** Editorial Director

Publishing for Consumer Dummies

> **Diane Graves Steele,** Vice President and Publisher

Composition Services

> **Gerry Fahey,** Vice President of Production Services

> **Debbie Stailey,** Director of Composition Services

Contents at a Glance

Table of Contents

Introduction

*R*elationships matter. Ever since the dawn of time, when caveman Fred asked caveman Barney whether there was any work down at the quarry, human beings have always networked. We're social creatures who like to reach out and talk to someone. As the Internet developed and grew in popularity, people rapidly took advantage of this new technology for communication, with e-mail, instant messaging, personal Web pages sharing voice, video, and data with each other, and lots of other applications to keep everybody connected. But how can the Internet help you do a better job with your professional networking? I'm glad you asked. Welcome to *LinkedIn For Dummies*.

LinkedIn was founded five years ago by a guy named Reid Hoffman, who felt that he could create a better way to handle your professional networking. Lots of Web sites let you build your own page and show it to the world, extolling your virtues and talents. But a lot of the popular Web sites focused more on the social aspects of your life and not that much on the professional side. LinkedIn changed all that with its approach of augmenting all the professional networking you do (or should do) on a daily basis. You don't have to be looking for a job to use LinkedIn, but if you're looking, LinkedIn should be a part of your search.

In short, LinkedIn allows you to coordinate your professional identity on the Internet and make you more effective in your career. The site is designed to make the aspects of networking less time-consuming and more powerful, so you can open doors with your professional connections and tap the connections of people you know who make up your extended network. LinkedIn does not require a huge amount of time or usage to be effective, and is focused on only providing tools that help your professional career.

Perhaps you've heard of LinkedIn, but you don't understand fully what it is, how it works, and most importantly, why you should care about it. Maybe you got an Invitation to join the LinkedIn Web site. Perhaps you've gotten multiple Invitations, or you keep hearing about it and want to find out more. Well, you're taking the right first step by reading this book. I talk about the Whys as well as the Hows. If you're looking to enhance your professional life, I truly believe you need to look at LinkedIn. If you want to go straight to the beach and retire, maybe this isn't the book for you!

This book covers LinkedIn from start to finish. In case you haven't already joined, I show you how you can sign up. If you've already joined, I show you how to build your identity and take advantage of LinkedIn's functionality. This book is useful regardless of your skill level, whether you want to join or you've been on LinkedIn for two years but feel stuck.

About This Book

This book covers all aspects of using the LinkedIn site: from signing up and building your profile, to growing your network of contacts, to taking advantage of some of the sophisticated options, and everything in between. I include a lot of advice and discussion of networking concepts, but you also find a lot of step-by-step instructions to get things done.

This book is organized as a guide; you can read each chapter one after the other or you can go straight to the chapter on the topic you're interested in. After you start using LinkedIn, think of this book as a reference where you can find the knowledge nugget you need to know and then be on your merry way. Lots of details are cross-referenced, so if you need to look elsewhere in the book for more information, you can easily find it.

How This Book Is Organized

I divide this book into six handy parts:

Part I: LinkedIn Basics

This part starts with the basics; I talk about the benefits of LinkedIn, how to sign up, and how to build your online profile.

Part II: Finding Others and Getting Connected

Here in Part II, I go a step further and discuss your network of connections. I show you how to search LinkedIn's database of tens of millions of professionals, how to introduce yourself to other people, and how to grow your own personal network.

Part III: Growing and Managing Your Network

This part starts to heat things up a bit by covering some of LinkedIn's built-in functionality, like getting and receiving Recommendations, adding LinkedIn toolbars to your e-mail and Web browser, and importing and exporting your network to other applications, such as Microsoft Outlook.

Part IV: Finding Employees, Jobs, and Services

Part IV takes everything I cover in the first three parts of the book and applies it to the top reasons why people use LinkedIn; namely, searching for a job, finding an employee, and finding a reputable service professional.

Part V: Using LinkedIn for Everyday Business

In this part, I continue the trend of showing the real application of LinkedIn by applying the site's capabilities to different professions. I talk about how to use LinkedIn for marketing, sales, venture capital and startup, and even some creative uses you may have never thought of doing with LinkedIn.

Part VI: The Part of Tens

Part VI is the traditional *For Dummies* Part of Tens — this part contains lists that detail a number of LinkedIn functions and resources you can find on the Internet to help you with your LinkedIn experience.

And Just Who Are You?

I assume that you know how to use your computer, at least for the basic operations, like checking e-mail, typing up a document, or surfing the great big World Wide Web. If you're worried that you need a Ph.D. in Computer Operations to handle LinkedIn, relax. If you can navigate your way through a Web site, you can use LinkedIn.

You may be utterly fresh on the idea of *social networking* or the specific ins and outs of a site like LinkedIn. LinkedIn allows you to do some really cool stuff and enhance your professional life. There's more to it, and this book is here to show you the ropes — and help you take full advantage of what LinkedIn has to offer.

This book assumes that you have a computer that can access the Internet; any PC or Macintosh line of computer will be fine, as well as Linux or any other operating system with a Web browser. All the main Web browsers can access LinkedIn just fine. In some parts of the book, I discuss specific applications such as Microsoft Outlook; if you have Outlook, I assume you know how to use it for the purposes of importing and exporting names from your address book.

Icons Used in This Book

As you go through this book, you'll see the following icons in the margins:

The Tip icon notifies you about something cool, handy, or nifty that I highly recommend. For example, "Here's a quicker way to do the described task the next time you have to do it."

Don't forget! When you see this icon, you can be sure that it points out something you should remember, possibly even something I said earlier that I'm repeating because it's very important. For example, "If you are only going to do one of my bullet point suggestions, do the last one because it's the most powerful."

Danger! Ah-oogah! Ah-oogah! When you see the Warning icon, pay careful attention to the text. This icon flags something that's bad or that could cause trouble. For example, "While you may be tempted to go into personal details in your profile, you should never post anything that could embarrass you in a future job interview."

This icon alerts you to something technical that I just cannot suppress the urge to share. For example, "It would be as ludicrous for me to recommend the 802.11q standard as it would be for me to insist that 1 is a prime number." Feel free to skip over this book's technical information as you please.

Where to Go from Here

You can start reading this book anywhere. Open the Table of Contents and pick a spot that amuses you or concerns you or has piqued your curiosity. Everything is explained in the text, and important details are cross-referenced so that you don't waste your time reading repeated information.

You can also visit my Web site at:

www.joelelad.com

Specific information for this book can be found on my Web site at

www.joelelad.com/linkedin

Finally, I enjoy hearing feedback. If you want to send me e-mail, my personal address is linkedin@joelelad.com. I'm happy to answer questions specific to this book or just say "Hello." Please be aware that I can't provide free troubleshooting or build your LinkedIn profile for you. If you need support, contact a computer professional. Thank you for understanding.

Good luck with LinkedIn. I'll see you on the site! Send me an Invitation!

Part I
LinkedIn Basics

The 5th Wave   By Rich Tennant

"Why am I the only one with vulture links on my profile page?"

In this part . . .

1t's like they say, "You gotta start somewhere." Well, of course you have to start somewhere, where else would you be? So, when you're ready to make that first step, that great leap for all of mankind, this is the place you want to be. And any other inspirational saying I can squeeze into this paragraph. . . .

This part covers the basics of using the LinkedIn Web site. I start with some background on the site and outline all the different features covered in this book. Then you move into the sign-up phase, where you can create your LinkedIn account, and end with building your LinkedIn profile, a Web page that details your professional and educational experience for all who want to see it — depending on who you want to see it, that is.

Chapter 1

Looking into LinkedIn

In This Chapter

▶ Getting to know your networking toolkit

▶ Understanding the different degrees of network connections

▶ Getting to know LinkedIn's features

▶ Comparing degrees of service

▶ Navigating around LinkedIn's menu system

*W*hen I hear the terms *social networking* and *business networking,* I always go back to one of my favorite phrases: "It's not what you know, it's who you know." Now imagine a Web site where both concepts are true, where you can demonstrate *what* you know and see the power of *who* you know. That's just one way of describing the Web site called LinkedIn, one of the top sites today that offers a place for you to do professional networking and so much more. Social networking has gotten a lot of attention over the years, and the two sites that everyone talks about are MySpace and Facebook. Let me state right now, in the first paragraph of the first chapter, that LinkedIn is *not* one of those sites. You can find some elements of similarity, but LinkedIn isn't the place to promote your garage band's next concert or show pictures of last Friday's beach bonfire.

LinkedIn is a place where Relationships Matter. (It's LinkedIn's slogan.) When you look at the mission statement, LinkedIn's goal "is to help you be more effective in your daily work and open doors to opportunities using the professional relationships you already have." This is *not* a Web site that requires a lot of constant work to be effective. It's designed to work in the background and help you reach out to whomever you need while learning and growing yourself. The key is to set up your online identity, build your network, and steadily take advantage of the opportunities that most affect you or greatly interest you.

In this chapter, I introduce you to LinkedIn and the basic services it has to offer. I answer the question "What is LinkedIn?" and, more importantly, "Why should I be using LinkedIn?" I talk about how LinkedIn fits in with the rest of your online activities, and then I move into the tangible benefits that LinkedIn can provide you, regardless of your profession or career situation. I discuss some of the premium account capabilities that you can pay to use, but rest assured, LinkedIn has a lot of features that are free. The last part of the chapter covers basic navigation of the LinkedIn site. I show you the different menus and navigation bars, which you use throughout this book.

Discovering Your New Contact Management and Networking Toolkit

When describing how people can be connected with each other, think of a *tangible* network. For example, roads connect cities. The Internet connects computers. A quilt is a series of connected pieces of fabric. But what about the *intangible* networks? You can describe the relations between members of our family by using a family tree metaphor. People now use the term *social network* to describe the intangible connections between them and other people, whether they're friends, co-workers, or acquaintances.

In the past, people relied on address books or contact organizers (like Personal Digital Assistants) to keep track of their social networks. With that method, you would grow your social networks by attending networking events or by being introduced in person to new contacts, and then you would continue to communicate with these new contacts, and eventually the new contacts were considered a part of your social network.

As people began to rely on technology, new tools were created to help people manage their social networks. Salespeople especially started using contact management systems like ACT! to keep track of their communication with various people. Phone calls replaced written letters, and cellular phones began to replace regular phones connected to wall jacks, also known as *landline* phones. E-mail has replaced phone calls and letters as a quicker way of handling communication, and because of the adoption of cell phones, short messages known as *text messages* are being increasingly used to handle short bursts of communication.

Recently, Internet tools have advanced to what people refer to as *Web 2.0 systems,* where online communication within your network is much more automated and accessible. Sites such as LinkedIn have started to replace the older ways of accessing your social network. Instead of asking your friend Michael to call his friend Eric to see whether Eric's friend has a job available, you can use LinkedIn to see whether Eric's friend works for a company you want to contact, and you can use LinkedIn to send a message through Michael to Eric (or in some cases, send a message direct to Eric's friend) to accomplish the same task.

Your collection of friends and other contacts is known as your social network. In the past, you had no way to view other people's social networks. Now, when everyone puts their social networks on a site like LinkedIn, you can see your friends' networks, and their friends' networks, and suddenly hidden opportunities start to become available to you.

This means you can spend more time doing research on potential opportunities (like finding a job or a new employee for your business) as well as receiving information from the larger network and not just your immediate friends. This makes the network more useful because you can literally see the map that connects you with other people.

Now, just because this information is more readily available, that doesn't mean there's no work anymore in networking. You still have to manage your connections and use the network to gain more connections or knowledge. LinkedIn simply works in the background to guide the way, so you spend your time more productively instead of making blind requests and relying solely on other people to make something happen.

Keeping track of your contacts

Does this situation sound familiar to you? You've made a connection with someone — suppose it's your roommate from college. It's graduation day; you give him your contact information, he gives you his information, and you tell him to keep in touch. As both of you move to different places, start new jobs, and live your lives, you eventually lose track of each other, and all your contact information grows out of date. How do you find this person again?

One of the benefits of LinkedIn is that, once you're connected with someone, you always have a live link to that person. When that person changes e-mail addresses, you'll be updated with that person's new e-mail address. In this sense, LinkedIn always keeps you connected with people in your network, regardless of how their lives change. LinkedIn shows you a list of your connections, as shown in Figure 1-1.

The different degrees of network connections

In the LinkedIn universe, the word *connection* specifically means a person who is connected to you through the site. The number of connections that you have simply means the number of people that are directly connected to you in your professional network.

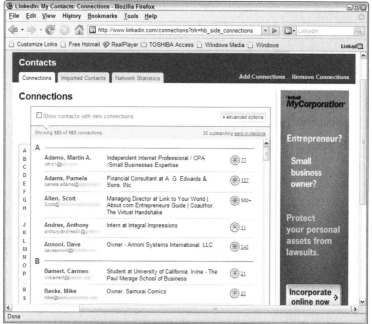

Figure 1-1:
See all
of your
connections
in one
centralized
list.

Specifically, though, there are different degrees of how you're connected with people on LinkedIn as follows:

- **First-degree connections** are people that you know personally; they have a direct relationship from their account to your account. These first-degree connections make up your immediate network and are usually your past colleagues, classmates, group members, friends, family, and close associates.

- **Second-degree network members** are made up of people who know at least one member of your first-degree network connections; in other words, the friends of your friends. These are also referred to as second-*degree* network members. You can reach any of your second-degree network members by asking your first-degree connection to introduce you to his or her friend.

- **Third-degree network members** are made up of people who know at least one of your second-degree network members; in other words, the friends of your friends of your friends. They're also referred to as third-*degree* network members. You can reach any of your third-degree network members by asking your friend to pass along an Introduction from you to his or her friend, who then passes it to his or her friend, who is the third-degree member.

The result of this is a large chain of connections and network members, with a core of trusted friends who help you reach out and tap your friends' networks and extended networks. If you take the concept of Six Degrees of Separation, where there are, on average, a chain of six people that can connect you to anyone else on Earth, and put everyone's network online, you have LinkedIn.

So, how powerful can these connections be? Let me show you a snapshot of someone's network on LinkedIn, as shown in Figure 1-2.

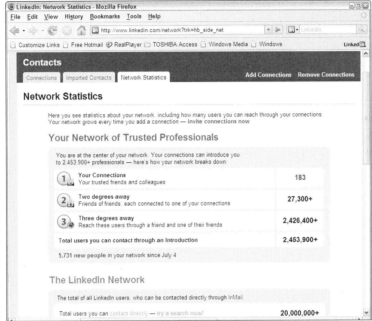

Figure 1-2:
Three
degrees of
separation
can give you
a network of
millions.

This account has 183 direct first-degree connections. When you add up all the network connections that each of these 183 people have, the user could reach over 27,300 different people on LinkedIn. When you go one step further and add in the third-degree network members, the user of this account could have access to almost 2.5 million members, part of a vast professional network that stretches across the world into companies and industries of all sizes. Such a network can help you (and you can help them) advance your career or professional goals.

The Things You Can Do with LinkedIn

After you find out about what LinkedIn is, the next step is to find out about what kinds of things you can do on LinkedIn. The following sections introduce you to the topics you need to know to get your foot in the LinkedIn door and really make the site start working for you.

The difference between a user and a LION

Given all this power and potential to reach people around the world, some people want to network with anyone and everyone who's eager to connect with them. These people are known as LinkedIn open networkers, or LIONs for short. Their goal is to network with as many people as possible, regardless of past interaction or communication with that person.

One of your most prominently displayed LinkedIn statistics is the number of first-degree connections that you have. After you surpass 500 connections, LinkedIn doesn't display your current count of first-degree connections, but rather it displays the message 500+. (It's kind of like how McDonald's stopped displaying the running total of hamburgers sold on their signs. Or am I the only one who remembers that?) Part of the reason LinkedIn stops displaying updated counts past 500 is to discourage people from collecting connections. Many LinkedIn LIONs have thousands or even tens of thousands of first-degree connections, and the 500+ statistic is a badge of honor to them.

LIONs encourage open networking (that is, the ability to connect with someone you have never met or worked with in the past) by advertising their e-mail address as part of their professional headline, so anyone can request this person to be added to their network. You can find more information at sites such as www. mylink500.com.

LinkedIn offers a formal program for people who are interested in networking with the larger community. It is called OpenLink, and it's a premium service you can sign up for at any time after you establish a premium account. When you enable the OpenLink feature, it allows you to send and receive messages with any other OpenLink member. I discuss this later in the chapter in the section "Understanding LinkedIn's Costs and Benefits."

I've been asked the following question many times: Is it okay to be a LION? Is there any meaning or benefit to having so many connections? The answer is: It depends. Some people use their high number of connections to get their name out so they can meet as many people as possible and find some quality hidden in the quantity. Other people just like to collect connections like they collect friends on MySpace; perhaps they see it as a popularity contest. Most people stick to using LinkedIn to cultivate the real quality connections they have, and they add a person to their network only after they get to know the person.

Build your brand and profile

One of the best ways to think about what you can do on LinkedIn is to recognize that LinkedIn can help you build your own brand. What do I mean by brand? Are you going to create a fancy cursive logo of your name like Coca-Cola and slap it on everything you own? No. (But hey, that does sound like fun if you have absolutely nothing else to do.) What I mean by *brand* is that your name, your identity, is like a brand in terms of what people think of when they think of you. It's your professional reputation. Companies spend billions to ensure you have a certain opinion of their products, and that opinion, that perception, is their brand image. You have your own brand image in your professional life, and it's up to you to own your brand, define your brand, and push your brand.

Most people today have different online representations of their personal brand. Some people have built their own Web sites, others have created and written their own blogs, and some others have created profile pages on sites like MySpace and Facebook. LinkedIn allows you to define a profile and build your own brand based on your professional and educational background; I use my profile as an example in Figure 1-3.

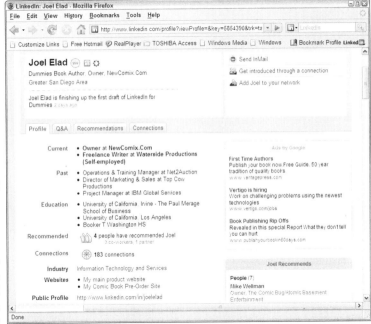

Figure 1-3: Create a unified profile page that details your entire professional history.

Your LinkedIn profile can become your jumping-off point where any visitor can get a rich and detailed idea of all the skills, experiences, and interests that you bring to the table. Unlike a resume, where you have to worry about page length and formatting, you can detail as much as you want on your LinkedIn profile, including any part-time, contract, non-profit, and consulting work in addition to traditional professional experience. You also have other options to consider. You can . . .

- ✔ Write your own summary.
- ✔ List any groups you belong to.
- ✔ Show any memberships or affiliations you have.
- ✔ Cite honors and awards you have received.

✔ Give and receive Recommendations from other people.

✔ Indicate your professional interests.

✔ Post Web site links to other parts of your professional identity, like a blog, a Web site, or an e-commerce store you operate.

The best part is that this is your professional identity and *you* control and shape it, not other people. You decide what the content should be. You decide what you emphasize and omit. You can decide how much of this information is visible to the world and how much is visible to your first-degree network connections. (I talk more about the power of your profile in Chapter 3.)

Looking for jobs now and later

Face it: At some point in your life, you'll probably have to look for a job. It may be today, it may be a year from now, it may be ten years from now. The job search is, in itself, a full-time job, and study after study shows that 60 to 80 percent of all jobs are found not through a job board like Monster.com, not through a newspaper classified ad, but rather by a formal or informal network of contacts where the job isn't even posted yet. LinkedIn makes it easier than before to do some of the following tedious job search tasks:

✔ **Finding the right person** at a target company, like a hiring manager in a certain department, to discuss immediate and future job openings

✔ **Getting a reference** from a past boss or co-worker to use for a future job application

✔ **Finding information** about a company and position before the interview

✔ **Searching posted job listings** on a job board like LinkedIn's job board

The hidden power of LinkedIn is that it helps you find jobs you weren't looking for or applying to directly. This is when you're a *passive job seeker,* currently employed but interested in the right opportunity. Currently, over 130,000 recruiters are members of LinkedIn, constantly using the search functions to go through the database and find skilled members that match their job search requirements. Instead of companies paying big money for resume books, they now have instant access to tens of millions of qualified professionals, each of which has a detailed profile with skills, experience, and recommendations already available.

This practice of finding passive job seekers is growing quickly on LinkedIn, mainly because of the following reasons:

✔ **Companies can run detailed searches** to find the absolute perfect candidate with all the right keywords and skills in his or her profile, and they then contact the person to see whether he or she is interested.

✔ **LinkedIn users demonstrate their capabilities** by answering other people's questions on the site, which gives companies insight into the passive job seeker's capabilities.

✔ **Companies can review a person's profile** to do reference checks ahead of time and interview only people they feel would be a great match with their corporate culture.

✔ **Currently employed individuals can quietly run their own searches** at any time to see what's available, and they can follow up online without taking off a day for an in-person or phone interview.

LinkedIn's research shows that "People with more than 20 connections are 34 times more likely to be approached with a job opportunity than people with less than 5 connections." Therefore, your connections definitely influence your active or passive job search.

Finding out all kinds of valuable information

You can use LinkedIn to find out more than just information about your job search. You can use this immense database of professionals to find out what skills seem to be the most popular within a certain industry and job title. You can learn how many project managers live within 50 miles of you. You can really learn more by finding past employees of a company and interviewing them about their previous job. LinkedIn now has thousands of detailed Company Profiles that not only show company statistics, but recent hires, promotions, changes, and lists of employees that are closely connected with you.

Imagine if you could pick the brains of tens of millions of professionals around the world about almost any topic. Well, now you can, using a system called LinkedIn Answers. With LinkedIn Answers, you can post a question about a certain topic, mostly business- or LinkedIn-related. Other LinkedIn members can browse the questions and write up free responses — from the one-line response to the three-page essay — to share their thoughts and answer your question the best they can. There's no think-tank to pay, no pre-qualifications or lag time in your data gathering. Typically, you start to see people responding within one to two business days. I talk more about LinkedIn Answers in Chapter 7.

Best of all, LinkedIn can help you find specific information on a variety of topics. You can do a search to find out the interests of your next sales prospect, the name of a former employee you can talk to about a company you like, or how you can join a start-up in your target industry by reaching out to the co-founder. You can sit back and skim the news, or you can dive in and hunt for the right facts. It all depends on what method best fits your goals.

Expand your network

You have your network today, but what about the future? Whether you want to move up in your industry, look for a new job, start your own company, or achieve some other goal, one way to achieve these goals is to expand your network. LinkedIn provides a fertile ground to reach like-minded and well-connected professionals who share a common interest, experience, or group membership. The site also provides several online mechanisms to reduce the friction of communication, so you can spend more time building your network instead of searching for the right person.

First and foremost, LinkedIn lets you identify and contact members of other people's professional networks, and best of all, you don't have to contact them via a cold call, but with your friend's Recommendation or Introduction. In addition, you can find out more about your new contact before you send the first message, so you don't have to waste time figuring out whether this is someone who could be beneficial to have in your network.

You can also meet new people through various groups on LinkedIn, whether it's an alumni group from your old school, a group of past employees from the same company, or a group of people interested in improving their public speaking skills and contacts. LinkedIn Groups are ways for you to identify with other like-minded members, search for specific group members, and share information about the Group with each other. I cover LinkedIn Groups in Chapter 14.

Understanding LinkedIn's Costs and Benefits

Signing up for LinkedIn is free, and many of the functions are open to all account holders, so you can take advantage of most of the opportunities that LinkedIn can create. You don't have to pay a setup or registration fee, but you can pay a monthly fee for a premium account in order to get additional functions or communication options. Finally, tailored solutions are available for corporations that want to use LinkedIn as a source for hiring quality candidates.

Free versus paid accounts

So, what's the difference between a free account and paid account on LinkedIn? The answer is not much. The basic account is anything but basic in usage.

Your free account with LinkedIn allows you to use most of LinkedIn's most popular features, including

✔ Build a network of connections with no limits on size or numbers.

✔ Reconnect with any member of the LinkedIn network, provided he or she knows you.

✔ Create a professional and detailed LinkedIn profile on the Web.

✔ Give and receive an unlimited number of Recommendations.

✔ Post up to ten questions and answer an unlimited amount of questions on LinkedIn Answers.

✔ Join or create a large number of LinkedIn Groups.

✔ Request up to five Introductions at one time. (After someone accepts an Introduction, you can request a new Introduction in its place.)

✔ Perform an unlimited number of searches for LinkedIn members in your extended network.

If you want to step up to a paid account, some of the main features include

✔ Sending a message to anyone in the LinkedIn community — regardless of whether he or she is in your extended network — through an InMail messaging service.

✔ Sending more Introductions out at any one given time than the basic account allows.

✔ Viewing more full profiles of people in your extended search results.

✔ Seeing more LinkedIn network profiles in your extended search results.

✔ Performing a Reference Search on someone.

✔ Membership in the OpenLink program and unlimited OpenLink messages. (See the sidebar elsewhere in this chapter, "The difference between a user and a LION.")

✔ Premium customer service channels with guaranteed response times.

Comparing the paid accounts

Currently, LinkedIn offers a few levels of paid accounts, each with a specific level of benefits as mentioned previously. For the most up-to-date packages that LinkedIn offers, check out the following LinkedIn page, which looks like Figure 1-4:

```
www.linkedin.com/static?key=business_info_more
```

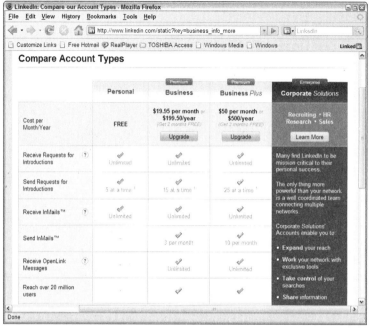

Figure 1-4:
Compare
different
paid
account
features on
LinkedIn.

Every premium account comes with certain benefits regardless of the level you choose. These benefits include

✔ Unlimited one-click reference searches

✔ OpenLink network membership

✔ Unlimited OpenLink messages

✔ Premium access content

✔ One-business-day customer service

As of this writing, LinkedIn offers three premium packages targeted at individual users, the Business, Business Plus, and Pro accounts. Each account level comes with a specific level of benefits:

✔ **Business accounts** cost $19.95 per month or $199.50 per year. This account includes

• Three InMails per month, with a seven-day response guarantee (Unused InMail credits roll over each month, up to a maximum of 9 credits. I discuss InMail specifically in Chapter 5.)

• Expanded Profile views for the top 100 search results outside your network

• Fifteen Introductions open at a time

✔ **Business Plus accounts** cost $50 per month or $500 per year. This account includes

- Ten InMails per month, with a seven-day response guarantee (Unused InMail credits roll over each month, up to a maximum of 30 credits. See Chapter 5 for more on InMail.)

- Expanded profile views for the top 150 search results outside your network

- Twenty-five Introductions open at a time

✔ **Pro accounts** cost $200 per month. This account includes

- Ten InMails per month, with a seven-day response guarantee (Unused InMail credits roll over each month, up to a maximum of 30 credits. I discuss InMail in detail in Chapter 5.)

- Expanded profile views for the top 200 search results outside your network

- Forty Introductions open at a time

How do I upgrade to a premium account?

I highly recommend starting out by creating your free account and using the various functions on LinkedIn. If you find that after some usage you need to reach the larger community and take advantage of some of the premium account features, you can always upgrade your account and keep all of your profile and network information that you previously defined.

If you're in charge of human resource functions at a small, medium, or large company and you are interested in using the Corporate Solutions functions for your company, do not follow the steps in this section. Instead, visit the following URL for more information:

```
www.linkedin.com/static?key=corporate_landing
```

To subscribe to a premium account, just follow these steps:

1. **You must have created a LinkedIn account already (see Chapter 2). Click the Account & Settings link near the top-right corner of the home page.**

   You see your Account & Settings page, like in Figure 1-5.

2. **Click the yellow Upgrade button from the Account section to bring up the premium account options, as shown in Figure 1-6.**

3. **Select the radio button for the premium level that you want to upgrade to for your account. Click the Continue button to go to the Billing Information screen, like the one shown in Figure 1-7.**

Figure 1-5:
Upgrade
your
account
from the
Account
& Settings
page.

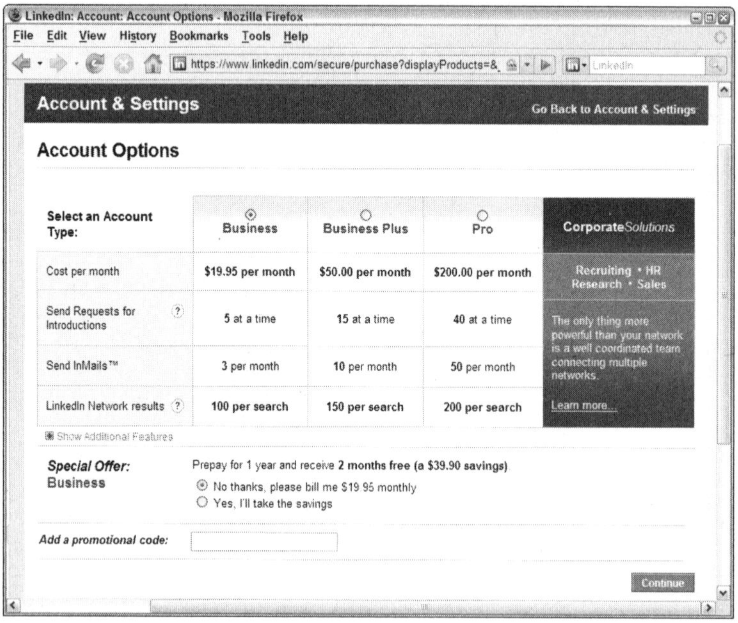

Figure 1-6:
Choose the
premium
account
that's right
for you.

4. **Fill in the appropriate billing information in the boxes provided.**

   LinkedIn accepts Visa, MasterCard, American Express, or Discover to pay for your premium account. Make sure the billing address you provide matches the credit card billing address on file.

5. **Select the check box to agree to automatic billing every month and LinkedIn's Terms and Conditions. Click the Buy Now button to upgrade your account.**

That's it! LinkedIn will pro-rate your first month's charge based on how many days were left in the billing cycle, and it will automatically charge your credit card each month afterwards for the full amount, unless you bought a yearly plan, for which the charges renew every 12 months.

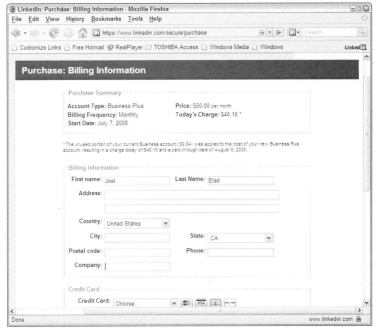

Figure 1-7:
Enter your billing information into the boxes provided.

Navigating around LinkedIn

When you're ready to get started, you can sign up for an account by checking out Chapter 2. Before you do, however, take a look at the following sections, which walk you through the different parts of LinkedIn's Web site so you know how to find all the cool features I discuss in this book.

After you've logged on to your LinkedIn account, you see the LinkedIn home page (www.linkedin.com), as shown in Figure 1-8. There are three important areas on your LinkedIn home page, which you'll use a lot, and I cover those areas in the following sections.

Top navigation bar   The Account Settings link

Left navigation menu

The top navigation bar

Every page on LinkedIn contains certain links to the major parts of the site, and I call this top set of links the top navigation bar throughout this book. As of this writing, the four major parts of the top navigation bar are

- ✔ **People:** Links to the different searches you can do on LinkedIn.
- ✔ **Jobs:** Links to the different job searches and postings you can do on LinkedIn.
- ✔ **Answers:** Links to the different pages within LinkedIn Answers.
- ✔ **Companies:** Links to a company or service provider search on LinkedIn.

When you click the drop-down arrow next to any of these words, you can see the various options within each section, like the People search shown in Figure 1-9.

Click to expand menu of options

Figure 1-9:
Click the drop-down arrow to see options for each section.

If you simply click the word, like People or Jobs, you're taken to the home page for that section of the Web site. You can also click the Advanced Search link to the right of the top navigation bar to bring up an Advanced People Search.

The left navigation menu

I call the menu of choices along the left side of the screen the left navigation menu throughout this book, and this menu helps you go straight to your various pages within LinkedIn.

When you first create your account, you may notice that none of the menu options are expanded, and it looks something like Figure 1-10. I recommend that you expand each menu section by clicking the + sign next to each section header so your menu looks more like Figure 1-11 below and you can access most of your functions with one click.

Figure 1-10:
Your left
navigation
menu may
be all con-
densed . . .

The Account & Settings page

If you ever need to update any aspect of your LinkedIn account, you can do so by accessing the Account & Settings page. You can always find a link to this page at the top right of any page within LinkedIn.

When you click that link, you see the Account & Settings page within LinkedIn, as shown in Figure 1-12. You first see the settings for your particular account level, especially if you chose a premium account.

Scroll down, however, and you see all the different settings you can update for your LinkedIn account, as shown in Figure 1-13.

The categories you can access from this page are

✔ **Profile Settings:** Here, you can update any part of your profile, add a profile photo, change your status and public profile settings, and manage your Recommendations.

✔ **Personal Information:** Here, you can update the personal information that LinkedIn has on file for you, including Name, Location, E-mail addresses, and passwords.

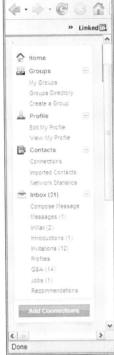

Figure 1-11:
... but I
recommend
expanding
your menu
so each
option is
easily
available.

✓ **Email Notifications:** Here, you set how you receive various communications from other LinkedIn members, like Introductions, InMail,
Invitations to Connect, and OpenLink messages, if applicable.

✓ **Privacy Settings:** Here, you decide how much of your profile is accessible by your contacts, and how much information you want to make
available to your network in terms of profile or status updates.

✓ **Home Page Settings:** Here, you decide how Network Updates and News
articles are displayed on your LinkedIn home page.

✓ **RSS Settings:** Here, you decide whether you want to enable something
called an RSS feed, which is a collection of any updates you make to your
profile that you can subscribe to and read without visiting LinkedIn.

✓ **Groups:** Here, you can update your settings for your memberships with
different LinkedIn Groups. You won't see this category until you join at
least one group.

✓ **My Network:** Here, you can update settings that will tell LinkedIn how you
plan to use the site. LinkedIn will then use this information to customize the
messages you see when using the site to help fit with your stated goals.

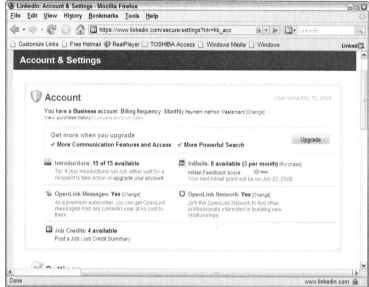

Figure 1-12:
See the
details
of your
LinkedIn
account.

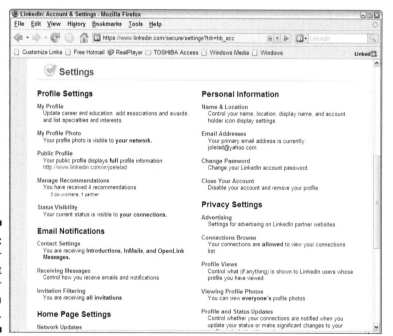

Figure 1-13:
Update your
account
settings for
LinkedIn
here.

Chapter 2

Sign Me Up!

*W*hen LinkedIn first launched, it grew primarily through invitations — you would join only if someone who was already a member invited you and encouraged you to join. Membership is open to anyone 18 years or over (as long as the user hasn't previously been suspended or removed from LinkedIn, of course). You can have only one active account, but you can attach multiple e-mail addresses, past and present, to your account so that people can more easily find you.

You will be presented with some configuration settings during the signup process that you may not know what to do with until you get more familiar with the system. Fortunately, you can customize all of those settings at a later time, but for now I suggest some initial settings. In addition, based on your initial settings, LinkedIn will recommend people to invite to your network. I discuss the ways you can grow your network more extensively in Chapter 6, but this chapter touches on the initial Recommendation process.

Joining LinkedIn

Many people join LinkedIn because a friend or colleague invited them. You can join just as easily without receiving an invitation. Everyone joins at the basic level, which is free (there are several levels of paid membership). That makes the signup process quite straightforward.

Joining with an invitation

When a friend or colleague invites you to join, you will receive an e-mail invitation. The e-mail will clearly identify the sender and have the words "Invitation to connect on LinkedIn," or a custom header that the sender wrote, that will hopefully have the word LinkedIn in the subject.

When you open the message, you see an invitation to join LinkedIn, like the message in Figure 2-1. There may be some extra text if the person inviting you has personalized the message. You'll also see a link that takes you back to LinkedIn to create your account. Simply click that link to start the process.

From here, your next step is to register, which is covered in the section "Registering with LinkedIn" a little later in this chapter.

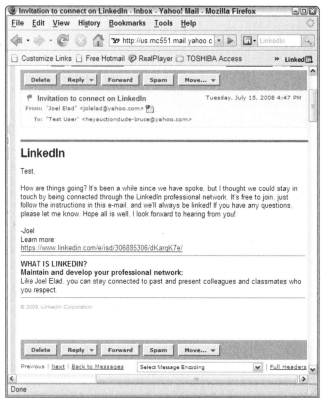

Figure 2-1:
An invitation
to connect
on LinkedIn.

Joining without an invitation

If you haven't gotten an invitation, don't let that turn you into a wallflower. You can join LinkedIn directly, without an invitation from an existing user.

Open Internet Explorer, Firefox, or another Web browser and make your way to www.linkedin.com.You see the initial LinkedIn homepage, as shown in Figure 2-2. It has a special link, "What is LinkedIn?" in the top-right corner, if you would like to read more information about LinkedIn. You simply need to provide your first name, last name, and your e-mail address, then click the Continue button to start the registration process. I cover the specifics of registration in the next section.

Figure 2-2:
The
LinkedIn
home page.

Registering with LinkedIn

The Registration page might vary in appearance, depending on whether you're signing up with or without an invitation, but the registration process is the same. On the Join LinkedIn page, which you can see in Figure 2-3, LinkedIn needs to collect some basic information about you to create your account.

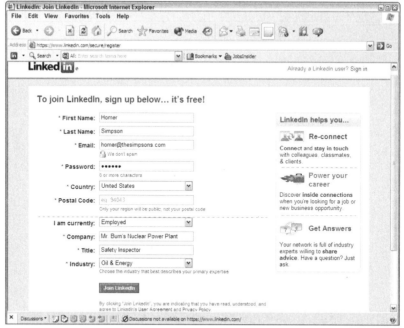

Figure 2-3:
Tell LinkedIn
a little about
yourself so
they can
create your
account!

Specifically, you need to provide the following information:

- ✔ **Your first name, last name, and e-mail address.** LinkedIn fills in this information, either from the invitation you received or the text you entered when you went to the home page.

- ✔ **A password for your LinkedIn account.** Your password needs to be at least 6 characters long, and should not be something another person could easily guess.

- ✔ **Your country and postal code.** LinkedIn will not display your ZIP code, but will use it to assign a Region to your profile, so others know the general area where you reside.

- ✔ **Your current employment status.** Click the drop-down box to indicate if you are employed, self-employed, looking for work, or a student.

- ✔ **Details about your status.** Depending on your status, LinkedIn will either ask for a Company, Job Title, and Industry if you are employed, or ask for Industry focus if you are looking for work, as shown in Figure 2-4.

If you find it hard to choose an industry that best describes your primary expertise, just choose one that's closest — you can always change the selection later.

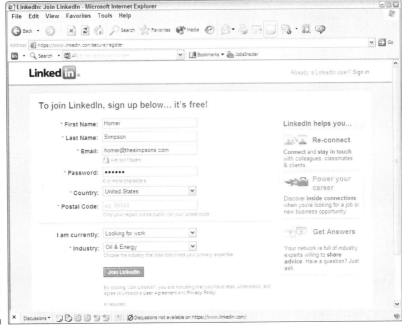

Figure 2-4:
Depending
on your
work status,
LinkedIn
may ask a
few less
questions.

Once you have completed the Join LinkedIn form, click the blue Join LinkedIn button to create your account.

If you're joining with an invitation, the Registration page will have a few slight differences, as shown in Figure 2-5:

✔ The top line of the screen includes the name of the person who invited you.

✔ You will see a right sidebar that includes some information about the network of the person who invited you, like their professional headline and their number of first-degree connections.

✔ Your name and e-mail address are displayed in the form based on what the inviter entered for you. Feel free to change it as you see fit.

If you want to be known on LinkedIn by another version of your name (say a nickname, maiden name, or proper name), or if you want to use a different e-mail address, you can change the details now in those fields — First Name, Last Name, E-mail.

Currently, when you click the Join button to create your LinkedIn account, LinkedIn states that by clicking the button, you are indicating that you have read, understood, and agree to LinkedIn's User Agreement and Privacy Policy. These are important documents, especially the sections of the User

Agreement on Termination (of your LinkedIn account) and User Conduct. The Privacy Policy contains important information about how LinkedIn will manage the information you provide and your activity online. You can read the documents online or print them out — each document prints out to about four pages of text. The User Agreement is also known as the Terms of Use. Simply click the links for User Agreement and Privacy Policy below the Join button, as indicated in Figure 2-6.

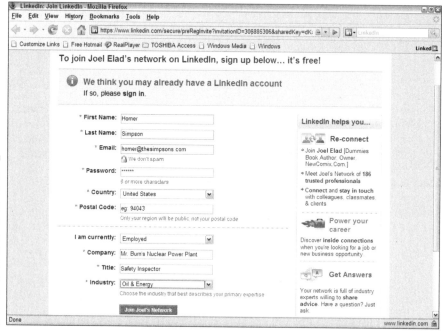

Figure 2-5: When someone invites you to LinkedIn, your Join LinkedIn screen has more information.

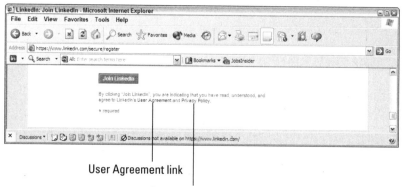

Figure 2-6: Click on the User Agreement and Privacy Policy links to pull up the right documents.

User Agreement link

Privacy Policy link

Before you click the Join button, double-check that you completed the required fields. Leaving any of the required fields empty or not choosing an industry in the Industry field returns an error message.

Deciding how you want to use LinkedIn

After you complete the registration and click the Join LinkedIn button, the LinkedIn: Contact Settings page asks you how you want to use LinkedIn, as shown in Figure 2-7.

You are asked to choose some options for the following:

✔ What you want the LinkedIn network to help you find

✔ What kinds of things you want to be contacted about via LinkedIn

The choices you make regarding how you want to be found will become what LinkedIn calls your Contact Settings. They help visitors to your LinkedIn Profile page understand your preferences for contact.

Notice that some of the check box items are already selected. These selections were made based on what you provided for your employment status on the Join page, under the "I am currently…" option. Make sure the selections are the ones you want. You may want to uncheck some that have already been selected and select some of the ones that aren't yet selected.

The selections you make are displayed on your LinkedIn Profile page. See Chapter 3 for suggestions on how to make the best use of your Profile page. Just for now, understand that:

✔ Your selection of items on this page determines the kinds of contact you have with other LinkedIn users.

✔ You can change your selections at any time and as often as you want.

An obvious example of what I'm talking about here is that if you're looking for a job, it clearly makes sense to select the Finding a Job option. That way any people who visit your profile can see you're on the hunt, and they would be able to tell that you'd welcome messages regarding job opportunities. If you aren't seeking a job, you don't want to receive messages about available jobs, and you'd want to leave the Finding a Job option deselected. As another example, in the To Be Found section, if you select the check box that indicates you want to be contacted about "Relevant requests for expertise about industries, products or companies," you need to be ready to welcome such requests.

For now, just select the check boxes for the items that seem to meet your needs. If in doubt, select less rather than more. When you've made your selections, press the Save Settings button.

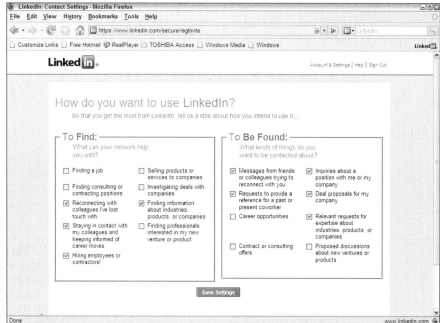

Finishing the LinkedIn registration process

If someone invited you to join LinkedIn, the Build Your Network page appears, as shown in Figure 2-8. This page provides some information and invites you to take several actions. LinkedIn informs you that your account has been created and the person who invited you is your first connection in your network. Additionally, it asks you to identify any people you consider trusted contacts, so LinkedIn can send them an invitation to join your account. Fill out the name and e-mail address fields if you think of people you want to invite immediately, and then click the Send invitations button. (I discuss how to grow your network in Chapter 6.) If you want to wait on sending out any invitations, click the small link marked Skip this step in the bottom-right corner of the screen.

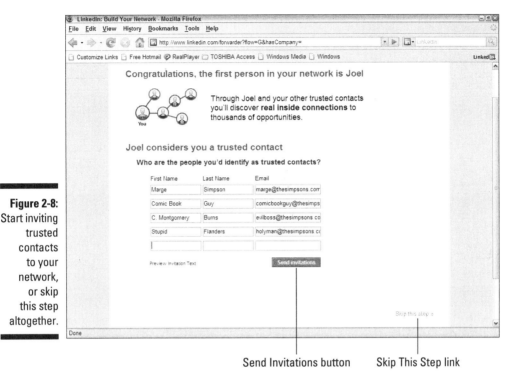

Figure 2-8:
Start inviting trusted contacts to your network, or skip this step altogether.

Send Invitations button   Skip This Step link

If you joined LinkedIn without an invitation, you will be taken to your new LinkedIn home page, as shown in Figure 2-9. First, at the top of the page, you can see a line of text that states your basic Contact Settings have been saved. In other words, the selections you just made on the previous page with the check boxes have now been incorporated into the online profile that LinkedIn is helping you build.

Privacy confidential

Keep in mind that when you provide LinkedIn with access to your existing contact lists, such as on Gmail or your Yahoo! mail, rest assured that LinkedIn respects your privacy.

LinkedIn is a licensee of the TRUSTe Privacy Program. In its Privacy Policy, LinkedIn declares its adherence to the following key privacy principles:

✔ LinkedIn will never rent or sell your personally identifiable information to third parties for marketing purposes.

✔ LinkedIn will never share your contact information with another user, without your consent.

✔ Any sensitive information that you provide will be secured with all industry standard protocols and technology.

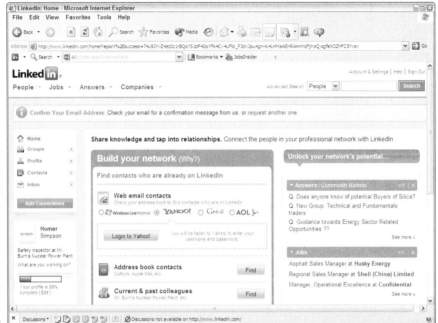

Figure 2-9:
LinkedIn
creates
your new
account and
asks you
to confirm
your e-mail
address.

Next, you are asked to check your e-mail for a confirmation message. Then, under the instruction to check your e-mail is the heading Build Your Network, with various options or tools. The practical thing to do first, before you start on the Build Your Network section, is to follow the instruction to check your e-mail for confirmation. This requires some action on your part before you return to the Build Your Network phase.

If you skip the step of confirming your e-mail with LinkedIn, you will be unable to invite any connections, use functions like LinkedIn Answers, apply for jobs on LinkedIn's job board, or take advantage of most other LinkedIn functions.

Open your e-mail program and look for an e-mail from LinkedIn Email Confirmation with the subject line Please confirm your e-mail address. When you open that e-mail, you should see an e-mail confirmation, as shown in Figure 2-10. Either click the link Click Here to Confirm Your Email Address or copy and paste the URL provided in the e-mail into your Web browser.

When you click the link, you are taken back to LinkedIn and asked to confirm your address, as seen in Figure 2-11. Click the Confirm button to confirm the e-mail address for your account. You will be asked to log in to your account, so simply provide your e-mail address and password when prompted.

After you've confirmed your e-mail address, you are taken back to the Build Your Network page with a thank-you message for confirming your e-mail.

Figure 2-10:
Click the
link, or copy
and paste
the link,
to confirm
your e-mail
address
with
LinkedIn.

Figure 2-11:
Click the
Confirm
button to
confirm
your e-mail
address
with
LinkedIn.

In the meantime, if you want to check your e-mail, you can find a "Welcome to LinkedIn!" message there from LinkedIn Updates, assuring you that you're now a registered LinkedIn user. The e-mail, as shown in Figure 2-12, has some useful links that you may want to explore later, including a tour of LinkedIn and how it works. The e-mail also offers some ways to find contacts, but you'll find the process simpler if you first use the Build Your Network system supplied in this process of signing up.

Figure 2-12: Welcome to LinkedIn!

Starting to Build Your Network

You're ready to look at how to build your network, with tools and forms provided by LinkedIn. Your first step is to decide who you want to invite to connect with you on LinkedIn.

Your profile is so important it got its own chapter (Chapter 3 if you really must know). Be sure to completely fill out your profile before you start inviting people to connect. Having a complete profile makes it easier to find former colleagues and classmates. After all, if you invite someone that you haven't spoken to recently, they will take a quick look at your profile before responding. If they don't see a part of your professional history where they know you, they will most likely ignore your invitation.

After you've joined LinkedIn, you may find yourself in one of the following situations:

- ✔ You feel compelled to start inviting friends and colleagues to connect with you right away, before working on your profile or thinking of a strategy.

- ✔ You get nervous and decide not to invite anybody beyond one or two close friends or family members.

- ✔ You wonder about the value of LinkedIn and leave your account alone for a long period of time with no activity.

I will admit, I have seen all three situations occur with various people who have joined LinkedIn, so don't feel bad if one of these is your natural reaction. Your best bet is to start using LinkedIn with some thought and planning, which is where I come in (along with this book, of course) with some advice. So, let's start by talking about who you would like to invite to your network.

LinkedIn provides a neat tool to help you identify, in your existing networks, people you know and trust well enough to feel confident about inviting them and expecting that they will accept.

The multi-faceted Build Your Network tool, as shown in Figure 2-13, is a part of your initial LinkedIn home page, and it is worth studying for a moment. The Build Your Network tool incorporates four basic options to identify and grow your network:

- ✔ Check your address book for contacts to invite with options for systems like Outlook and Apple Mail.

- ✔ Check your address book for an e-mail system only available on the Web, like Yahoo!, Gmail, and AOL.

- ✔ Reconnect with past colleagues.

- ✔ Find former classmates.

We cover these techniques in greater detail in Chapter 6. I recommend that you spend a little time thinking about who you want to invite, then focus on getting your profile set up first and then inviting people.

LinkedIn makes it very easy for you to send invitations in bulk — to your entire contact list if you want. However, even though it's easy to do, it's not necessarily a good idea. It can have negative social implications and can even potentially get you suspended from LinkedIn (and you wouldn't want that!). Exercising some discretion with regards to the people you invite (and how — see Chapter 5) will serve you better in the long run.

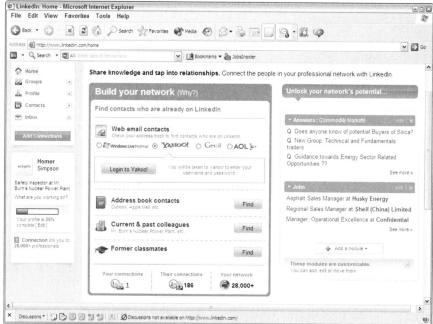

Figure 2-13:
The Build
Your
Network
tool as part
of your
home page.

Chapter 3

Building Your Own Profile

After you've registered with LinkedIn and worked to build your network by looking outward, it's time to look inward by focusing on your profile. Think of your LinkedIn profile as your personal home page to the business world: This profile exists to give anyone a complete picture of your background, qualifications, and skills, as well as paint a picture of who you are beyond the numbers and bullet points.

In this chapter, I walk you through all the different sections of your profile and explain how to update them and put the right information in a concise and appealing manner. I take you through the steps of adding information at each stage, so you can update your profile now or down the road (say, when you finish that amazing project or get that spiffy promotion you've been working towards).

At any time, you can go to www.linkedin.com and click the Profile link in the top-left corner to access your LinkedIn profile to view or make changes.

Determining the Contact Settings for Your Profile

Before you dive right in and start updating your profile, stop and think about what kind of profile you want to construct and show to the world. Specifically, think about the ways in which you want to use LinkedIn. For example, some people just want to add to their network, but others are actively looking for a job. You can have many reasons for using LinkedIn, and you can identify yourself through setting up your Contact Settings on LinkedIn. The ones you choose mainly depend on what you plan to use LinkedIn for, as discussed in Chapter 2. You can always go back and update your contact settings as your situation changes.

You can select from eight main contact settings in your LinkedIn profile. Each describes a type of opportunity that lets other people know what they can approach you with on the site:

- **Career opportunities:** If you're looking to augment your skill set so you can advance your career, or if you want to network with people that could approach you with a career opportunity now or in the future, you'd want to select this setting.

- **Expertise requests:** If you're available to provide expertise on your main subject areas to someone with a question or opportunity, select this setting.

- **Consulting offers:** If you want to be open to receiving offers to do consulting work for another company or individual, you'd want to select this setting. You can always accept or reject offers as they come in, but selecting this setting means you're open for consideration.

- **Business deals:** If you're open to doing a business deal, either for your main job or your entrepreneurial venture, you'd want to select this setting. Deals here could range from supplier/vendor requests, launching a new line of products, or doing a joint venture.

- **New ventures:** If you're interested in participating in a new company, either as an employee, co-owner, financier, or anything else, select this setting.

- **Personal reference requests:** If you're open to providing references for your first-degree connections when someone asks for one, you'd want to select this setting.

- **Job inquiries:** If you're open to receiving job offers or interests from other companies, you'd want to select this setting.

- **Requests to reconnect:** If you're interested in old friends, colleagues, and classmates, to send you a request to connect with you on LinkedIn, select this setting.

After you select your settings, they show up as a bulleted list on your profile. In addition, they help determine or block the type of communication that you receive on LinkedIn. For example, if you aren't interested in job inquiries, you shouldn't receive any direct solicitations to apply for a job.

Adding Your Summary to LinkedIn

Your LinkedIn profile's Summary section, which appears in the top third of your profile, should give any reader a quick idea of who you are, what you've accomplished, and most importantly, what you're looking for on LinkedIn. Some people think of their summary as their "elevator pitch," or their 30-second introduction of themselves that they tell to any new contact. Other people think of their summary as simply their resume summary, which gives a high-level overview of their experience and job goals. Each summary is as individual as the person writing it, but there are right ways and wrong ways to prepare and update your summary.

LinkedIn has split up the Summary section into four distinct parts:

- ✔ **Your professional "headline."** Think of this as your job title. This is displayed underneath your name on LinkedIn, in search results, connections lists, and on your profile. Therefore, you want a headline that grabs people's attention. Some people put their job title; other people add some colorful adjectives and include two or three different professions. For example, I entered "Dummies Book Author; Owner, NewComix.Com," indicating two of my main professions.

- ✔ **Your primary industry of experience.** This is a list of industries you can choose from to indicate your main industry affiliation.

- ✔ **Your professional experience and goals.** This is typically a one-paragraph summary of your current and past accomplishments and future goals. See the next section for more on how to construct the right paragraph for this part.

- ✔ **Your specialties in your industry of expertise.** This is a list of your specific skills and talents. This is separate from your professional experience in that this section allows you to list specific job skills (for example, contract negotiation or writing HTML software code) as opposed to the daily responsibilities or accomplishments from your job that you would list in the professional experience and goals paragraph.

Writing your summary first

Before you plan to update your summary on LinkedIn, we advise writing it out, using a program like Microsoft Word so that you can easily copy and paste it once written. This will allow you to organize your thoughts, decide on the right order of your statements, and pick and choose the most important statements to put in your summary.

Of course, the goals of your summary should be the same as your goals for using LinkedIn, because your summary is the starting point for most people when they read your profile. As you write out your summary, keep these points in mind:

- ✔ **Be concise.** Remember, this is a summary, not a 300-page memoir of your life. Most summaries are one paragraph long, with a separate paragraph to list your skills and/or specialties. Give the highlights of what you've done and are planning to do. Save the detailed information for when you add your individual employment positions to your profile.

- ✔ **Pick three to five of your most important accomplishments.** Your profile can have lots of detail regarding your jobs, skill sets, education, and honors, but your summary needs to reflect the three to five items throughout your career that you most want people to know. Think of it this way: If someone were introducing you to another person, what would you want this new person to know about you right away?

    Depending on your goals for LinkedIn, the accomplishments you put in your summary may not be your biggest accomplishments overall. For example, if you're trying to use LinkedIn to get a new job, your summary should include accomplishments that matter most to an employer in your desired field.

- ✔ **Organize your summary in a Who, What, Goals format.** Typically, the first sentence of your summary should be a statement of *Who* you are currently, meaning your current profession or status. (For example, "Software project manager with extensive experience in Fortune 500 firms.") The next few sentences should focus on *What* you've done so far in your career, and the end of your summary should focus on your *Goals* for the future.

- ✔ **Use the right keywords in your summary.** Keywords are especially important if you're looking for a new job or hoping to pick up some consulting work. Although you should use a few keywords in your professional experience paragraph, you should really use all the appropriate keywords for skills you've acquired when you write the Specialties section of your summary. Potential employers will scan that section looking for the right qualifications first, before making any contact.

- ✔ **Be honest with your specialties, but don't be shy**. Your Specialties section is your opportunity to list any skill or trade that you feel you've learned and demonstrated with some ability. Some people see it as a chance to list out the "hottest" skills for their industry, in hopes of impressing a potential employer. Typically, a prospective employer will detect this during the interview phase, which wastes everybody's time. Conversely, however, some people don't list a skill here unless they feel they're an expert at it. You should list any skill or specialty where you believe you are above the level of a novice or pure beginner.

TIP

If you need help coming up with your various summary sections, click the link See Examples below each section header to see LinkedIn-provided examples, or you can view profiles of other people in similar industries.

Updating your LinkedIn profile's Summary section

When you have an idea of what you want to put in your profile's Summary section, it's time to go into LinkedIn and plug that data into the correct fields. When you're ready, follow these steps:

1. **Go to LinkedIn and log in. Click the Profile link in the left navigation menu.**

   You're taken to the Profile page.

2. **Scroll down to the Summary section and click the Edit link below the Summary section header.**

   You now see the Professional Summary page, as shown in Figure 3-1.

   The first step is to input your professional headline, which is to say your main job title. You can put any job title here, but make sure it conveys your main role as you want others to see it.

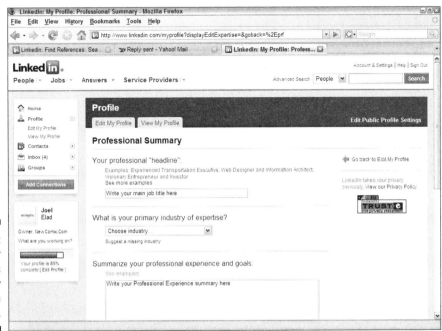

Figure 3-1:
Update your
profile's
Summary
section
here.

3. **Click the drop-down arrow under the text What Is Your Primary Industry of Experience? and select the industry you most associate with your career.**

   There are over 140 different designations, so take a few moments to do a quick scan of the list. Note that some of the industries listed are more specific than others. You want to pick the best match possible. For instance, if you create custom graphics for Web sites, you could select Internet as your industry, but an even better choice would be Online Media.

4. **In the Summarize Your Professional Experience and Goals text box, enter a paragraph that sums you up professionally (as discussed in the previous section).**

   Although there is a 2,000 character limit, you can benefit from writing a concise and focused paragraph.

5. **Scroll down to the final section of the Professional Summary page, as shown in Figure 3-2, and enter your skills and/or specialties in the text box provided.**

   Remember to separate each item with a comma, and don't put any punctuation after the last item in your list. You don't need to press Enter between skills.

6. **When you're done, click the Save Changes button to save your summary.**

   You're taken back to your Profile page.

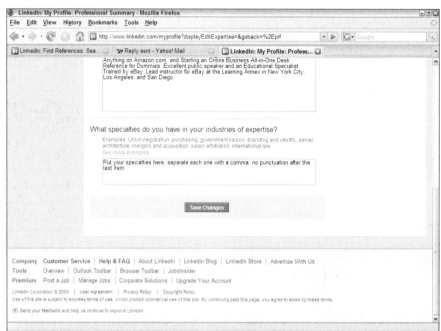

Figure 3-2:
List your
various
specialties
in the box
provided.

The $5,000 profile update

I have a great example of why you should update your profile. Jefre Outlaw's LinkedIn profile says that he's a "portfolio entrepreneur." His profile didn't mention, however, that Mr. Outlaw spent more than 20 years as a real estate investor and developer, nor that he had recently obtained his own real estate license and joined his cousin Blake's agency, Outlaw Real Estate Group. He realized a golden opportunity was available to him through LinkedIn.

Outlaw was interviewed for the LinkedIntelligence blog (www.linked intelligence.com/the-5000-profile-update). "At first I completely forgot about updating my LinkedIn profile," he said. "But I got a request to forward an introduction, and it reminded me that I should probably go update my profile to include my new gig as a realtor."

This turned out to be a valuable update for Outlaw.

Several weeks later, someone from his extended network was using LinkedIn to search for realtors and saw Outlaw's profile.

This person contacted Outlaw about listing a home for sale. Well, the potential client signed up with Outlaw's agency, who was able to sell the house quickly for $170,000. When you do the math, $170,000 home × 3% commission = about $5,000 to the brokerage.

As Outlaw relayed his experience to LinkedIntelligence, he wanted his story to be clear. "Let's not overstate what happened," said Outlaw. "Being on LinkedIn didn't get me the business. We [Outlaw's real estate agency] were one of several realtors the client talked to, and I brought in my cousin, who's a great closer and more experienced than I, to meet with the client. But the fact that I was in [LinkedIn], that my profile was up-to-date, that I have over 20 really good Recommendations on my profile — all that put us on the short list."

The moral of the story is simple. Keep your profile up to date on everything you're doing. If your profile isn't up to date, plan to update it right away — you may never know what opportunities you're missing out of by ignoring your profile.

Adding a Position to Your LinkedIn Profile

One of the most important aspects of your LinkedIn profile is the list of positions you've held over the years, including your current job. This list is especially important if you're using LinkedIn to find a new or different career or to reconnect with past colleagues. Hiring managers want to see your complete history to know what skills you can offer, and past colleagues can't find you as easily through LinkedIn if the job they knew you from isn't on your profile. Therefore, it's critical to make sure you have all the positions posted on your profile with the correct information.

For a company that's in LinkedIn's directory, you need to fill in the following fields:

- Company name (and display name, if your company goes by more than one name)

 ✔ Your job title while working for the company

 ✔ The time period you worked for the company

 ✔ Description of your job duties

If your company is *not* listed in LinkedIn's directory, you need to fill in the industry, type, size, and stock ticker symbol for the company.

You may want to have a copy of your resume handy when completing this section, because most resumes have all or most of the information required.

To add a position to your LinkedIn profile, follow these steps:

1. **Go to LinkedIn and log in. Click the Profile link in the left navigation menu.**

   This step takes you to the Profile page.

2. **Scroll down your profile until you see the Experience header and click the Add Position button.**

   You're now taken to the Add Position page, as shown in Figure 3-3.

3. **In the text boxes provided, enter the information about your position, including company, title, time period, and job description.**

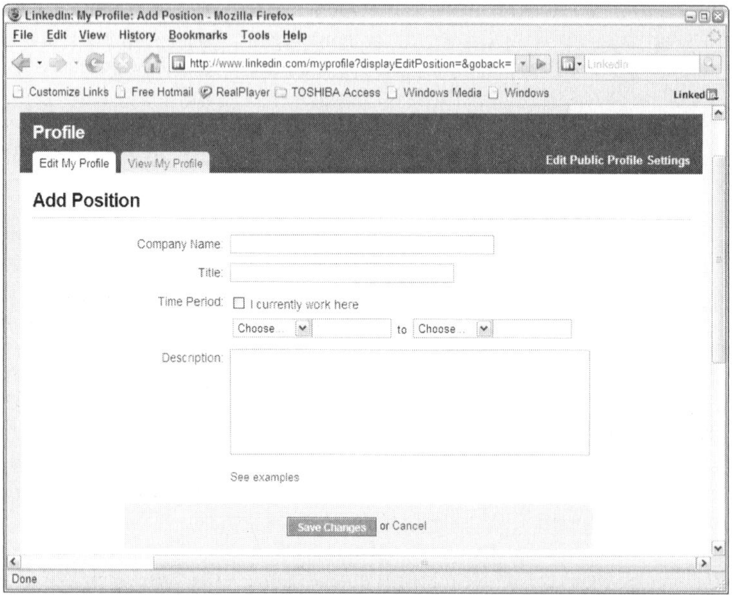

Figure 3-3:
Enter
your job
information
on this
page.

When you type in your company information, LinkedIn checks that name against a database of thousands of companies from their records, and you see suggested company names as you type. If you see your company name in that list, click the name, and LinkedIn automatically fills in all the company detail information for you.

4. **When you're done entering information, click the Save Changes button.**

   This adds the newly entered position into your profile, and you're taken back to your Profile page.

5. **Repeat Steps 2 through 4 for any additional position you want to enter.**

To edit a position you already have listed, simply click the Edit link next to that record, instead of clicking the Add Position button.

The Experience section isn't just for paid full-time employment. You can add position information for any contract work, non-profit assignments, or other valid work experience you did that added to your skill set. If you've written a book, maintain a blog, or have a regular magazine column, you might want to list that as a separate position.

If you have most of the information that LinkedIn asks for a given position but you're missing a few details in the description, go ahead and add whatever you've got. (You must provide a job title, company, and time period to save the position in your profile.) You can always come back later and fill in any missing information. In addition, if you make your profile public (as discussed later in this chapter in the section "Setting your Profile URL and public view"), then make sure any position information you enter is something you don't mind the whole world — including past employers — seeing on your profile.

Reporting Your Education on Your Profile

After you've documented your past and current jobs, it's time to move onto the next part of your profile, namely Education. After all, besides at your jobs, where else are you going to meet and stay in touch with so many people? At school, of course! Your Education section says a lot about you, especially to potential employers and to former schoolmates who are looking to reconnect with you.

When you signed up with LinkedIn, you were asked to provide your basic education information. However, you may have more than one school to list, or perhaps you didn't create a full listing for the schools you put down upon registration. In either case, whenever you find a moment, you can go back to make sure that your profile is up to date and has all your education listed.

Some people ask how much education you should list on your profile. Although you could theoretically go all the way back to preschool or kindergarten, most people start with high school or undergraduate education. This is up to you, but keep in mind that the more items you list, the greater the opportunity that your past schoolmates can locate and contact you.

This section isn't limited to high school, undergraduate, and post-graduate education. You should also list any vocational education, certification courses, and any other stint at an educational institution that matters to your career or personal direction.

When you're ready to update or add your education information, follow these steps:

1. **Go to LinkedIn and log in. Click the Profile link in the left navigation menu.**

2. **Scroll down your profile until you see the Education header. Click the Add Education button to continue.**

   The Add Education page appears, as shown in Figure 3-4. This is the page where you enter the information about your school.

3. **From the drop-down lists provided, select the Country and State where your school was located.**

   LinkedIn then displays a drop-down list of schools.

4. **Look through the alphabetized list to find your school and select it. If your school name doesn't appear, select Other and then type in the school name in the new text box provided.**

5. **Complete the degree information about your education.**

   This includes filling in your degree type, fields of study (if applicable), and the years you attended this institution. For your degree type, you can either provide an abbreviation (BS, BA, and so on) or write out the entire degree name (Masters of Science, Doctorate, and so on). The Fields of Study text box is optional, but if you had a specific major or emphasis, this is the box to put that information in. Finally, for dates attended, if you're still attending this institution, simply fill in your expected graduation date.

6. **Scroll down to the Activities and Societies text box and fill it in.**

   This is the place to enter any extracurricular activities you participated in while attending this school. Enter any clubs or organizations you belonged to (including any officer positions you held in those clubs) and any societies you joined or were given membership to, such as honor societies, fraternities, or sororities.

   Don't forget to separate each of your activities with a comma.

7. **Scroll down to the Additional Notes text box and enter any additional information about your education experience.**

   This is the place to enter any awards or honors received from this school, as well as any special events or experiences that did not fit in the Activities and Societies box, such as studying abroad, events you organized, or committees that you served on at this school. You can separate each item with a period.

   You should also list all your awards and honors under the appropriate field in Additional Information, which I cover in the next section.

8. **When you're done entering information, scroll down and click the Save Changes button.**

   This step adds the newly entered education listing into your profile, and you will be taken back to your Profile page.

9. **Repeat Steps 2 through 8 for any additional education listings you want to enter.**

   If you want to edit an existing education record, click the Edit link next to that record, instead of the Add Education button.

Completing the Additional Information for Your Profile

Whenever you meet someone, the most common questions you ask are, "So, what do you do?" and "Where did you go to school?" However, there's more to you than your jobs and education, and LinkedIn has created an Additional Information section to reflect that and to tie your LinkedIn profile to your other Internet and real-life identities.

The Additional Information section allows you to provide lots of information in these areas:

- ✔ **Web sites:** LinkedIn allows you to add up to three different Web site links, which will point from your LinkedIn profile to whatever Web site(s) you designate, such as your personal Web site, your company Web site, a blog, an RSS feed, or any other promotional mechanisms you use online.

  When you add a link from your LinkedIn profile to your other Web sites, this helps the search engine rankings for those pages because those rankings are partially determined by the quantity and quality of Web pages that link to them, and LinkedIn is a high-quality site as far as the search engines are concerned. You must make your profile public to receive these benefits.

- ✔ **Interests:** This section is designed to highlight your extracurricular activities and what you like to do in your spare time. It allows potential contacts to see what else they may have in common with you (favorite hobbies or sports) and gives potential employers a glimpse into what else interests you outside a job.

- ✔ **Groups and Associations:** This section is designed to illustrate what organizations you belong to and what formal activities you do in your spare time. Many people use this section to highlight any charity work they participate in, any networking groups they belong to, or any religious or political groups where they attend services or rallies.

- ✔ **Honors and Awards:** This section is designed to announce to the world any distinctions or awards you have earned throughout your career. This could be work-related, like Salesman of the Year; education-related, like Summa Cum Laude or Dean's List; group-related, like Best Fundraiser; or even sports-related, like 1st Place Men's Singles in the City Tennis Tournament.

These items are completely optional for you to complete, but a strong, well-rounded profile usually helps you in your career or networking goals because it gives you more opportunities to connect with someone ("Hey, Joel's a big travel fan. So am I!") or allows people to identify with your situation.

When you're ready to update the rest of the information on your profile, simply follow these steps:

1. **Go to LinkedIn and log in. Click the Profile link in the left navigation menu.**

   You're taken to the Profile page.

2. **Scroll down your profile until you see the Additional Information section header.**

   You should see an Edit link below that header. Click that link to continue.

   You are now taken to the Additional Information page, as shown in Figure 3-5. This is the page where you enter the additional information about yourself, from associated Web sites to interests, groups, and awards.

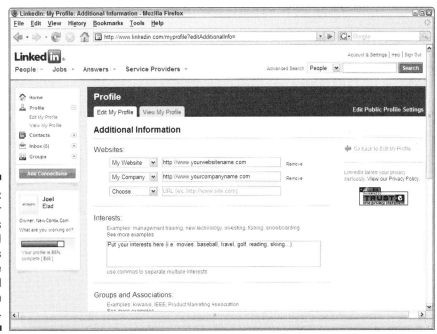

Figure 3-5:
Enter your
Web sites
and
interests
in the
Additional
Information
window.

3. **Under Websites, in the drop-down lists on the left, select short descriptions for the sites you intend to display.**

   You can pick from the predefined list of descriptions (like My Company, My Website, and so on), or you can pick Other and, in the blank text box that appears, type in a brief custom description for your Web site link (like My Rotary Club page or My eBay page).

This description is what's going to appear as a link on your profile — the reader isn't going to see the site's URL.

Search engines look at the text used in these links when calculating rankings. So if there are certain keywords for which you want your site to rank higher, you may want to include them in the link text. So for example, you might want to say "Springfield Toastmasters" rather than "My Toastmasters Club."

4. **Still in the Websites section, in the text boxes to the right, enter the URLs of the Web sites you want to list on your profile, corresponding to the correct descriptions on the left.**

   You can add up to three URLs to your LinkedIn profile, so use them wisely.

This might seem obvious, but, well, people are going to be able to click those links and check out your Web sites. Sure, that's the point, but do you remember that hilarious yet embarrassing picture of yourself you added to your personal site, or that tirade you posted in your blog about a co-worker or tough project? Before you link to a site from your LinkedIn profile, scour it and make sure you won't end up scaring off your contacts.

5. **Complete the Interests text box.**

   This is your chance to tell the world a little more about you besides your jobs and education. Make sure to separate each interest with a comma.

You probably want to omit any interests that a potential employer wouldn't like to see. For instance, if you work in the entertainment industry, talking about how you love to download pirated movies will not make any hiring manager happy. Talk instead about how you love to watch licensed content from approved sources like iTunes or Amazon Unbox!

6. **Scroll down to the Groups and Associations text box, as shown in Figure 3-6, and fill it in.**

   This is the text box where you can list your groups not listed under any school, such as any charity groups, religious organizations, alumni associations, rotary clubs, and so on.

7. **Scroll down to the Honors and Awards text box and fill it in.**

   This is where you can list your accolades from jobs, school, or any extracurricular activity. Even if you listed an award under your Education section, feel free to repeat it here.

8. **When you're done entering information, click the Save Changes button.**

   This step updates your Additional Information section in your profile, and you're taken back to your Profile page.

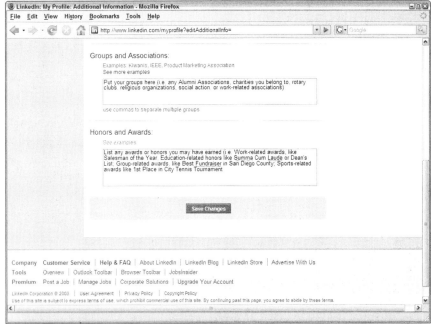

Reviewing Your LinkedIn Profile

After you've gone through the various sections of your LinkedIn profile and added the critical information, you should review your profile and make sure it appears exactly the way you want other people to see it, as well as decide how much information is visible to the public and what others on LinkedIn can contact you about in what regard.

Viewing your profile as others see it

As you're updating your LinkedIn profile, you may want to view your profile to see how it will be displayed on the computer screen when anyone clicks to view your profile. You have several ways of accomplishing this:

✔ In the left navigation menu, click the View My Profile link under the Profile link to see your profile as it would appear. (If your left navigation menu isn't expanded, click the plus sign next to the word Profile in the menu.) The link whisks you away to the Profile page, and there you can see that the View My Profile tab is selected and waiting for your review.

✔ While editing your profile, you can see two tabs under the Profile header in the middle of the screen, Edit My Profile, and View My Profile, as shown in Figure 3-7. Click the View My Profile tab to see your profile.

View My Profile tab

Figure 3-7:
You have several options for viewing your LinkedIn profile in action.

Setting your profile URL and public view

After you've fully updated your LinkedIn profile, your next goal is probably to share it with the entire world, not just your LinkedIn network. The best way to accomplish this is to set up your profile so that your full profile is available for public viewing.

Setting your profile to full public view gives you several advantages:

✔ Anyone looking for you has a better chance of finding you because of the increased information tied to your name.

✔ When you make your profile public, it gets indexed in both the Google and Yahoo! search databases. This makes your online identity accessible and controlled by your access to LinkedIn.

✔ You give increased exposure to any companies, projects, or initiatives that you're working on by having that credit published on your LinkedIn profile.

When you're ready to set your profile to Public, just follow these steps:

1. **Go to LinkedIn and log in. Click the Profile link in the left navigation menu.**

   You arrive at the Profile page. Look to the right of the Edit my Profile and View My Profile tabs, for a link that says Edit Public Profile Settings, like in Figure 3-8.

Edit Public Profile Settings link

Figure 3-8:
Here's where you can edit your LinkedIn profile settings.

2. **Click the Edit Public Profile Settings link.**

   This step takes you to the Public Profile settings page, as shown in Figure 3-9.

3. **(Optional) If you want to set a custom URL for your LinkedIn profile, fill in the text box next to the Set Address button.**

   You can enter anywhere between 5 and 30 numbers or letters, but don't put in any spaces, symbols, or special characters. When you've picked your custom address, click the Set Address button to save your changes.

   After you set a custom URL, this text box will be hidden if you come back to this process. You should keep your URL changes to a minimum (preferably, just set it once and leave it), so everyone will know how to get to your profile, especially the search engines. Otherwise, you'll have different versions of your profile with different URL's in different places on the Internet.

4. Scroll down the main Public Profile section on the page and determine what parts of your LinkedIn profile you want to be available for public viewing.

You have the option of picking which sections of your LinkedIn profile are public. To reveal a section on your public profile, simply select the check box next to that given section, as shown in Figure 3-10. Your basic information is already selected for you by default, but you can decide whether to add your education, positions, groups, or any other indicated section. As you check off more sections, a preview of your Profile page on the right side of the page gets updated.

5. When you're done, click the Save Changes button to save your selections.

You're taken back to your Public Profile settings page, and you should see a confirmation message at the top of the screen.

Whenever you're editing your profile, you can scroll down and click the link next to the Public Profile header to see your public profile. On that page, you can click a button to view your full profile. This way, you can see the difference between your public and full profiles.

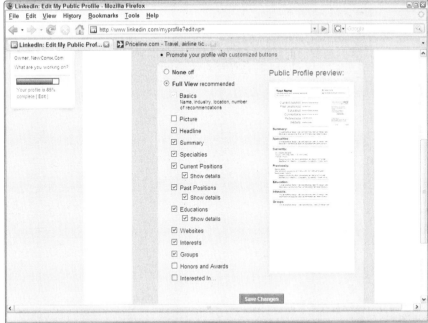

Figure 3-10:
You decide
what
elements
to add to
your public
Linked
profile (on
the left)
and the
preview (on
the right)
shows your
changes
instantly.

Checking your contact settings

You definitely want to make sure that you've selected the correct contact
settings for your LinkedIn profile. After all, if you're looking for a new job,
for example, you want to make sure that the option for Career Opportunities
has been checked off. (I go into plenty of detail about the eight main contact
settings in the earlier section "Determining the Contact Settings for Your
Profile.") When you're ready to check your contact settings, just follow these
steps:

1. **Go to LinkedIn and log in. Click the Profile link in the left navigation
   menu.**

   Your browser presents you with the Profile page.

2. **Scroll down the page to the bottom of your profile. Under the Contact
   Settings section header, click the Edit link.**

   This brings you to the Contact Settings page, as shown in Figure 3-11.

3. **Select an option under the What Type of Messages Will You Accept?
   question.**

   If you want to receive InMail e-mails from people who aren't direct connections in your network, make sure the option I'll Accept Introductions
   and InMail is selected.

Otherwise, select the I'll Accept Only Introductions option to block anyone sending you InMail. Your first-level (direct) connections will always be able to send you a message through LinkedIn.

4. **Make sure the correct options are selected in the Opportunity Preferences section.**

   The items you have selected here show up as a bulleted list in your profile and will limit (or allow) the ways in which other LinkedIn members can contact you. If you don't want to receive any InMail or Introductions from other LinkedIn users, you can uncheck all those boxes and no options to contact you will be displayed on your profile.

5. **(Optional) If you want to give special instructions on how people can contact you, fill in that information in the indicated text box.**

   For example, if you require a few pieces of information from someone before you will add them to your network, you can indicate that in this text box. You can also indicate whether this is a good time to contact you, or what projects or subject areas you're currently involved in.

6. **When you're done updating this page, click the Save Changes button to save your selections.**

   You're taken to your Account & Settings page.

Part II
Finding Others and Getting Connected

The 5th Wave   By Rich Tennant

"Hold on, Barbara. Let me post this question
and see what my connections have to say."

In this part . . .

There are days when I'm amazed at how small the world is — for instance, when I find out that someone I met randomly while I was 3,000 miles from home is related to a good friend of mine from California. The more you ask around and get involved, the more you realize that all these great connections are out there, just waiting to be discovered. Maybe Kevin Bacon is less than six degrees apart from me. But I digress. . . .

This part covers the essentials of building and growing your network of connections on LinkedIn. I start by talking about how you can search the database far and wide for the person or people you know, and then I tell you how you can send them invitations or use a friend to send an Introduction to someone new. I go through a lot of tips and advice on how to grow your network, using LinkedIn functionality and your own ingenuity. I end the part by talking about one of the great ways to see others and be seen on the site, the LinkedIn Answers section, where you can share and gather knowledge on all sorts of topics.

Chapter 4

Searching LinkedIn

*A*fter you've signed up for LinkedIn and built your profile (see Chapters 2 and 3, respectively, for more on that), it's time to go forth and find connections! As you start searching your own immediate network and your first, second, and third degrees of connection's networks as well, you can see just how valuable LinkedIn can be to you. LinkedIn is the embodiment of the Six Degrees of Separation concept because in most cases you can connect to any other person in the network whether you already know her or not.

In this chapter, I demonstrate the different ways you can search the LinkedIn network. By that, I mean your ever-growing personal network and the greater LinkedIn member network. I talk about viewing your own network, searching within the second and third levels of your network, and performing searches on LinkedIn using different types of criteria or search terms.

Viewing Your Connections

I seem to recall an old saying: "Before you know where you can go, you have to know where you are" or something like that. This holds true even for LinkedIn. Before you start searching throughout the network, it's helpful to understand the reach of your own immediate network and how your first-degree connection's networks add up to keep you connected with a lot of people. The first thing you should do is get familiar with your own LinkedIn network.

To view your LinkedIn network and also some nifty statistics about your network, just follow these steps:

1. **Log in to LinkedIn. From the left navigation menu, click the plus button next to the Contacts link and then click the Connections link.**

   This brings up a list of your current Connections on the Contacts page, as shown in Figure 4-1. You can scroll through the list or click the letter of the alphabet (located along the left side) to go straight to that section of your Connections list.

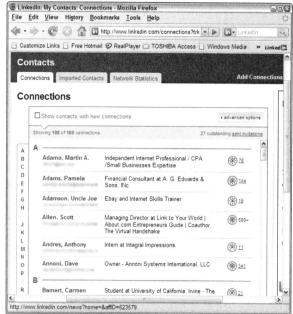

Figure 4-1: An alphabetical list of your connections.

2. **Click the Advanced Options link to filter your list of connections by location or industry.**

   For example, if you click the Advanced Options button, you bring up the two filter drop-down lists (as shown in Figure 4-2): the Filter by Location and Filter by Industry drop-down lists. With these filters, you can display a list of your connections that live in a greater metropolitan area of a certain city or work in a particular industry. The drop-down lists only contain options for people who are your first-level direct contacts. Suppose you're looking for Internet professionals in the Austin, Texas area. LinkedIn can show you who in your network matches that request! If you don't see Austin, TX in the list, that means none of your first-level connections reside in Austin.

Figure 4-2:
Generate
a targeted
list of your
connections
based on
location or
industry.

3. **Click the Network Statistics tab to see the overall summary of your network.**

When you click the Network Statistics tab, you see a page like the one in Figure 4-3. Not only does this have the current count of your Connections, but it shows how many people are considered your second-degree connections (a friend of one of your connections) or third-degree connections (a friend of a friend of your friend) that you can search or reach through an Introduction.

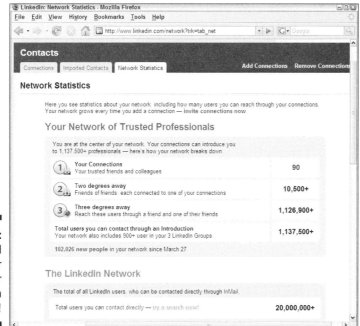

Figure 4-3:
Behold
the power
of your
LinkedIn
network!

4. **Scroll down this page to the Regional Access and Industry Access sections to see a breakdown of where the folks in your network are located and what they do.**

The last two sections on the Network Statistics tab are Regional Access and Industry Access, as shown in Figure 4-4. LinkedIn shows you the percentage breakdown of which regions are the most popular in your network and which industries are represented in your extended network of first-, second-, and third-degree connections.

Figure 4-4:
See the region and industry breakdown of your network.

If you click any of the top five regions or industries on this page, LinkedIn automatically performs a search of your network with that criteria. So, if you want to see your network contacts that live in the greater New York City area, click the Greater New York City Area link in the Regional Access list.

Searching the LinkedIn Network

When you're ready to find a specific person, it's time to get to know the LinkedIn search engine, which allows you to scan the tens of millions of LinkedIn members based on keywords you provide. Currently, you have two main ways to search the network: a basic search and the Advanced Search.

At the top-right corner of every page on LinkedIn, you can find a simple search form. This feature performs a keyword search on the LinkedIn database. Generally, it works just fine if you're searching only for a specific name, employees of a particular company, or people with a specific job title In fact, you'll get a lot of results with the basic search because you're searching each LinkedIn member's entire profile for your keywords, not just one field. For example, if you type **Mike Jones** in the basic search box, as opposed to searching by the name Mike Jones (see the section "Searching by Name" later in this chapter), you get a larger set of results because you will see every profile where the words Mike and Jones were anywhere in the profile. (When you search by Name, LinkedIn will only search everyone's Name field.) Keep this in mind when you do your search, and pick the method you want based on your goals.

Now, in some situations, the simple search just doesn't cut it because you want to specify whether you're searching for someone's name, title, employer, industry, skills, location, or some combination thereof. In those cases, you need the Advanced Search function, which you can access in several ways:

✔ From almost any page on LinkedIn, you can click the link Advanced Search, near the top-right corner of the page, to bring up the search page. If you're using LinkedIn Jobs or LinkedIn Answers, clicking this link brings up the Job Search or Advanced Answers search page, respectively.

✔ You can click the drop-down arrow next to People in the top-left corner of the LinkedIn home page, to bring up links to the Advanced People Search, Name Search, and Reference Search, as shown in Figure 4-5.

✔ If you download one of the toolbars or companion software (as discussed in Chapter 10), you can perform a search from the search box in that toolbar or software program.

The examples in the rest of this chapter assume you are clicking the Advanced Search link from the top right of the page. However, feel free to pick the method of search you're most comfortable with!

Advanced People Search   Advanced Search link

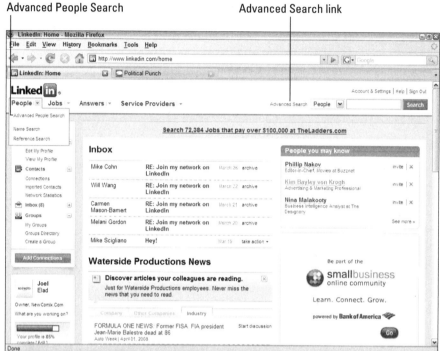

Sorting your advanced search results

Whenever you do an advanced search, LinkedIn defaults to sorting your search results by the keywords you provided in your search. However, that is not your only option. When you're setting up your advanced search, you see an option entitled Sort By with a drop-down list containing four options. (If you've already generated search results, you can click the link refine search results to bring up this option.) You can sort your search results by picking from these four methods:

- ✔ **Degrees and Recommendations:** This sort method gives the top spots on the search result to people who are not only closely connected to you, but people who have received Recommendations from other LinkedIn members. This sort result helps you find the most recommended person who is closely connected to you, as opposed to the Degrees away from you method, which simply shows the closest connected person in terms of degrees of separation.

- ✔ **Degrees away from you:** This sort method shows you the people who are closely connected to you at the top of the list. This is incredibly helpful if you're searching for someone that you plan to contact, because you have a better chance of connecting with someone who is only two or three degrees away from you, in which case you can be introduced by one of your connections.

✔ **Number of connections:** This sort method shows you the people with the greatest number of connections on LinkedIn at the top of the list. This sort result helps you when your search involves looking for someone who needs to have a large network of first-degree connections.

✔ **Keyword relevance:** This sort method is currently the default when you search on LinkedIn, and it simply returns the people whose profiles have the keywords you inputted in your search. Therefore, this sort result may put people at the top of the list who simply have the keywords in their profile multiple times. It gives some weight to members who are featured on LinkedIn, which means they have premium accounts or have OpenLink membership. Typically, the default search results show up under the Your Network tab (which appears directly above the first name in your results list) to get sort results that only contain your first-, second-, or third-degree connections on the list. This search is intended for situations where the keyword is more critical than the person.

Searching by keyword

Quick. Who do you know that knows how to write software code in PHP? Who do you know that enjoys mountain climbing or hiking? Do you know anybody that gives presentations on a regular basis? Well, with LinkedIn's search capabilities, you can find out the answers to these questions, and more, when you search by keyword.

When you search by keyword, LinkedIn analyzes everyone else's profiles to find that matching word. You can put any sort of skill, buzzword, interest, or other keyword that would be present in someone's profile, and see who in your network is a match. To search by keyword, just follow these steps:

1. **While logged in to LinkedIn, click the Advanced Search link at the top right of the page.**

   You're taken to the People page, and the Advanced People Search tab is selected.

2. **Enter the keyword(s) in the Keywords text box provided.**

   In Figure 4-6, you can see that I decided to search for Six Sigma Operations. If you enter multiple keywords like I did, LinkedIn looks for members that have all of the keywords in their profile.

   I recommend tacking on additional search criteria, such as picking one or more industries, location information (country and ZIP/postal code), or perhaps a job title, so you can get a more meaningful search result. Otherwise, your result list will be long and unhelpful.

If you're searching for a specific keyword phrase, like Six Sigma, put those words in quotation marks so LinkedIn will search for the exact phrase. Otherwise, LinkedIn searches each individual word, and you might get a result like mine in Figure 4-7, where I have the words *six* and *Sigma* in different places in my profile. Because LinkedIn found both words in my profile, even though those words didn't appear together in one phrase, I came up on the search results page.

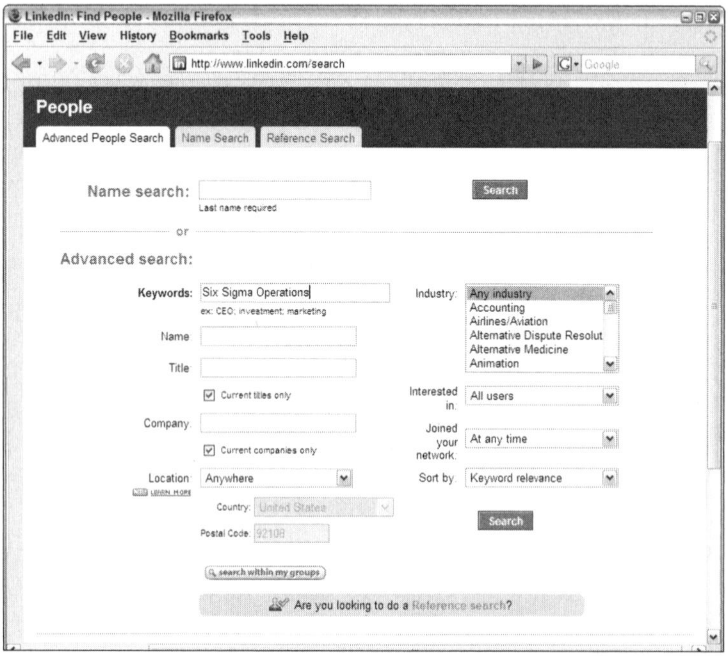

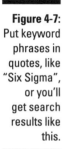

Figure 4-6: Search for people by the keywords in their profile.

Figure 4-7: Put keyword phrases in quotes, like "Six Sigma", or you'll get search results like this.

3. When you're ready, click the blue Search button to start your search.

You see the people in your extended network that have those keywords in their profile.

4. If you want to get better results, click the Refine Search Results button.

The results window expands, and you can enter more information, like additional keywords, job titles, user types, or location information into the boxes provided, as shown in Figure 4-8. When you're finished, click the Search button to run a more precise search that narrows down the list.

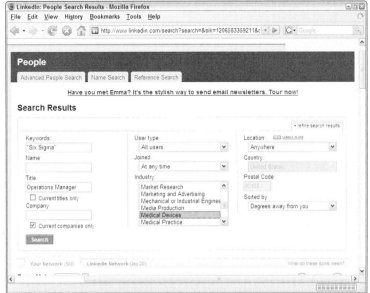

Figure 4-8: Add more information to get a more targeted list of matching people.

Searching by name

When you want to find a specific person on LinkedIn, you can search by name. LinkedIn has developed a special Name Search box that will help you find that person. When you search by name, you are required to enter the last name, and you can enter the first name, too.

When you're ready to search by name, just follow these steps:

1. While logged in to LinkedIn, click the Advanced Search link at the top right of the page.

You're taken to the People page, and the Advanced People Search tab is selected.

2. Click the Name Search tab along the top of the page.

On the Name Search tab, enter the last name (and first name, if you know it) into the text box provided (see Figure 4-9).

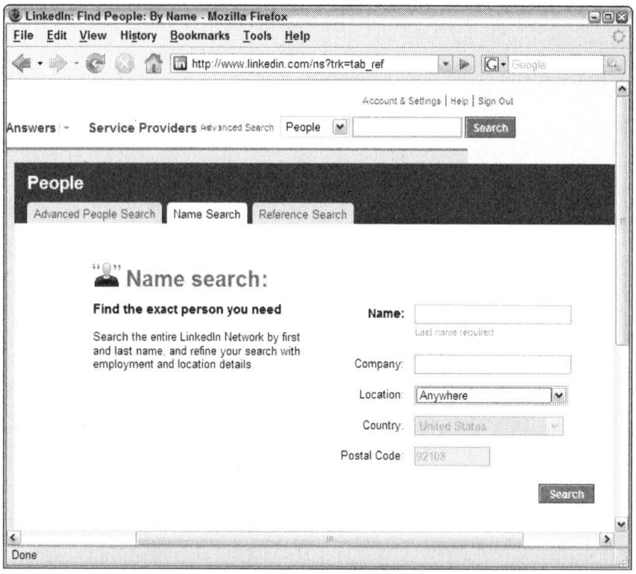

Figure 4-9:
Search
LinkedIn by
someone's
name.

3. **(Optional) You can input additional information to help identify the exact person you're looking for.**

   If you know a company where the person used to work or is currently employed, you can input a company name into the box provided.

4. **If you know the approximate location of this person, use the Location drop-down list to select the Located In or Near option. Then use the Country drop-down list and fill in the Postal Code text box.**

   Only after you select Located In or Near can you pick a country from the next drop-down list and input a ZIP code in the box indicated, as shown in Figure 4-10.

5. **When you're ready, click the Search button.**

   You see a results list of people, sorted by the degrees of connection in your overall LinkedIn network. (For example, people who are second-level connections appear above people who are third-level connections.)

6. **If you want to get better results, click the Refine Search Results button.**

   You can enter a full name, company name, or location information into the boxes provided. Then click the Search button.

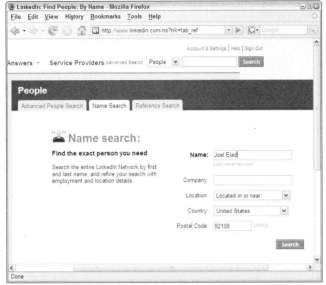

Searching by company

Sometimes, you might need to search by company. Maybe you're thinking of applying to a company, and you want to see who you know (or, rather, who is in your extended network) that works for that company, so you can approach them to ask some questions or get a referral. Perhaps you're looking for a decision maker at a company that can help you with a deal, or you're curious how active a particular company's employees are on LinkedIn.

Whatever the reason, LinkedIn is an excellent place for searching detailed corporate profiles of specific companies. When you're ready to search by company, just follow these steps:

1. **While logged in to LinkedIn, click the Advanced Search link at the top right of the page.**

   You're taken to the People page, and the Advanced People Search tab is selected.

2. **Enter the name of the company in the Company text box provided (as shown in Figure 4-11).**

   If you want to search for only current employees of the company, leave the Current Companies Only check box selected. If you deselect it, your search results will include all the people who have ever worked for that company.

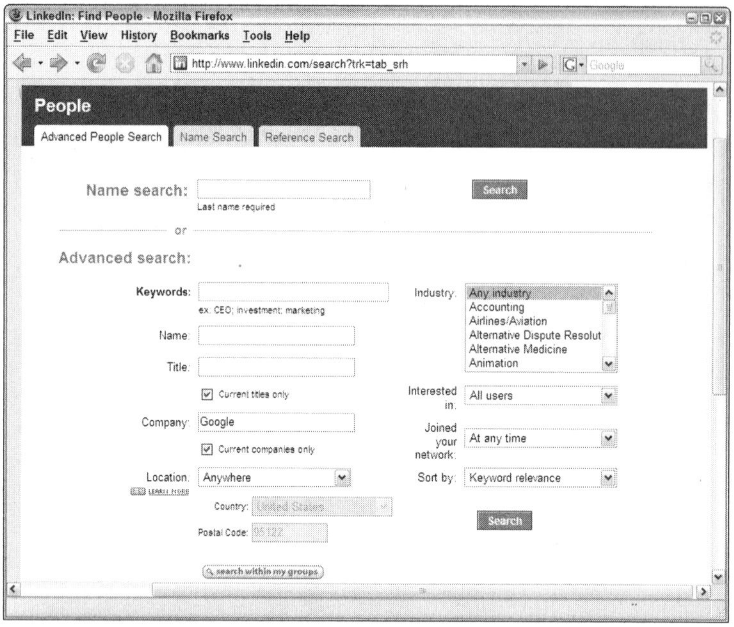

Figure 4-11:
Search
for people
by the
company
where they
work(ed).

3. **Click the Search button to start your search.**

   You see up to 500 results that match your company and exist somewhere in your extended network. (If you have paid for a premium account, you see the first 500 results on this page.)

4. **If you click the LinkedIn Network (Top 20) link, you see a list of the top 20 results within the entire LinkedIn system, as shown in Figure 4-12.**

   Notice that, in this list, you see the person's professional headline, but not the person's name. Because this person is not in your network, her name is private, and you have to send her an InMail to find out her name. (InMail is covered in Chapter 5.)

5. **If you want to get better results, click the Refine Search Results button.**

   You can enter more information, like job titles, user types, or location information into the boxes provided. Click the Search button when you're finished.

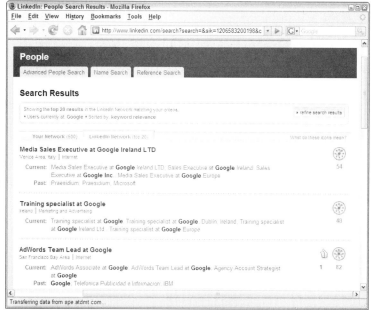

Searching by job title

Sometimes you might need to look for someone in a specific position rather than for a specific person. After all, who knows what you go through better than other people with the same job, right? Who better to give advice on a topic like Search Engine Optimization (SEO) than someone whose job relates to SEO, correct?

Therefore, LinkedIn gives you the ability to search by job title instead of person. When you're ready to search by job title, just follow these steps:

1. **While logged in to LinkedIn, click the Advanced Search link at the top right of the page.**

   You're taken to the People page, and the Advanced People Search tab is selected.

2. **Enter the job title in the Title box provided (Figure 4-13 shows Project Manager entered).**

   If you want to search for only people who currently have that title, leave Current Titles Only check box selected. If you deselect the box, your search results will include all the people who have ever held that job title.

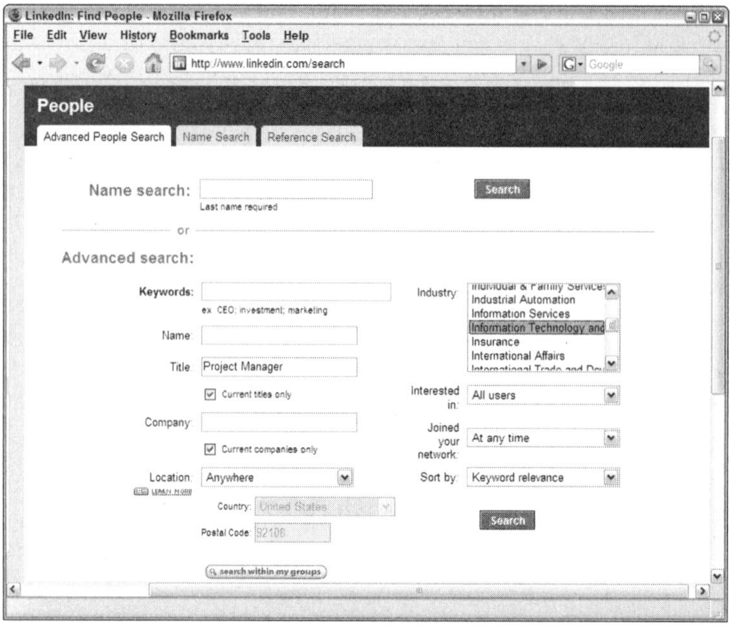

Figure 4-13:
Search for
people by
their current
or previous
job title.

3. **(Optional, but do it anyway if you can) Select at least one Industry from the list provided, so your search results are relevant to the job title search.**

   I highly recommend doing this step. After all, a Project Manager in Construction is completely different from a Project Manager in Computer Software.

   You can actually select multiple industries from the list. On a PC, hold down the Ctrl button and click to select each industry you want to add to your search. On a Mac, hold down the ⌘ button and click to select each industry.

4. **When you're ready, click the Search button to see your results.**

   You see a set of results that match your job title request. You can always click on the Refine Search Results button to add more information and get a highly targeted list.

Performing a Reference search

One of the benefits of LinkedIn is that it allows you to search for someone who might have worked with someone you're researching. Perhaps you're about to hire someone but would like to speak with someone else who knows your potential candidate because they worked together in the past. You could be deciding to hire a consultant for a project but want to contact someone who has hired this consultant in the past, to get a better idea of his work quality. Maybe you're about to enter a business deal and want some information from someone who knows your potential new partner.

LinkedIn has created the Reference search to give you a better window into the person or company. All you need is the company name and the range of years someone has worked there, and LinkedIn searches your network and shows you the people who match that search and how closely they're connected to you.

To perform a Reference search, just follow these steps:

1. **Click the Advanced Search link at the top right of the LinkedIn home page.**

   You're taken to the People page, and the Advanced People Search tab is selected.

2. **Click the Reference Search tab along the top of the page.**

   The Reference Search tab is shown in Figure 4-14.

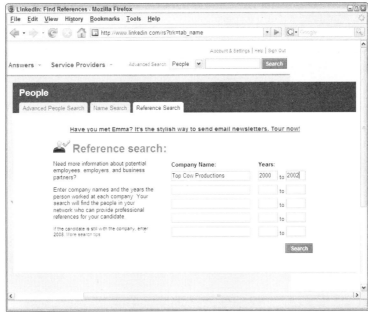

Figure 4-14: Search LinkedIn for potential references for someone.

3. **Enter the name of the company and a date range into the boxes provided.**

   For example, suppose you have a job candidate who claims to have worked for Top Cow Productions from 2000 to 2002. You would enter that company name and date range into the boxes provided.

You can enter more than one company and date range, and you will get a list of potential references who worked at any of the companies on your search.

4. **When you're ready, click the Search button to start your search.**

If you have the basic account, you see a Summary page like the one shown in Figure 4-15. This gives you an idea of how many potential connections exist and how many are connected to your immediate network. If you have a Business or Pro account, you would see a list of people (like in a name or job title search) that worked at the designated company in that timeframe and have the ability to contact them. (For more on the different account types, take a gander at Chapter 1.)

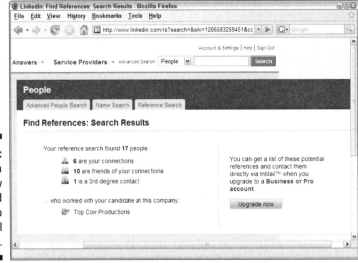

Figure 4-15:
Get an idea of how connected you are to potential references.

Chapter 5

Managing Introductions and InMail

*O*ne of the goals of using LinkedIn is to expand your personal network and of friends and colleagues by seeing who is connected to you at each degree level. When you can see your second and third degree of your network, your next goal is to start interacting with these people and see how they might fit into your network, goals, or ambitions. However, the whole system of contacting people requires some order and decorum (otherwise, nobody would feel comfortable signing up for the site in the first place). Therefore, LinkedIn offers two methods for meeting and connecting with people outside your immediate network: Introductions and InMail. Not so coincidentally, I cover Introductions and InMail in this very chapter.

Introductions are simply where you ask to be introduced to a friend of a friend, and your friend can decide whether or not to pass along your Introduction to the intended target. InMail allows you to directly communicate with anyone in the LinkedIn network through a private LinkedIn message. I also cover what to do when you get a request from a connection on LinkedIn.

InMail versus Introductions

Your first question is, most likely, "What's the difference between Introductions and InMail?" (Figure 5-1 shows an example of both.) The answer depends on how involved your common friend or colleague is in connecting you with this new contact.

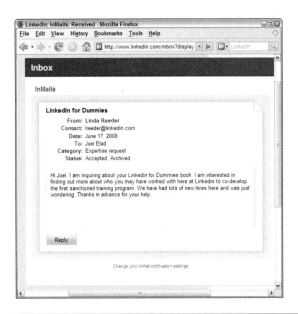

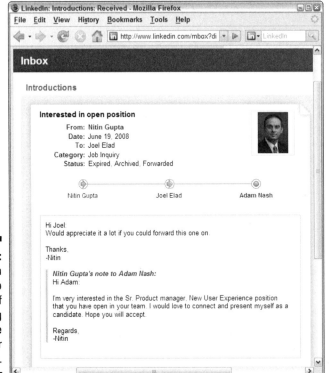

Figure 5-1:
LinkedIn
offers two
ways of
connecting
with people
outside your
network.

Every LinkedIn user decides on his own contact level, and it's possible for a user to not allow any Introduction or InMail to reach him, regardless of sender. If you don't want to receive any Introductions or InMail, simply deselect all the Contact Settings options. (See Chapter 3 for the section on checking your contact Settings.) If you don't want any InMail, go to the Account & Settings page, find the Contact Settings section, and unselect the InMail option.

Understanding Introductions

In the real world, if you're at a party with your friend Michael, you might say to him, "You know, I'd really like to meet someone who can help me with some software tasks for my company." In that case, Michael would look around, see his other friend James, and he would introduce you to James by saying, "Hello, James. This is my entrepreneur friend from business school, [Your Name Here]. [Your Name Here], this is my old buddy James. He and I studied computer science together in college." After that, Michael might give some more background information about each person to the other.

On LinkedIn, an *Introduction* is very similar to my real-world example. You send a request to someone in your immediate first-degree network (Michael) and ask that person to introduce you to someone in his or her network (James) by forwarding your request to the intended party. In some cases, if you're trying to reach someone in your third-degree network (maybe James has a programming buddy you should talk to), your Introduction request would have to go to two different parties before reaching the intended recipient.

Here are some benefits of using Introductions:

- ✔ **You're represented by someone close.** Instead of sending a random, unexpected e-mail to a stranger, you're introduced by somebody who knows the intended party, even if that introduction is done with an e-mail. That gives your Introduction request a much higher chance of being read and getting a response.

- ✔ **You get your network involved.** When you ask people in your network to get involved, they learn more about you and your intentions, and sometimes you might find what you're looking for is closer than you think. In addition, when you ask them to pass along your Introduction request, you can offer to facilitate an Introduction on their behalf as well, which helps both parties.

- ✔ **You leverage the power of your network.** By using LinkedIn, you not only expand your network by using your first-degree connections to help you meet new people, but you can decide who would make the Introduction for you. I recommend that you read up on your friend's profile and your intended party's profile and see what they have in common.

✔ **You can have multiple Introductions going on at one time.** With a LinkedIn free account, you can have up to five open Introductions going at any one time. When you get introduced to your intended party, that spot opens up and you can make another Introduction request. InMail, in all cases, costs money, either on a per-mail basis or as part of a premium paid account. (So even someone with a free basic account can use InMail, for a cost.)

Getting to know InMail

Because everyone on LinkedIn has a profile and a secure e-mail Inbox within LinkedIn, communicating with other people online is easy. LinkedIn allows you to send InMail directly to an intended party, regardless of whether he is directly or indirectly connected with you. The e-mail gets immediately delivered to the recipient's e-mail address and LinkedIn Inbox, without the sender learning of this address, so each party has some privacy. The recipient can read your profile and decide whether or not to respond.

The cost of using InMail depends on whether you subscribe to a premium account. You can purchase InMail credits (one credit allows you to send one message) at a cost of $10 per InMail message. Premium accounts, such as the Business account for $19.99/month, come with a set number of InMail credits per month that roll over to the next month if unused. The Business account gets 3 credits per month, the Business Plus account gets 10 credits per month, and the Pro account gets 50 credits per month.

Here are some benefits of using InMail:

✔ **Instant delivery.** With InMail, you simply write your message or request and send it directly to the intended party. There's no delay as a request gets passed from person to person and waits for approval or forwarding.

✔ **You owe no favors.** Sometimes, you just want to reach somebody without asking your friends to vouch for you. InMail allows you to send a request to someone new without involving anyone else.

✔ **It's sure to be delivered.** With Introductions, the party(ies) involved in the middle could choose to deny your request and not pass along the message. With InMail, you know that the intended party will get a copy of your message in his or her e-mail account and LinkedIn Inbox.

Setting Up an Introduction

When you want to bring two (or more) parties together, you usually need to apply some thought to the process, whether it's figuring out what both parties have in common, thinking up the words you'll use to introduce party A to party B, or coming up with the timing of exactly when and where you plan to make the Introduction. On LinkedIn, you should do your best to make sure the Introduction process goes smoothly — but don't worry, there's not nearly as much social pressure. The following sections give you tips and pointers for setting up an Introduction.

Approaching each party in the Introduction

When you want to send out an Introduction request, spend some time planning out your request before you log on to LinkedIn to generate and send it. Preparing a quality and proper Introduction goes a long way towards keeping your network in a helpful and enthusiastic mood, and it increases your chances of making a new and valuable connection.

You need to prepare two messages: one for your intended recipient and one for your connection/friend. Each of these messages needs to perform a specific objective. Start with the message to your friend and keep the following tips in mind when you're writing it:

- ✔ **Be honest and upfront.** Say exactly what you hope to achieve so there are no surprises. If you tell your friend that you're hoping her contact will be a new bowling buddy for you, but when you reach that contact, you ask for funding for your new business plan, then you're in trouble. Your friend will probably never forward another request again, and the contact, who expected one type of interaction and got another, will see you as untrustworthy and be unlikely and/or unwilling to help on this request or any in the future.

- ✔ **Be polite and courteous.** Remember, you're asking your friend to vouch for you or back you up when your request goes to the intended party. So be polite when making your request and show your gratitude regardless of the outcome.

- ✔ **Be ready to give in order to get.** One of the best ways to go far with your network is to offer some sort of reciprocal favor when you want someone to do a favor for you. Perhaps you can introduce your friend to one of your other contacts in exchange for your friend accepting your Introduction request.

✔ **Be patient.** Although you may be eager and under a deadline, your friends probably operate on different schedules and different levels of urgency. Some people are online all the time, other people log in to LinkedIn infrequently, and most people are completely disconnected at times, like when they're on vacation or behind on a project. Asking your friend every 20 minutes whether she forwarded your request is an almost sure-fire way of getting that request bounced back to you.

When writing your message to your intended recipient, keep these tips in mind:

✔ **Be honest and upfront.** Just like with your friend, when you have a specific goal or request in mind, make it known in the message. The recipient is most likely busy and doesn't know you, so if he spends the time to talk to you and finds out that you have an ulterior motive, he feels like his time was wasted and that he was deceived, which are NOT good feelings to create when trying to get help from someone.

✔ **Be succinct.** You're asking someone for his time, resources, or advice, so don't beat around the bush too much. You should introduce yourself in your first sentence or two. Then you should explain why you're contacting the recipient and how you hope he can help you.

✔ **Be original.** If you stick to the sample text that LinkedIn gives you, your message has an air of "Hey, I want to talk to you, but I don't have a few seconds to really tell you what I'm after." When you customize your message, you have a greater chance of capturing the other person's attention. If your intended recipient gets a lot of requests, you'll stand out if you show some effort to rise above the daily noise this person encounters.

✔ **Be ready to give in order to get.** You're asking for help of some sort, so be ready to give something, whether it's gratitude, a reciprocal favor, or something more tangible. Most people are eager to help out, especially when they understand the situation, but having something to offer in exchange rarely hurts. Explain how you might provide something useful in return.

Sending an Introduction

When you've prepared your messages (one to your contact and one to the recipient) and you're all ready to send an Introduction request, just follow these steps:

1. **While logged in to LinkedIn, search for the person you'd like to meet.**

   You can use the Search box in the top-right corner of any LinkedIn page, or you can click on your Connections and search your friend's networks. (See Chapter 4 for the lowdown on searching LinkedIn.)

2. **From the list of search results, click the name of the person you want to contact. (If you didn't find the person you're looking for, try another search.)**

   This step takes you to the recipient's profile page, where you should see two things: a chart along the right side of the page showing how you're connected to this person and a link entitled Get Introduced through a Connection. (If you don't have anyone in your network yet, you won't see the chart or the link.)

   Suppose I'm hoping to be introduced to Patrick Crane, VP of Marketing & Advertising over at LinkedIn. When I get to Patrick's profile page, I see that I have a connection to him (see Figure 5-2) in the form of an old high school buddy who now works with Patrick at LinkedIn.

Get Introduced through a Connection link.

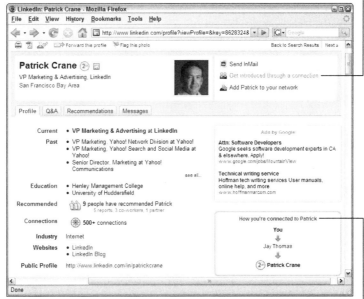

Figure 5-2:
See how you're connected to your intended recipient via LinkedIn!

This tells you how you're connected to your recipient.

3. **On the person's profile page, click the Get Introduced through a Connection link to start the Introduction process.**

   You're taken to the Request an Introduction page, as shown in Figure 5-3. Fill out the contact information section that you would like to share with this individual. Then pick a category and subject for this request. Write a short but informative message as to why you want to meet this person. (See the preceding section, "Approaching each party," for more about writing this message.)

4. **Scroll down and add a message for the person who will be passing on your Introduction.**

   It's required to add a note here (see Figure 5-4), so the facilitator (the person who receives this Introduction request from you) knows why you want to reach the other party. After all, this facilitator is going to vouch for you when he sends this request to the intended party, so the more information you give, the better. (See the preceding section, "Approaching each party," for more about writing this message.)

5. **Click the Send button to send the request.**

   You see a green confirmation message as you're taken back to your main LinkedIn page, and your first-degree connection will receive this Introduction request in his LinkedIn Inbox.

   After that, your facilitator friend will accept or decline your request, and you'll get a notification about the facilitator's decision.

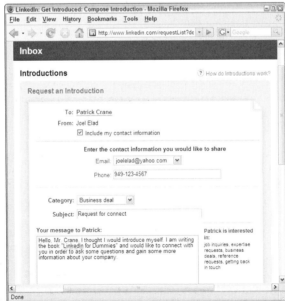

Figure 5-3:
Fill out the
Request
for an
Introduction
form . . .

Figure 5-4:
. . . and tell
your friend
why you're
requesting
an Intro-
duction.

You may want to send an e-mail to your facilitator friend first before starting the Request for Introduction, especially if you think he may not want to forward your request or the intended recipient may be too busy to receive an Introduction request.

Sending InMail

If you're looking to connect with someone right away and you don't have an immediate or secondary connection with someone, you can use a LinkedIn feature called InMail to send a message directly to another LinkedIn member without anyone else getting involved.

This feature is currently available to paid members of LinkedIn who have InMail credits available. If you're using a free account, you would have to pay for individual InMail credits to reach other members through InMail. Consult the LinkedIn Help section for more information (http://linkedin.custhelp.com/).

InMail is basically a private e-mail message that enables you to reach other members, but it protects those members' privacy and e-mail address information. If your message is accepted, you will see the other party's name and e-mail address, and you can communicate further. (In some cases, you see only the other person's professional headline first, and then you see the person's name after he or she accepts the InMail message)

When you're ready to send someone an InMail, just follow these steps:

1. **While logged in to LinkedIn, search for the person you'd like to meet.**

   You can use the Search box in the top-right corner of any LinkedIn page, or you can click on your Connections and search your friend's networks. (Chapter 4 has all sorts of details for you about searching LinkedIn.)

2. **From the list of search results, click the name of the person you want to contact. (If you didn't find the person you're looking for, try another search.)**

   You're taken to the person's profile page.

3. **Click the link that says Send InMail.**

   For example, suppose that I want to connect with Lynn Dralle, the Queen of Auctions, who can not only teach you how to sell on eBay, but sells over $100,000 a year in antiques and collectibles herself. When I look at her profile (see Figure 5-5), I see the Send InMail link, which means she is open to receiving InMail. I would click the Send InMail link to send her a message.

   Now you can start filling out the Compose Your Message form.

4. **Select or deselect the Include My Contact Information check box, depending on your preference.**

   You're asked whether to provide contact information that your recipient can use to contact you, in the form of e-mail and/or a phone number. Simply select the Include My Contact Information check box (as shown in Figure 5-6) if you want to send contact information.

Send InMail link

Figure 5-5:
Find the person who you want to contact and click Send InMail.

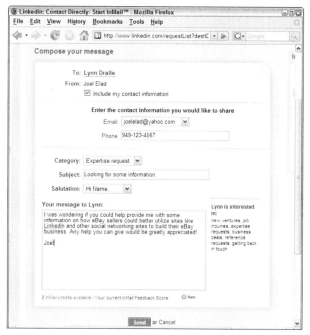

Figure 5-6:
Compose
your InMail
message.

5. **Complete the Category, Subject, and Salutation fields and then enter a message in the box provided.**

   Your Salutation options are these: Dear Name, Hi Name, Name, or no salutation. As with an Introduction, keep your message focused on why you would like to talk with this person, and/or what information you were hoping to exchange. (The earlier section, "Approaching each party in the Introduction," contains advice about writing to an intended recipient that applies to InMail messages as well.) If you look at Figure 5-6, you can see how many InMail credits you have — you need at least one to send this message.

6. **When you're ready, click the Send button to send off your InMail.**

   Your recipient receives this InMail in his LinkedIn Inbox and can decide whether to accept it. If your message is accepted, it's up to the recipient to contact you in return. Be patient. While you're waiting, I recommend a game of Connect Four or Internet Chess.

Managing Introduction Requests

What if someone in your network is looking for your help to meet someone in your network? You can facilitate the introduction between your LinkedIn first-degree connections. Now that your reputation is on the line too, you should spend some time thinking about and processing any and all Introduction requests that come your way.

You really have only two options for handling an Introduction request:

✔ Accept it and forward it on to the party it's intended for.

✔ Decline it (politely!).

I cover these two options in more detail in the following sections.

However you decide to handle the request, keep these tips in mind:

✔ **Act or reply quickly.** The reason LinkedIn works so well is that people are active with their networks and build upon their profile by answering questions, meeting new people, or joining groups. When you get an Introduction request, you should either act on it or respond to the person with the reason why you won't act on it. Ignoring it is not a productive use of the LinkedIn system and makes you look very unprofessional.

✔ **Don't be afraid to ask for clarification.** Sometimes you might need someone to remind you exactly how you're connected with her. Hopefully, in the note you get from this person, she includes some reminder or thought that helps you place her. If not, don't be afraid to shoot back a message and ask for clarification or a gentle reminder.

✔ **Read your friend's request before forwarding.** Chances are good that the person to whom you forward this request might come back to you and ask, "Hey, why did I get this?" or "What do you really think about this person?" If you don't know the details of your friend's request, the intended party may think you're a quick rubber-stamper who sends stuff off without offering to screen anything, and that lowers this person's impression of you.

Accepting requests and forwarding the Introduction

When you're ready to accept your friend's request and forward her Introduction, follow these steps:

1. **Click the plus (+) sign next to the Inbox link in the left navigation menu.**

    This expands your Inbox options, allowing you to go straight to your Messages, InMail, Introductions, Invitations, and so on.

2. **Click the Introductions link to see your requests.**

   This brings up your Introductions page, as shown in Figure 5-7. Here you can see Introduction requests from fellow members (Received Introductions), as well as the results from Introductions you have requested yourself (Sent Introductions).

   In Figure 5-7, you can see some little flags. A small yellow flag means the message hasn't been addressed yet.

3. **In the Subject column, click the link of the request you're evaluating.**

   In this example, I clicked Hello! from David Nakayama, a friend of mine who's a comic book artist. Doing so brings up the Introduction request, as shown in Figure 5-8.

   Read the full text before acting on the request. Don't just skim it — you might miss an important detail.

4. **If you accept the request, click the Forward Introduction button.**

   A new window opens where you can compose your message to the recipient, as shown in Figure 5-9. The text box in the middle contains the note from your friend to you, which you can supplement with a note to the intended recipient. Be sure to add your own comments, like I did in Figure 5-9, to help connect the two people properly.

5. **Click the Forward Message button to send the request.**

Figure 5-7: See your Introduction requests in one place.

Figure 5-8:
Read the
Introduction
request
from your
contact.

Figure 5-9:
Compose a
message to
send to the
intended
recipient.

In this case, Joe Benitez will get the Introduction request from me on behalf of David Nakayama. David will never see Joe's direct e-mail address, and Joe can decide whether or not to reach out to David and form a connection.

Gracefully declining requests

There may come a point when you receive an Introduction request that you just don't feel comfortable sending on to the recipient. Perhaps you don't know enough about your contact who made the request, or you're unclear about that person's true motivations. Or maybe your connection with the recipient isn't at the stage where you feel you can introduce other people to this person.

Whatever the reason, the best response is simply to gracefully decline the request. Here are some tips on how to respond:

- ✔ **It's not you, it's me.** The most common way to decline is to simply inform the initial contact that you're not that deeply connected with the intended recipient, and you really don't feel comfortable passing on a request to someone who isn't a strong contact. Often, you might have first-degree connections in your network that are "weak links" or people who you're acquainted with but aren't particularly close to or tight with.

- ✔ **The recipient doesn't respond well to this approach.** You can respond that you know the intended recipient, and you know what she's going to say, either from past requests or other experiences with that person. Because you know or feel that the intended recipient wouldn't be interested, you would rather not waste anyone's time in sending on the request.

- ✔ **I just don't feel comfortable passing the request along.** It's best to be honest and simply state that you don't feel right passing on the request you've received. After all, if the original contact doesn't understand your hesitation, he'll probably keep asking, and LinkedIn will want you to follow up on any unresolved Introduction. Just as in life, honesty is usually the best policy.

- ✔ **I think your request needs work.** Because you're vouching for this person, you don't want to pass along a shoddy or questionable request that could reflect badly on you. In this case, simply respond that you think the request needs to be reworded or clarified, and offer concrete suggestions on what should be said as well as what requests you feel comfortable forwarding.

When you're ready to decline the request, follow these steps:

1. **Click the + sign next to the Inbox link in the left navigation menu.**

   More links show up under the Inbox link.

2. **Click the Introductions link and then click the subject line of the request.**

   You see the Introduction request.

3. **Click the Decline to Forward button.**

   The Not Interested in Forwarding page appears, as shown in Figure 5-10.

4. **Pick a reason for not forwarding the request, or click the Other option and write a message why you're declining to forward.**

   If you pick any of the main options, like "I know X, and this message is not a good fit," you don't have to provide any additional message. Unless one of these options really states your case, you should probably select Other and write a custom message (or send a separate e-mail message giving more information).

5. **Click the Send button to decline the request.**

   The original contact receives an e-mail and a message in his LinkedIn inbox.

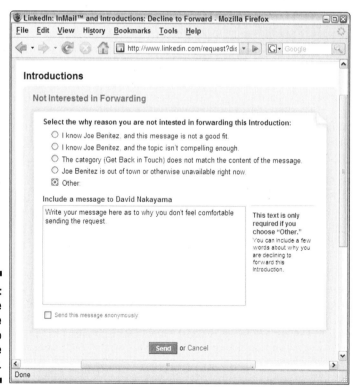

Figure 5-10:
Describe why you're declining to forward the request.

Chapter 6

Growing Your Network

*M*aybe by now you've signed onto LinkedIn, created your profile, searched through the network, and started inviting people to connect to you, and you're wondering, what's next? You certainly shouldn't be sitting around on your hands, waiting for responses to your Invitations. LinkedIn is designed to open doors to opportunities using the professional relationships you already have (and, with luck, by creating new ones). The best use of it, therefore, is to capture as much of your professional network as possible in the form of first-degree connections to your LinkedIn network so that you can discover those inside leads, as well as those friends of friends who can help you out.

In this chapter, I discuss how you can grow your LinkedIn network. You find out some guidelines to keep in mind when growing your network. I also cover various search tools for you to use to stay on top of LinkedIn's growing membership and how others may relate to you.

Of course, to expand your network, you need to know how to send Invitations, as well as how to attract LinkedIn members and your contacts who haven't yet taken the plunge into LinkedIn membership, so you find all that out here, too. And finally, this chapter helps you deal with the etiquette of accepting or declining Invitations that you receive, and shows you how to remove connections that you no longer want to keep in your network.

Building a Meaningful Network

When you build a house, you start with some blueprints. When you start an organization, you usually have some sort of mission statement or guiding principles. Likewise, when you start to grow your LinkedIn network, you should keep in mind some of the keys to having and growing your own professional network. These guiding principles will help you make decisions regarding whom to invite to your network, whom to search for and introduce yourself to, and how much time to spend on LinkedIn.

You may have heard of the highly popular social networking sites such as Facebook and MySpace. LinkedIn is different from these sites because it focuses on business networking in a professional manner, rather than encourage users to post pictures of their latest beach party. The best use of LinkedIn involves maintaining a professional network of connections, not sending someone a Super Hug.

That said, there is a lot of variety in the types of networks that people maintain on LinkedIn, and much of that has to do with each person's definition of a meaningful network. Some of the key elements of a "meaningful" network are the following:

✔ **Quality versus quantity:** As mentioned in Chapter 1, some people use LinkedIn with the goal of gaining the highest number of connections possible, thereby emphasizing quantity over the quality of their LinkedIn connections. Those people are typically referred to as LinkedIn Open Networkers, or LIONs. At the other end of the spectrum are people who use LinkedIn only to keep their closest, most tightly knit connections together without striving to enlarge their network. Most people fall somewhere in between these two aims, and the question of whether you're after quality or quantity is something to keep in mind every time you look to invite someone. LinkedIn strongly recommends that you should connect only with people you know, so its advice is to stick to quality connections. Here are some questions to ask yourself to help you figure out your purpose:

  • Are you looking to manage a network of *only* people you personally know?

  • Are you looking to manage a network of people you know or who might help you find new opportunities in a specific industry?

  • Are you looking to maximize your chances of being able to reach someone with a new opportunity or job offering, regardless of personal interaction?

✔ **Depth versus breadth:** Some people want to focus on building a network of only the most relevant or new connections — people from their current job or industry who could play a role in one's professional development in that particular industry. Other people like to include a wide diversity of connections that include anyone they have ever professionally interacted with, whether through work, education, or any kind of group or association, in hopes that anyone who knows them at all can potentially lead to future opportunities. For these LinkedIn users, it doesn't matter that most of the people in their network don't know 99 percent of their other connections. Most people fall somewhere in between these two poles, but lean toward including more people in their network. Here are some questions to keep in mind regarding this question:

- Are you looking to build or maintain a specific in-depth network of thought leaders regarding one topic, job, or industry?

- Are you looking to build a broad network of connections who can help you with different aspects of your career or professional life?

- Do you want to add only people to your network who may offer an immediate benefit to some aspect of your professional life, or are you looking to add a professional contact now and figure out later how that person might fit with your long-term goals?

✔ **Strong versus weak link:** I'm not referring to the game show "The Weakest Link" but rather to the strength of your connection with someone. Beyond the issue of quality versus quantity, you'll want to keep differing levels of quality in mind. Some people invite someone after meeting them once at a cocktail party, hoping to strengthen the link as time goes on. Others work to create strong links first and then invite those people to connect on LinkedIn afterward. This issue comes down to how much you want LinkedIn itself to play a role in your business network's development, meaning, do you see your LinkedIn network as a work in progress or as a virtual room in which to gather only your closest allies? Here are some questions to keep in mind:

- What level of interaction needs to have occurred for you to feel comfortable asking someone to connect to you on LinkedIn? A face-to-face meeting? Phone conversations only? A stream of e-mails?

- What length of time do you need to know someone before you feel that you can connect to him or her? Or, does time matter less if you have had a high-quality interaction just once?

- Does membership in a specific group or association count as a good enough reference for you to add someone to your network? (For example, if you've met someone only briefly once, but he or she is an alumnus of your school, does that tie serve as a sufficient reference?)

✔ **Specific versus general goals:** Some people like to maintain a strong network of people mainly to talk about work and job-related issues. Other people like to discuss all matters relating to their network, whether it's professional, personal, or social. Most people fall somewhere in between, and herein lies what I mean by the "purpose" of your network. Do you want to simply catalog your entire network, regardless of industry, because LinkedIn will act as your complete contact management system and because you can use LinkedIn to reach different parts of your network at varying times? Or do you want to focus your LinkedIn network on a specific goal, using your profile to attract and retain the "right kind" of contact that furthers that goal? Here are some more questions to ask yourself:

- Do you have any requirements in mind for someone before you add them to your network? That is, are you looking to invite only people with certain qualities or experience?

- Does the way you know or met someone influence your decision to connect to that person on LinkedIn?

- What information do you need to know about someone before you want to add them to your network?

By the way, this has not been a quiz — there is no one right answer to any of these questions. It's totally up to you to decide what you want to accomplish through your LinkedIn network, and how you want to go from there. Also keep in mind that although you may start LinkedIn with one goal in mind, as with most other things in life, your usage and experience may shift you to a different way of using the site. If that happens, just go with it, as long as it fits with your current goals.

Understanding Linking Strategies

After you've established why you want to link to other people, you can start looking for and reaching out to those people. In this section, I point you to a number of linking strategies that can help you reach your goals for your network. When you started on LinkedIn, completing your profile helped you get your first round of connections, and you were prompted to enter whatever names you could remember to offer an Invitation for them to connect with you. Now you're ready to generate your next round of connections, and to get into the habit of making this a continual process as you use the site.

Checking for new LinkedIn members

When you fill out your LinkedIn profile, you create a the opportunity to check for colleagues and classmates, as well as to import any potential contact and invite that person to connect with you and stay in touch using LinkedIn. However, that search happens only after you define your profile (and when you update or add to your profile). After that, it's up to you to routinely check the LinkedIn network to see whether there are new members on the site who may want to connect with you or with whom you might want to connect. Fortunately, LinkedIn provides a few tools that help you quickly scan the system to see whether a recently joined member is a past colleague or classmate of yours. In addition, it never hurts to use your friends to check for new members, as I discuss in a little bit.

Every time you send an Invitation to someone, you may see one of the following functions pop up automatically. Feel free to click the link and take advantage of the reminder to keep your network current.

Finding newly added colleagues

If you've worked at least one job in a medium-size or large company, you're probably familiar with the concept of the farewell lunch. The staff goes out to lunch, reminiscences about the good old days, and wishes the departing employee well as that person gives out his or her e-mail address, phone number, and says to keep in touch. But as time goes on, jobs change, people move around, and it's easy to lose touch with that co-worker. Thankfully, LinkedIn allows you to stay connected regardless of moves.

Sometimes people you've fallen out of contact with have joined LinkedIn since the last time you checked, so it's important to do an occasional search to see whether you know any newly added colleagues.

When you want to do a search for newly added colleagues (and add them to your network, if you choose), just follow these steps:

1. **While logged in to your LinkedIn account, click the Add Connections button below the left navigation menu.**

   The Add Connections window opens.

2. **Click the Colleagues tab below the Add Connections blue title bar.**

   The Colleagues window, shown in Figure 6-1, appears.

3. **Pick an employer (current or past) from the list presented.**

   If you've previously looked over the list of colleagues for an employer, two buttons are available: Find New and View All. To check for just the latest additions, you want to click the yellow Find New button, as I've done under NewComix.com in Figure 6-1. If you have never checked an employer's list, only one button is available for you to click, as Figure 6-1 shows under Waterside Productions. Clicking the View All Waterside Productions link brings up the new colleagues list shown in Figure 6-2.

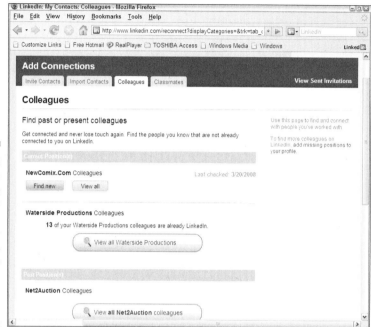

Figure 6-1:
The Colleagues window shows you whether any of your former colleagues are on LinkedIn.

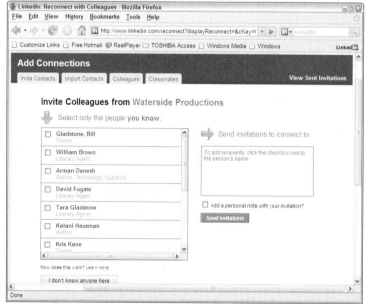

Figure 6-2:
A list of former colleagues who are now on LinkedIn.

4. **Go through the list of names and see if there is anyone you recognize or wish to connect with on LinkedIn.**

   You can click a name to see the person's profile for more information. If you see someone you want to invite to your network, select the check box next to the person's name, and it should appear in the right window, as shown in Figure 6-3.

Figure 6-3: Invite one or more colleagues to your network.

   I encourage you to select the Add a Personal Note to Your Invitation? check box and add some text to help the contact remember who you are.

5. **After you've finished selecting the names, click the blue Send Invitations button.**

   Each person on your list will receive an Invitation to join your network. If you don't know or want to invite anyone on the list, click the gray I Don't Know Anyone Here button to cancel the entire process. You'll see up to 50 names; if you don't see any company names on this page, it's because you didn't add any companies to your profile.

Finding newly added classmates

No matter how much time goes by since my graduation from college, I still remember my school years well. I met a lot of cool and interesting people, folks I wanted to stay in contact with because of common goals, interests, or experiences. As time progressed and people moved on to new lives after graduation, it was all too easy to lose touch and not be able to reconnect.

Through LinkedIn, though, you can reconnect with them and maintain that tie through your network, no matter where anyone moves on to. For you to find them to begin with, of course, your former classmates have to properly list their dates of receiving education. And, just as with the search for former colleagues, it's important to do an occasional search to see what classmates of yours have recently joined LinkedIn.

1. **While logged in to your LinkedIn account, click the green Add Connections button below your left navigation menu.**

    The Add Connections window opens.

2. **Click the Classmates tab.**

    The Classmates window appears, as shown in Figure 6-4. If it is blank, that is because you have not yet added any education entries to your profile.

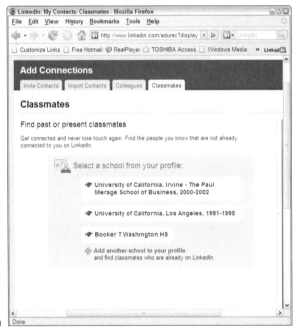

Figure 6-4: The schools you identified in your profile appear in the Classmates window.

3. **Look over the list of schools and click the name of the one you attended.**

    Clicking the list brings up a list of potential classmates, as shown in Figure 6-5.

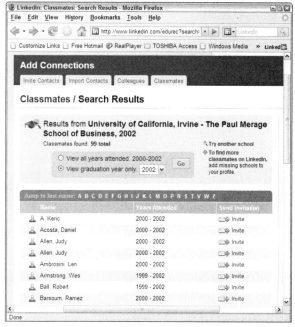

Figure 6-5:
Finding
former
classmates
on LinkedIn.

4. Go through the list of names to see whether you find someone you want to add to your network.

You can view this list by graduation year only (which means you see only people who graduated the same year as you) or you can switch the view to all the years you attended the school by clicking that radio button. When you find someone, click the Invite link that's on the same line as the person's name (and appears in the Send Invitation column) to bring up an Invitation for that person, as shown in Figure 6-6.

Before you invite people, click their name to read their profiles and see what they've been doing. Why ask them what they've been doing when you can read it for yourself? By doing your homework first, your Invitation will sound more natural and be more likely to be accepted.

5. Write up a personal Invitation (using the one in Figure 6-6 as an example, if you need some ideas) and click the blue Send Invitation button.

Your Invitation is sent and a page appears like the one shown in Figure 6-7. If you want to invite more classmates, simply click the yellow Find Classmates button and repeat Steps 3 and 4.

I cover more about sending invitations later in this chapter, in the "Sending Connection Requests" section.

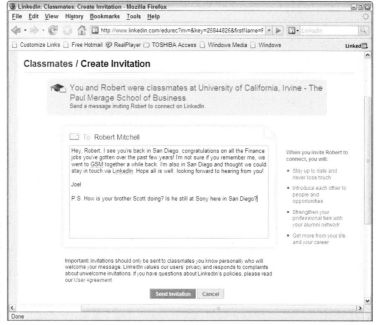

Figure 6-6:
Invite an old classmate to network with you!

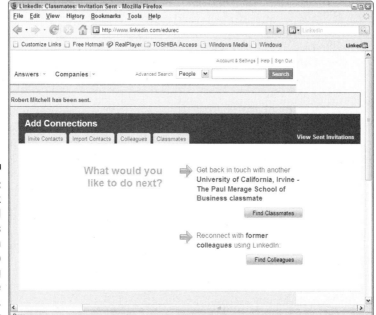

Figure 6-7:
Click the Find Classmates button to keep searching for more people.

There's another way to keep on top of newly added colleagues and class-mates. When you go to your LinkedIn home page, you can find a section enti-tled Just Joined LinkedIn. This section tells you how many new colleagues and classmates have joined LinkedIn since the last time you logged on to the site. You can click the link to view the names of these people.

Browsing your connections' networks

Although it's helpful for LinkedIn to help you search the network, sometimes nothing gives as good results as some good old-fashioned investigation. From time to time, I like to browse the network of one of my first-degree connec-tions to see whether he or she has a contact that should be a part of my net-work. I don't recommend spending a lot of your time this way, but a "spot check" by picking a few friends at random can yield some nice results.

Why is this type of research effective? Lots of reasons, including these:

- ✔ **You travel in the same circles.** If someone is a part of your network, you know that person from a past experience, whether you worked together, learned together, spoke at a conference together, or lived next door to each other. Whatever that experience was, you and this contact spent time with other people, so chances are you will have shared connections or, better yet, you will find people in that person's network who need to be a part of your network.

- ✔ **You may find someone newly connected.** Say that you've already spent some time searching all your undergraduate alumni contacts and adding as many people as you could find. As time passes, someone new may connect to one of your friends.

    One effective way to keep updated about who your connections have recently added is to review your Network Updates (which I discuss back in Chapter 1).

- ✔ **You may recognize someone whose name you didn't fully remember.** Many of us have that contact whom we feel we know well, have fun talk-ing to, and really trust, but for some reason, we can't remember that person's last name. Then, for some reason, when you search a common contact's network and see the temporarily forgotten name and job title, you suddenly remember. Now you can invite that person to join your network. Another common experience is seeing a the name and job title of a contact whose last name changed after she got married and you knew her only from her former name and chosen profession.

- ✔ **You may see someone you've wanted to get to know better.** Have you ever watched a friend talking to someone whom you wanted to add to your network? Maybe your friend already introduced you, so the other person knows your name, but you consider this person a casual acquaintance at best. When you see that person's name listed in your friend's LinkedIn net-work, you can take the opportunity to deepen that connection. Having a friend in common who can recommend you can help smooth the way.

To browse the network of one of your connections, follow these steps:

1. **Click the Connections link in the expanded left navigation menu to bring up your network.**

2. **Click the name of a first-degree connection (or you can search for the name from the search box on the home page and then, on the search results page, click the name you want).**

   When you have the person's profile, look for tabs like Profile and Connections below the name and professional headline. If you don't see a tab marked Connections, you can't proceed with this process because that person has chosen to make their connection list private. If that's the case, you need to select another of your first-degree connections.

3. **Click the Connections tab of the connection.**

   For the example in these steps, I've picked a friend and associate, Michael Wellman, of the Comic Bug in Redondo Beach, California, and his connection list is shown in Figure 6-8.

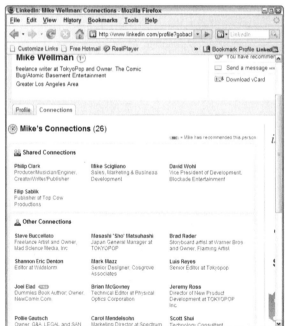

Figure 6-8:
You can look through your friend's network.

4. **Look through the list to see whether you'd like to send an Invitation to anyone and, if so, click the person's name to pull up his or her profile.**

When I scan through Mike's list, I notice that his wife, Carol Mendolsohn, is in his network. I spoke with her once about some questions she had regarding search engine optimization (SEO), so I clicked her name to bring up her profile, which is shown in Figure 6-9.

Click here to add a person to your network.

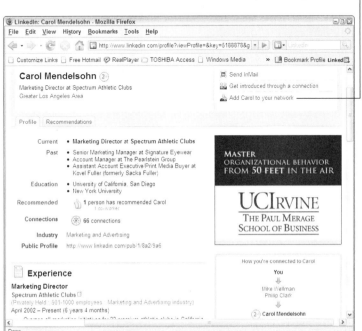

Figure 6-9:
Pull up the person's profile to add her to your network.

5. **Click the Add *Person's Name* to Your Network** link, which appears at the top right of the page.

   The Invitation page appears, as shown in Figure 6-10.

6. **Select the option that best describes your connection to this person.**

   It's a good idea to enter some text in the box under Include a Personal Note. This text customizes your Invitation and you can use it to remind the person of you and why you'd like to connect.

7. **Click the blue Send button to send off the Invitation.**

Presto! You're all done.

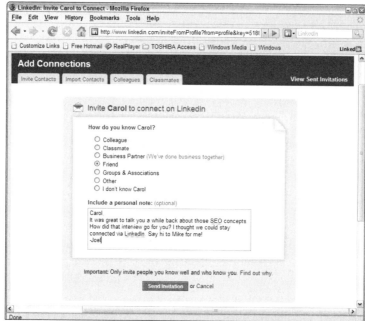

Figure 6-10:
Send a
custom
Invitation to
your new
contact.

Sending Connection Requests

You can check out previous sections of this chapter to find out how to use LinkedIn to search the entire user network and find people you want to invite to join your personal network. In the following sections, I focus on sending out the Invitation, including how to go about inviting people who haven't yet decided to join LinkedIn.

Sending requests to existing members

When you're on a LinkedIn page and spot the name of a member whom you want to invite to your network, you can follow these steps to send that person a Connection Request to add him to your network:

1. **Click the person's name to go to his profile page.**

   You might find people to invite using one of the methods described in the "Understanding Linking Strategies" section earlier this chapter. You might also find them while browsing LinkedIn Answers (which I cover in more detail in Chapter 7) or the Advanced People Search, which I cover in Chapter 4. Figure 6-11 shows the profile page of a LinkedIn member.

Click here to add a person to your network.

Figure 6-11:
Adding a
person to
your
network
from that
person's
profile page.

2. **Click the Add *Person's Name* to your Network link (where *Person's Name* is, of course, the real name of the person you're adding).**

   The Invitation page appears, as shown in Figure 6-12.

3. **From the list of connection reasons, choose the option that best describes your relationship to this person.**

   In some cases, you may have to input the person's e-mail address to help prove that you actually know the person. If you select the I Don't Know *Person's Name* option, LinkedIn will deny the request, so keep that in mind. If you pick a category such as Colleague or Classmate, LinkedIn will display a drop-down list of options based on your profile. For example, if you pick Colleague, LinkedIn displays a drop-down list of your positions. You need to pick the position you held when you knew this person.

4. **Enter your Invitation text in the box that appears under Include a Personal Note.**

   I highly recommend that you compose a custom Invitation rather than use the standard text, "I'd like to add you to my professional network on LinkedIn." In my example in Figure 6-12, I remind the person how we recently met, acknowledge one of his achievements, and ask him to connect.

Figure 6-12:
Here is
where you
can invite
someone
to connect
with you!

5. Click the blue Send Invitation button to send the Invitation.

You will be notified by e-mail when the other party accepts your connection request.

Why you shouldn't use canned Invitations

You might be very tempted to look at the "canned" Invitation that LinkedIn displays when you go to the Invitation Request page, especially if you're having a rough or busy day, and just send off the Invitation without adding to or replacing the canned Invitation with some custom text. We all have things to do and goals to accomplish, so stopping to write a note for each Invitation may seem tedious. However, it's becoming increasingly important, for the following reasons, to replace that text with something that speaks to the recipient:

 ✔ **The other person may not remember you.** Quite simply, your recipient may take one look at your name, see no additional information in the note that accompanied it, and think, "Who is that guy (or gal)?" A few may click your name to read your profile and try to figure it out, but most people are busy and won't take the time to investigate. They are likely to ignore your request.

 ✔ **The other person could report you as someone they don't know.** Having someone ignore your request is not the worst possibility. The worst thing pertains to a button that recipients of the Invitation see, the I Don't Know This Person button. If several people click this button from an Invitation you've sent, LinkedIn will consider you a spammer and will suspend and possibly even remove your profile and account from the site!

✔ **You offer no motivation for a mutually beneficial relationship.** When people get an Invitation request, they understand pretty clearly that you want something from them, whether it's access to them or to their network. If you've sent a canned Invitation, what they can't answer is the question, "What is in it for me?" A canned Invitation gives no motivation for or potential benefit of being connected to you. A custom note explaining that you'd love to swap resources or introduce them to others is usually enough to encourage an acceptance.

✔ **A canned Invite implies you don't care.** Some people will look at your Invitation request with a canned Invitation and think, "This person doesn't have 30 to 60 seconds to write a quick note introducing herself? She must not think much of me." That impression will quickly kill your chances of getting more connections.

Sending requests to nonmembers

Only members of LinkedIn can be part of anyone's network. Therefore, if you want to send a Connection Request to someone who has not yet joined LinkedIn, you must invite that person to create a LinkedIn account first. To do so, you can either send your invitee an e-mail directly, asking him or her to join, or you can use a LinkedIn function that generates the e-mail Invitation that includes a link to join LinkedIn.

Either way, you need to have the nonmember's e-mail address, and you'll probably have to provide your invitee with some incentive by offering reasons to take advantage of LinkedIn and create an account. (I give you some tips for doing that in the next section of this chapter.)

When you're ready to send your request using LinkedIn, just follow these steps:

1. **Click the Add Connections button below the left navigation menu.**

   The Add Connections window appears.

2. **Fill in the names and e-mail addresses of the people you want to invite to LinkedIn in the boxes provided, as shown in Figure 6-13.**

3. **Click the link Edit/Preview Invitation Text link to bring up a preview pane within the same page.**

4. **Write a custom Invitation in the text box provided**

   You'll send this Invitation to everyone on your list.

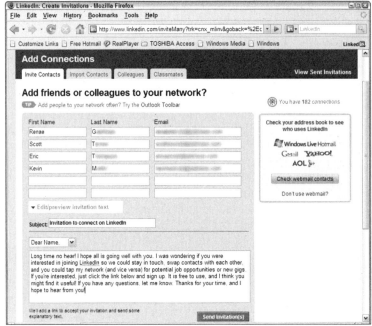

5. Click the blue Send Invitation button.

You're returned to the Add Connections page, where you see a green confirmation message on the screen. From here, you can invite additional people to your network.

Communicating the value of joining LinkedIn

Okay, you want to add some people to your LinkedIn network, but they haven't yet taken the plunge of signing up for the site. If you want them to accept your request by setting up their account, you may need to communicate the value of LinkedIn to your contact. After all, recommendations are one of the most powerful sales tools, which is why all types of businesses — from e-commerce stores and retail businesses to service directories and social networking Web sites — use recommendations so often.

So, how do you make the "sale"? (I use that term figuratively, of course; as you know, a basic LinkedIn account is free, — a feature that you should definitely not neglect to mention to your invitees!) If you send a super-long thesis on the merits of LinkedIn, it'll most likely be ignored. If you send a simple "C'mon! You know you wanna. . . ." request, that may or may not work. (You know your friends better than me.) You could buy them a copy of this book, but that could get expensive. (But I would be thrilled! C'mon! You know you wanna. . . .) The simplest way is to mention some of the benefits they could enjoy from joining the site, such as:

- ✔ **LinkedIn members always stay in touch with their connections.** If people you know move, change their e-mail address, or change jobs, you still have a live link to them via LinkedIn. You will always be able to see their new e-mail address if you're connected (assuming that they provide it, of course).

- ✔ **LinkedIn members can tap into their friends' networks for jobs or opportunities, now or later.** Although someone may not need a job now, he or she will eventually need help, so why not access thousands or millions of potential leads? LinkedIn has tens of millions of members in all sorts of industries, and people have obtained consulting leads, contract jobs, new careers, and even startup venture capital or funding for a new film! After all, it's all about "who you know."

- ✔ **LinkedIn can help you build your own brand.** LinkedIn members get a free profile page to build their online presence, and can to link to up to three of their own Web sites, such as a blog, personal Web site, or e-commerce store. The search engines love LinkedIn pages, which have high page rankings — and this can only be a boost to your online identity.

- ✔ **LinkedIn can help you do all sorts of research.** You might need to know more about a company before an interview, or you're looking for a certain person to help your business, or you're curious what people's opinions would be regarding an idea you have. LinkedIn is a great resource in all these situations. You can use LinkedIn to get free advice and information, all from the comfort of your own computer.

- ✔ **A basic LinkedIn account is free, and joining LinkedIn is easy.** There are a lot of misconceptions that users have to pay a monthly fee or spend a lot of time updating their LinkedIn profiles. Simply remind people that joining is free, and after they set up their profiles, LinkedIn is designed to take up very little of their time to keep an active profile and get some usefulness from having an account there.

Removing people from your network

There may come a time when you feel you need to remove someone from your network. Perhaps you added the person in haste, or he or she repeatedly asks you for favors or Introduction requests, or sends messages that you don't want to respond to. Not to worry — you're not doomed to suffer forever; you can simply remove the connection. When you do so, that person can no longer view your network or send you messages, unless he or she pays to send you an InMail message.

To remove a connection from your network, just follow these steps:

1. **While logged in to your LinkedIn account, click the Connections link in the expanded left navigation menu to bring up your list of connections.**

2. **Click the Remove Connections link that appears on the right side of the page, as shown in Figure 6-14.**

Remove Connections link

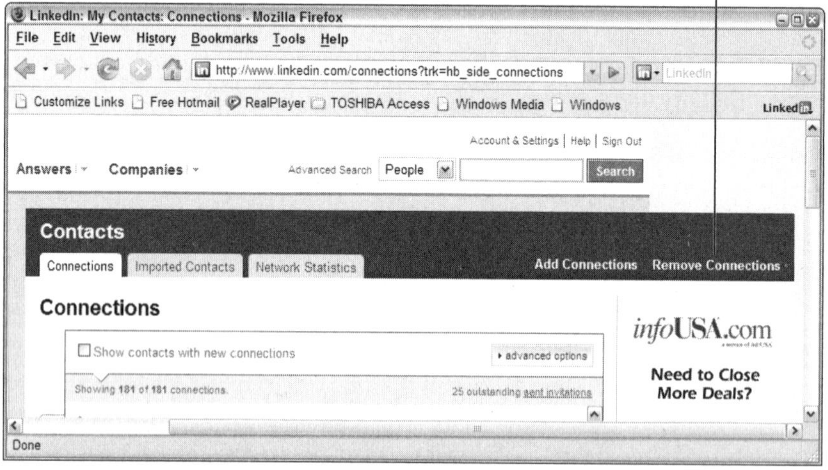

Figure 6-14:
Click the
Remove
Connections
link on the
Connections
page.

3. **On the Remove Connections page that appears, select the check box next to the name of anyone in your connections list whom you want to remove, as shown in Figure 6-15.**

   Any names you select appear on the right side of the page under Remove These Connections, as shown in Figure 6-16.

4. **When you're done selecting names, click the Remove Connections button to remove them from your network.**

   Your removed connections won't be notified of the removal.

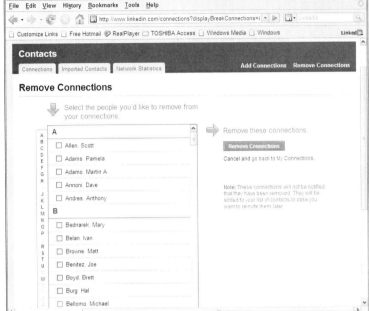

Figure 6-15:
Select the
check box
next to the
names of
contacts
you want to
remove.

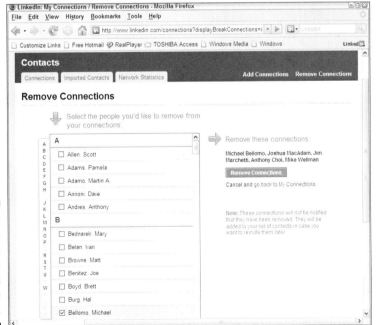

Figure 6-16:
Make sure
you have
selected all
the names
you want to
remove.

Accepting Invitations (or Gracefully Declining)

In this chapter, I talk a lot about how and why you might send out Invitations and add people to your network, and even covered what to do when you need to remove someone from your network. But what about the flip side of that coin — that is, being the invitee? In this section, I offer some guidance on what to do when you're faced with an Invitation and you have to decide whether to happily accept or gracefully decline it.

When you receive an Invitation to join someone's network of connections and you're not whether to accept or decline the Invitation, ask yourself these questions:

   ✔ **How well do you know this person?** With any luck, the inviter has included a custom message clueing you in to who he or she is, in case you don't remember. You can, of course, click their name to read their profile, which usually helps in triggering your memory. If this is somebody you don't know or remember, you probably don't want to add him to your network just yet. If you do know him, you need to consider whether he's worth adding to your network.

   ✔ **Does this person fit with the goals of your network?** As I mention early in this chapter, it's easier to put together a network when you've established a sense of the purpose you want it to serve. When you're looking at this Invitation, simply ask yourself, "Does accepting this Invitation help further my goals?"

   ✔ **Is this someone you want to communicate with and include in your network?** If you don't like someone or don't want to do business with them, you should certainly not feel obligated to accept his or her Invitation. Keep in mind that these people will have access to your network and can hit you up with Introduction and Recommendation requests (see Chapters 5 and 8, respectively).

If you're thinking of declining an Invitation, here are some tips to help you do so gracefully:

   ✔ **Respond quickly.** If you wait to respond to the Invitation, and then decide to go ahead and decline the invite, the other person may be even more offended and confused. Respond quickly so that this issue isn't hanging over anyone's head.

✔ **If necessary, ask for more information.** If you feel uncomfortable because you don't know the person well but want to consider the invitation before you decline, respond with a request for more information, such as, "I appreciate your interest, but I am having trouble placing our previous meetings. What is your specific interest in connecting with me on LinkedIn? Please let me know how we know each other and what your goals are for LinkedIn. Thanks again."

✔ **Respond politely but with a firm no.** You can simply write something along the lines of, "Thank you for your interest; I appreciate your eagerness. Unfortunately, since I am not familiar with you, I am not interested in connecting with you on LinkedIn just yet." Then, if you want, you can spell out the terms on which you may be interested in connecting, such as if the opportunity ever arises to get to know the person better or if he or she is referred to you by a friend.

Chapter 7

Using LinkedIn Answers

*I*f you believe the phrase, "Knowledge is power," you'll find the LinkedIn Answers feature to be a very powerful tool. Imagine being able to ask your network or the entire LinkedIn network a question and draw on the expertise and experiences of a potential pool of tens of millions of users. This is exactly what LinkedIn Answers was designed for, and it's a free service available to any LinkedIn user!

In this chapter, I discuss how to use LinkedIn Answers properly. I start by helping you find questions you can answer, and then I walk you through how to put together an answer and post it on the LinkedIn Answers site. Then, I shift gears and focus on the ability to ask questions. You find out how to phrase your question, how to determine what kind of information is the best to request, and then how to post your question on the site.

How LinkedIn Helps You Find Answers to Your Questions

The goal of LinkedIn Answers is to allow professionals to exchange expertise. Now, upon hearing that, your first question may be: "Well, what kind of question can I ask on LinkedIn Answers?" Glad you asked! LinkedIn members have a lot of personal and professional experiences to share, so there's no end to the questions you can pose. Plus the network makes it easy to organize and gather information.

You should NOT use LinkedIn Answers to simply forge connections, create a personal advertisement, or run a group poll. Users can flag inappropriate questions, which moderators can then review and possibly remove from the site. If your questions keep getting flagged, you won't be able to use this feature anymore. Inappropriate questions include asking for direct contact, posting just an advertisement for your business, or posting inappropriate content not suitable for public viewing.

Therefore, to encourage an orderly and productive exchange, LinkedIn organizes questions into the following categories:

- **Administration:** Do you have questions about rules and regulations? Are you putting together your small business benefits package? Or are you planning to move your business to a bigger building and need some ideas on how to pick the right facility? With topics that run from business insurance to purchasing and facilities management, you can post a question on LinkedIn and draw on expertise from company administrators, commercial real estate agents, and even customer service professionals.

- **Business Operations:** From supply chain and inventory issues to manufacturing, packaging, and quality management concerns, this category is your area to ask operations-related questions and read questions from other like-minded professionals, whether it's project management issues or something on your shop floor.

- **Business Travel:** Because many professionals still have to travel for their jobs or personal enjoyment, this category is dedicated to letting you ask all those questions about air travel, hotels, car rentals, and the different travel tools out there. Ask a question about the best place to host a business dinner in a certain city, or how people save money while booking travel on the Internet.

- **Career and Education:** Because lifelong learning and the eternal job search are two important benefits of using LinkedIn, this category is dedicated to questions for everything from resume writing, professional networks, and job searches to getting certifications and licenses, coaching, freelancing, and contracting.

- **Conferences and Event Planning:** Before you rack your brain figuring out how to plan the perfect conference or event for your company, you can use LinkedIn to ask others about this topic. This category is dedicated to questions regarding conference planning, conference venues, and event marketing and promotions. So, if you need help picking the right facility to accommodate your staff, or how to get the word out about your software development seminars, this is the place to do so!

- **Finance and Accounting:** From Accounting 101 to Risk Management, anything you were afraid to ask your Microeconomics Professor is fair game here. There are subsections devoted to corporate debt and taxes, budgeting, and mergers and acquisitions, and your questions could be answered by an entrepreneur or a CFO from a Fortune 500 company.

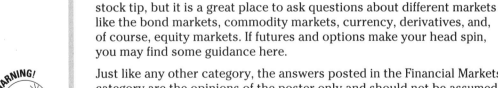

✓ **Financial Markets:** This isn't the place to hope to find that next hot stock tip, but it is a great place to ask questions about different markets like the bond markets, commodity markets, currency, derivatives, and, of course, equity markets. If futures and options make your head spin, you may find some guidance here.

Just like any other category, the answers posted in the Financial Markets category are the opinions of the poster only and should not be assumed as fact. Check with your financial expert or attorney before acting on any advice you receive here.

✓ **Government:** When you deal with government entities, each country has their own guidelines. Therefore, why not bounce some questions off folks who work in those arenas and benefit from their experience and guidance? Unclear about government policy? Ask a question and see whether a fellow LinkedIn member has dealt with it or can point you to the person, document, or Web site that can help.

✓ **Hiring and Human Resources:** While Donald Trump can make HR look easy with two famous words, the world of Human Resources is full of staffing, recruiting, policies, and benefits rules and regulations that are always changing and sometimes complex. Use the Answers section to find someone who knows his way around a 401k plan so you can focus on your main job.

✓ **International:** Thinking of doing business outside your country? Reach out with LinkedIn to ask questions of people who live in your target areas. Or ask questions of fellow countrymen (and women) who have entered those new areas, and find out what works and what doesn't. From customs to exporting to outsourcing, if you need to understand the ins and outs of International Law you can get all the answers you need in this category.

✓ **Law and Legal:** No matter what you do in the business world (not to mention the real world), you're bound to have a legal question sooner rather than later. Whether it concerns corporate, tax, or employment/ labor laws, see what fellow business owners or legal experts have to say about your legal question.

✓ **Management:** When you're the boss, or running your own division, tap the expertise of fellow managers when you're stuck with a question or curious about some of the newest trends or practices. This category has subsections devoted to labor relations, business analytics, and organizational development. When you have a planning or governance question, why not poll the community and see what other leaders have to say.

✓ **Marketing and Sales:** Still trying to sell that refrigerator to someone in the Arctic Circle? From advertising to business development to writing and sales, you can pose your question to a potential pool of millions of eager networkers and gain insight, anecdotes, and some valuable advice from marketers, salespeople, and management who may not share the same product line, but probably have faced the same issues.

✔ **Non-Profit:** When you deal with non-profit entities, there are plenty of rules about what the organization can and cannot do with their funds. Therefore, this category is dedicated to answering your questions about topics like fundraising, managing a non-profit organization, and philanthropy, as well as the growing area of social entrepreneurship. If you've got a question about innovative ways to have a fundraiser event, filing for your 501c3 government status with the IRS, or how you can encourage overseas entrepreneurs with small micro-loans, you can post something in this section.

✔ **Personal Finance:** What if you have a question about your bank account, your investments, or your retirement goals? You can pose a question on anything from wealth management to debt management, and odds are good that, regardless of your current status, there are LinkedIn members who can relate and share some advice or stories.

✔ **Product Management:** This is probably one of the most exciting categories. This category is presented to a worldwide audience, and you can now benefit from the ideas, opinions, and perspectives of potential customers and business partners. I profile one company who used this category for market research (see the sidebar "How LinkedIn made Mahalo a better search engine" later in the chapter), but you can also get advice on everything from positioning to pricing.

✔ **Professional Development:** As you grow in your career, your success will partially be determined by the amount of lifetime learning and skills development you undergo as you do your job. You have to grow your skills to keep up with new technology and new processes, and this category is dedicated to help you with topics like career management, ethics, professional books, communications and public speaking, and professional organizations.

✔ **Startups and Small Businesses:** The life of an entrepreneur can feel lonely sometimes, but now with millions of entrepreneurs all looking for the next step, you have an audience to pose questions on a wide range of issues from your business plan and incorporation steps to everyday small business concerns.

✔ **Sustainability:** A key concern for almost every business is how that business deals with their energy usage and how the company affects the environment. This category is dedicated to handling questions regarding energy and development, green business, and green eco-friendly products. If you are wondering about such concepts as carbon footprints, offset credits, or alternative energy, this is the category to post your question.

✔ **Technology:** With the ever-changing world of technology, you need to be able to get information fast without scratching your head over how to use the newest gee-whiz device in your business. You can post a question or share your knowledge about the newest, latest, and greatest software development techniques, Internet and e-commerce tips, blogging advice. You can even gain insight into ever-changing areas like biotechnology and wireless communications.

✔ **Using LinkedIn:** As LinkedIn develops and adds new functionality (and users), it's great to have a place where new members can ask questions. Questions posted here are typically answered by established members who have clicked and connected their way around LinkedIn and can offer friendly guidance to those just starting out.

Finding Questions to Answer

When you're ready to contribute some knowledge, you can start by checking out the LinkedIn Answers home page. Click the Answers link from the top menu on any LinkedIn page to get to the Answers home page. (See Figure 7-1.) This is the hub for LinkedIn Answers.

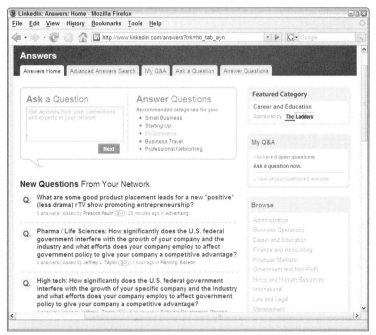

Figure 7-1:
Get all your questions answered with LinkedIn Answers!

When you go to find a question to answer, you have several ways to search for one that's right for you:

✔ **Browse the Open Questions section.** You can click the Answer Questions tab and browse through all the current open questions, with the default sort being questions from people in your LinkedIn network.

✔ **Browse by category.** You can browse through the categories listed on the Answers home page and go through subcategories until you find a question that's right up your alley.

Each category has its own RSS feed, which you can use to monitor categories in your RSS reader or personalized home page such as My Yahoo! or iGoogle. You can find out more about RSS by searching online, or you can get more in-depth information about how to subscribe to RSS feeds (a popular activity when reading blogs) in *Blogging For Dummies,* 2nd Edition by Susannah Gardner and Shane Birley, or *Syndicating Web Sites with RSS Feeds For Dummies* by Ellen Finkelstein (both published by Wiley).

✔ **Use Advanced Answers Search.** You can click the Advanced Answers Search tab and search through the Answers database (see Figure 7-2). Based on the criteria you enter on the search page, you can limit yourself to a specific category, or you can go after completely unanswered questions.

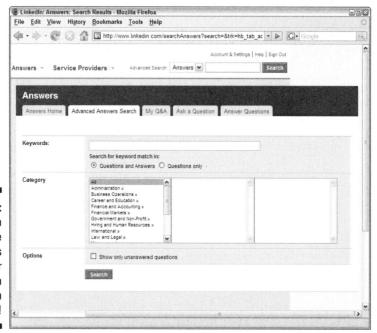

Figure 7-2: Search through the Answers database for a question only you can answer!

To get a better idea of what questions are being asked and how people are answering them, spend some time looking through the list of questions. When you're ready to contribute, it's time to post your answer!

Answering a Question

As you go through LinkedIn Answers, you may see a question that you would love to contribute an answer to, whether it's to help someone avoid the same mistake you made about something, or a topic you enjoy discussing. Perhaps you want to share your knowledge, hoping the person who posed the question will want to work with you further on their problem. Whatever the reason, when you are ready to answer a question, just follow these steps:

1. **Locate a question you can answer. Click Answers on the top menu of the home page to get to the main Answers page, as shown in Figure 7-1 in the previous section.**

2. **Click the Answer Questions tab to browse the categories of open questions.**

   You see an Open Questions list, as shown in Figure 7-3.

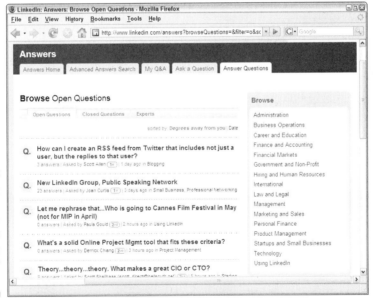

Figure 7-3:
See the list of open questions waiting for your answer!

3. **Click a category name in the pane on the right.**

   This step narrows down the Open Questions list. Suppose you choose the Startups and Small Businesses category. You see the Open Questions list for that category, as shown in Figure 7-4. You also see a new pane of sub-categories on the right.

4. **(Optional) If you need to, click a sub-category on the right to narrow down your search even further.**

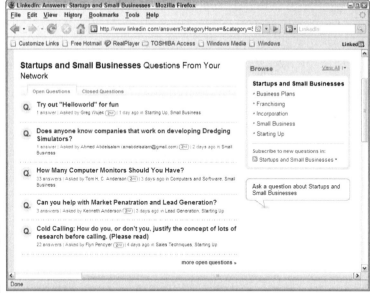

Figure 7-4:
There has
to be a
question I
can answer
somewhere
around
here.

5. **When you find a question you want to answer, click the link for that question.**

   This brings up the Question page, as shown in Figure 7-5. Read through the specifics of what the person is asking.

   Scroll down to see what answers, if any, have already been given. This way, you can incorporate their information into your answer so you're not repeating the same thing and you are providing new, helpful information.

Figure 7-5:
Read
through
the entire
question
and speci-
fications
before you
provide your
answer.

6. **Click the Answer button to start preparing your response.**

   The Your Answer form smoothly pops open right in the middle of the page you're looking at, like in Figure 7-6. How's that for sleek?

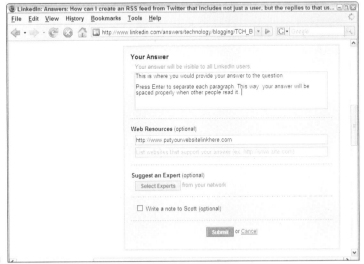

Figure 7-6:
Type your
answer in
the box
provided.

If you don't see the Answer button, it could be that this question has been closed by the person who posted the question, meaning that person isn't looking for any more answers to this question. It could also be that the question automatically closed after seven days of being on LinkedIn. You can only contribute to open questions.

7. **Type your response in the Your Answer text box.**

   Additionally, you can enter Web sites that are part of your answer, into the boxes provided. You can also suggest up to three experts who could further expand on your answer. (See the Tip right after these steps for more info on this.)

8. **When you have your answer ready, click the Submit button to send it in.**

   You're taken back to the Question posting page, but now, your answer is posted along with any other answers given already. The person who posted the question will be notified that a new answer has been posted.

If you feel like you can't provide a quality answer, but you know someone who should be able to give an expert answer, click the Select Experts button in the Your Answer form. This opens up a window (Figure 7-7 shows an example), where you can pick up to three people from your network by clicking the Select Experts button. In addition, you can add a note in the About the Expert(s) field, to let the question owner know why you think your suggested expert is qualified to answer this question. You can also select the check box to write a private note to the person who posted the question.

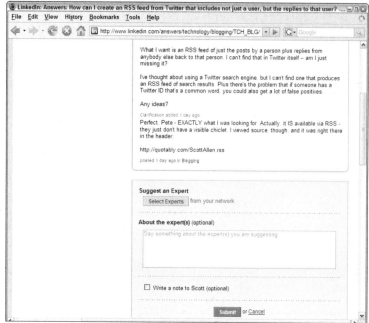

🔵 LinkedIn: Answers: How can I create an RSS feed from Twitter that includes not just a user, but the replies to that user? ....

Figure 7-7:
Suggest an
Expert to
answer the
question if
you do
not know
the right
information.

Asking a Question

Technology can be overwhelming. For example, has your boss ever asked you to figure out how to set up something for the business like an RSS feed? (And your first question was something like "What the heck is an RSS feed?") Imagine that you can put the question to your connections and the rest of the LinkedIn network, drawing from the knowledge of a potential pool of up to tens of millions of professionals. Whether it's a question pertaining to what you do, what you're planning to start, or something that you need some fresh insight on, LinkedIn allows you to post your question to be answered by the community.

Your LinkedIn question is available for up to seven days from the time you post your question on the site. You can always reopen your question later for more answers, but typically one week is enough for members of the community to start responding. Sometimes, a question gets anywhere from one to five responses. You might get anywhere from 10 to 20 answers for a popular question, while others may get 30, 50, 70, or more answers if lots of people have something to say.

How LinkedIn made Mahalo a better search engine

Imagine you're the head of a new human-edited search company called Mahalo. This was the case for Jason Calacanis, who started this company and built it up. He got to the point where he was looking for people's opinions about where the company should proceed and focus. Therefore, he turned to LinkedIn and posted the following question:

What would you do next if you were the CEO of Mahalo.com?

Background:

1. We've got a great team: tech, admin, research, and editorial.

2. We've got an amazing server setup and can handle massive traffic.

3. We've got 4,000 (Web) pages done and can do 500 per week.

4. The public hs suggested links already (if you do a search for apple, iPhone, a car, or a TV show, you'll fine some suggested links).

5. Folks are not chatting on the message board yet.

6. We have a very stable and robust technology platform (MediaWiki).

   So, given what we've got . . . what would you do next?!?!?

What he got was 88 responses, ranging from thoughtful insight, in-depth advice, balanced critique, to even a few requests to work at Mahalo! Not only did Jason make his network aware of Mahalo, but he got a lot of valuable insight and some in-depth "consulting" work just by posting a question!

The kinds of questions to ask

Now, you don't have to ask a giant question (like Jason Calacanis did in the sidebar "How LinkedIn made Mahalo a better search engine") but LinkedIn Answers are more useful to you if you think about the kind of question you want to ask and make sure it's something appropriate that can be answered by the community you're posting the question to.

Here are some questions to ask yourself before you . . . well, ask a question on LinkedIn Answers:

- ✔ **Is your question really a comment or opinion?** It can be tempting to post an opinion, a comment, or something designed to get a response, but that's not the intent of this function. Try to pose a question that can be answered by an expert.

- ✔ **Is your question non-trivial or useful?** Remember, the goal of LinkedIn Answers is to exchange useful information that matters to other people using the site. Try to keep the question focused on something business or professionally related.

✔ **Is your question worded clearly?** If you're hoping for some helpful replies, people need to clearly understand what it is you want to know. You can provide additional details about your question, but make sure the actual question is clear, concise, and simply put.

✔ **Is your question an appropriate question?** Some people try to post spam or generic advertising messages, or simply make negative, philosophical, bizarre, or highly personal statements. Make sure that this question is something you would feel comfortable asking of a person in a networking group or a fellow colleague.

LinkedIn prohibits using the Answers page for posting jobs, announcing your job search, or openly requesting people to connect with you. If you post such things, the questions will be deleted and your account may be subject to suspension or closure.

Getting the most and best responses

After you come up with your question, take a moment to consider the best way to present your question, so as many people as possible provide useful responses for you.

✔ **Provide as much detail as you can.** After you pose your question, you can (and should) fill out a details section that lets people know exactly what kind of answer you're hoping to receive. Add whatever detail is necessary for someone to properly answer your question. Include links to relevant Web sites that could help answer the question. If you already know a part of the solution, state that in the detail section so people don't waste their time answering something you've already figured out. Also be sure to provide clarification if people ask for it. If you need to know more about how to clarify your question, see the section, "Adding clarification to a posted question" later in this chapter.

✔ **Use the right keywords in your question.** As LinkedIn Answers continues to grow and expand, more people are using the search engine to find questions to answer instead of browsing open questions or categories. Therefore, if you need an expert in a certain subject matter, make sure the right keywords of that subject are in the question so it shows up in search results.

✔ **Use the right category(ies) for your question.** Since many people search LinkedIn Answers by category, it is important to pick the right category for your question. Go through the different categories, see what previous questions match your question the best, and keep in mind that you can assign up to two categories per question, in case you need information that doesn't fit neatly into one specific category.

✔ **Keep your question as simple as possible.** It can be tempting to get on a roll and start asking multiple questions that seem related in one posting. If people see a massive or highly complex question being asked, they typically are more reluctant to answer it, or they may answer a minor question and ignore the major one you really wanted an answer for.

✔ **Engage your audience.** Sometimes, the point of your question is to make your audience members think about a topic and share their opinions or advice in that situation. Therefore, provide some focus to your question but leave it open-ended (meaning a question that cannot be answered in a few words) to generate different perspectives when people answer your question. (For example, "How would you do X in this situation?")

✔ **Keep your question clean and readable.** Nothing can distract your audience quite like an obvious spelling or grammatical error. Before you post your question, take a minute or two to make sure the question and detail sections flow and are visually clean. Reword your question if necessary to make that first sentence as logical as possible to anyone who would read it.

The 20-year-old question — and 12 LinkedIn Answers

Tom Clifford is an award-winning corporate filmmaker who goes by the moniker "Director Tom." For over 20 years, Director Tom has helped companies large and small tell their stories through documentary videos. These videos relate the purpose of their companies, and Tom makes sure the videos are "energetic, engaging, compelling, meaningful and authentic."

On a guest blog entry, Clifford relates one aspect of his career: "No one has ever successfully answered a question I've been seeking in over 20 years. So, I asked the folks on LinkedIn for their thoughts." Clifford posted the following question on LinkedIn Answers:

ROI Using Corporate Videos?

Is there a way to measure or express the return on investment with corporate videos . . . financial or otherwise?

My experience has taught me that the ROI on a video is easier to calculate after it is produced vs. before production begins . . . especially for non-commercial productions like raising awareness of issues or corporate culture and values.

Perhaps, in a way, this is an unanswerable question. But, clearly, the corporate video market is a huge industry and one that continues to expand yearly.

So, how does this industry continue to expand without a clear model for ROI?

By posting his question to a wide audience, Clifford gained some fresh insights from the LinkedIn community. Twelve answers came in, each taking a different perspective. Today, Clifford credits his LinkedIn colleagues with providing him "a goldmine of information" that he uses in presentations about his business. Sometimes, all it takes is the right audience!

Posting your question on LinkedIn Answers

Okay, you've thought about the right question, prepared enough detail to help someone prepare a good answer for your question, and now you want to put your question on LinkedIn. To post your question, just follow these steps:

1. **On the LinkedIn home page, click the Answers link in the main menu along the top.**

   You're taken to the LinkedIn Answers home page (refer to Figure 7-1 earlier in this chapter).

2. **Start by clicking the Ask a Question tab to prepare your full question.**

   You end up at the Ask a Question page, as shown in Figure 7-8.

   On the Answers home page, you can also fill in the text box under Ask a Question and then click Next. That would also take you to the Ask a Question page, and your question would already be filled in.

3. **Type your question in the box below the Ask a Question text.**

4. **(Optional) If you want your question to go only to designated contacts, select the Only Share This Question with Connections I Select check box.**

   Please be aware that selecting this option makes your question completely private and only available to your designated 1st degree connections. No other LinkedIn user will be able to access or answer this question.

   The Only Share This Question with Connections I Select box is intended to relay the main question you're asking. Don't try to squeeze in every detail — you have a detail section for that information.

5. **Type any additional details for your question in the Add Details text box provided.**

   The Add Details box is optional, but I recommend using it to give readers a more complete idea of what kind of response you're seeking, and any additional information they may need to answer your question.

6. **Under Categorize Your Question, pick a category for your question and then a sub-category.**

   You're presented with a list of categories, where you can assign one to your question. When you click the category that most represents your category, the box to its right may appear with sub-category options. Continue to select sub-categories that best represent the topic of your question. (You might even be able to pick a sub-sub-category in the rightmost box.) When you've selected a valid category, you see the full category name represented below the boxes, as shown in Figure 7-9.

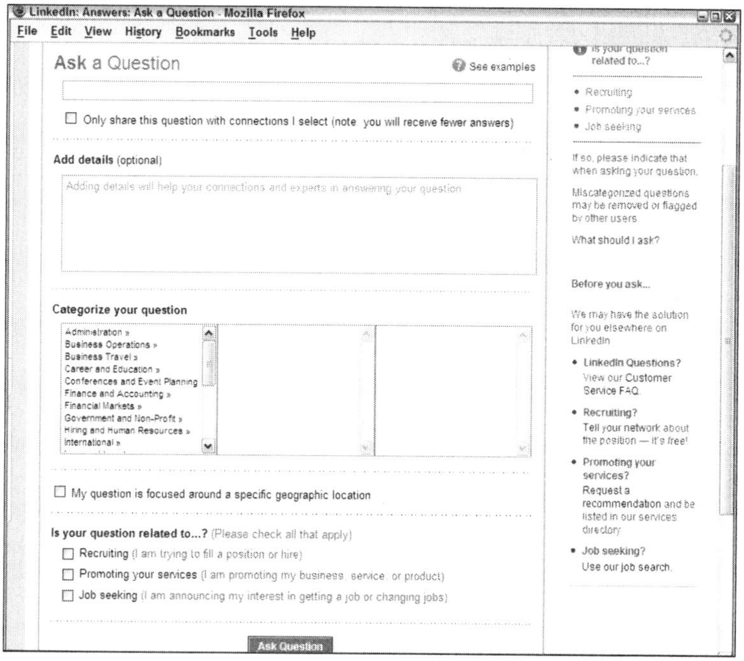

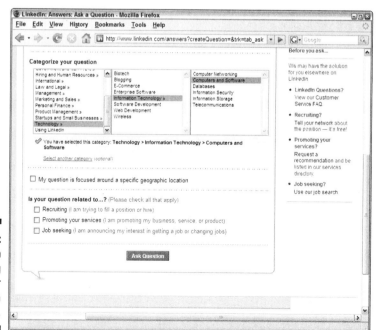

Figure 7-8:
Post your
question
for LinkedIn
Answers
here.

Figure 7-9:
Finish
preparing
your
question
posting.

Sometimes a question overlaps categories, such as when an entrepreneur asks about funding strategies from mergers as well as venture capital. If your question applies to more than one category, you can add a second category to expand the readership of your question and get different answers.

7. Select any check boxes relating to your question (regarding location and/or question content).

LinkedIn asks you to identify whether your question relates to a specific geographic location. If so, click that check box. In addition, if your question relates to recruiting, specific promotions, or a job search, select the appropriate check box so LinkedIn can flag the question and display it appropriately.

8. When you're ready, click the Ask Question button to post your question to LinkedIn Answers.

You see a confirmation bar (see Figure 7-10) telling you that your question has been posted and will remain open for seven days to gather answers. You also see a new screen that gives you the option to send your question to your LinkedIn network.

Green confirmation bar

Figure 7-10: Let your LinkedIn network know about your open question!

9. **Fill out the form to send your question to connections and then click the Send button, or just click the Skip link.**

Click the Select Connections button to pick people from your network to receive a copy of your question sent to their Inbox. When you're ready, click the Send button to distribute your question to your network.

You can customize the subject line and details of your message before you send out your question. After you click the Send button or the Skip button, your question is posted to the community.

The more people you send this to, the more interest and response you should get in your question. Balance that, though, with some consideration of the people in your network and send it to the people you feel it would be most relevant to and who would likely provide a thoughtful answer. Remember, though, that these will be the ONLY people who receive this question and can answer it, so choose your connections wisely.

Adding clarification to a posted question

After you've posted your question and people have started to respond, you may notice some things:

✔ You've thought about additional information you forgot to put in your post.

✔ The answers being posted aren't targeting the correct area for your question.

✔ The people posting answers are asking for follow-up information.

In any of these cases, or for whatever reason, you may need to post a clarification to your original question. If that's the case, just follow these steps:

1. **On the LinkedIn home page, click Answers from the main menu.**

2. **Click the My Q&A tab to bring up your list of questions.**

When you see your list of questions, select the question you need to update to bring up the question details.

3. **From the question detail page, click the link Clarify My Question to add any extra detail to your original question.**

You cannot edit your original question, so the only way to change your question is to add information through clarifying your question.

4. **On the Clarify Your Question page, add your clarification into the text box provided and click the Clarify Question button to add your message to your original question.**

Selecting a Best Answer for your question

After your question has been on LinkedIn and you start receiving responses from the community, at some point you should go back into your question and review the answers you've received. At this stage, LinkedIn gives you the option to identify the Best Answer to your question, so anyone reading your question in the future can understand what you felt to be the most appropriate answer.

As you scroll through the answers that people have submitted, pick the answer that best defines your question and assign it as a Best Answer. Doing this helps LinkedIn recognize experts in these different categories and can be your way of rewarding the person who spent time answering your question most effectively.

I recommend waiting until either the question automatically closes in seven days or waiting until you have several great answers and you feel ready to close the question on your end.

I also recommend that you select at least one Good Answer on top of the Best Answer. This way, you are rewarding members who took the time to rate your question, because this designation will show up on their profile, whether you rated them Best Answer or Good Answer.

Part III

Growing and Managing Your Network

The 5th Wave   By Rich Tennant

If Grond want more connections, me recommend Contact Box.

In this part . . .

The ball is rolling, you feel some traction, and you're raring for more. Many people get to a certain level, look around, and go, "Ok, great, but what's the next step?" Well, I'm here to say that there are a lot of next steps and ways that you can save time while using LinkedIn even more.

This part talks about the steps you can take to really raise your LinkedIn identity to the next level. I cover the ins and outs of LinkedIn's Recommendations feature, which can help you earn trust and maybe even a new job. I also talk about the LinkedIn Web site some more and how you can access some of the functions, like the Inbox, to be more efficient as you handle more activity. Finally, I talk about some cool little add-ons you can plug into your Internet experience that give you lots of data on other people, courtesy of LinkedIn, as well as some ways to tie your e-mail system and LinkedIn together.

Chapter 8

Exploring the Power of Recommendations

*E*ndorsements and testimonials have long been a mainstay of traditional marketing. But really, how much value is there in reading testimonials on someone's own Web site, like

> *"Maria is a great divorce attorney — I'd definitely use her again."*
>
> Elizabeth T. London

or

> *"Jack is a fine lobbyist — a man of impeccable character."*
>
> Emanuel R. Seattle

Without knowing who these people are, anyone reading the testimonials tends to be highly skeptical about them. At the very least, the reader wants to know that they're real people who have some degree of accountability for those endorsements.

The reader is looking for something called *social validation*. Basically, that's just a fancy shmancy term meaning that a person feels better about his decision to conduct business with someone if other people in his extended network are pleased with that person's work. The reader knows that people are putting their own reputations at stake, even if just to a small degree, by making a public Recommendation of another person.

As this chapter shows you, LinkedIn's Recommendations feature offers you a powerful tool for finding out more about the people you're considering doing business with, as well as a means to build your own reputation in a way that's publicly visible. I walk through all the steps needed to create a Recommendation for someone else, request a Recommendation for your profile, and how to manage your existing Recommendations.

Understanding Recommendations

The LinkedIn Recommendation process starts in one of three ways:

✔ **Unsolicited:** When viewing the profile of any of your direct connections, a Recommend This Person link is clearly displayed at the top of the profile, as shown in Figure 8-1. (For more information on connections, see Chapter 6.) By clicking that link, you can give an unsolicited Recommendation.

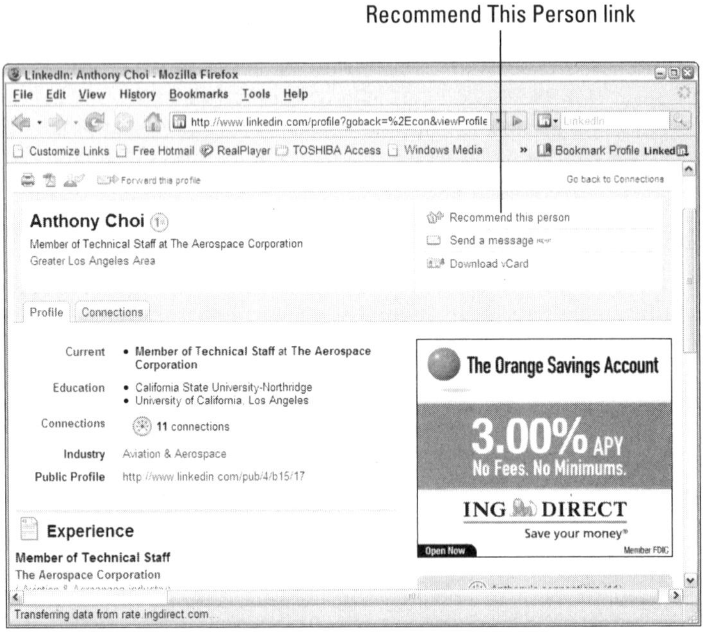

Recommend This Person link

Figure 8-1: You can start a Recommendation with any first-level connection.

✔ **Requested:** You can request Recommendations from your direct connections. You might send such a request at the end of a successful project, for example, or maybe ask for a Recommendation from your boss before you plan to transition to a new job.

> ✔ **Reciprocated:** Whenever you accept a Recommendation from some-
> one, LinkedIn presents you with the option of recommending that
> person in return. Some people do this as a thank you for receiving the
> Recommendation, other people reciprocate only because they didn't
> realize they could leave a Recommendation until someone left them one,
> and there are some people that do not feel comfortable reciprocating
> unless they truly believe the person deserves one. You should decide in
> each circumstance whether you want to reciprocate.

After the Recommendation is written, it's not posted immediately. It goes to
the recipient for review, and he has the option to accept it, reject it, or request
a revision. So even though the majority of Recommendations you see on
LinkedIn are genuine, they're also almost entirely positive because they have
to be accepted by the recipient.

With LinkedIn, you can use Recommendations in several ways:

> ✔ **On your profile page:** LinkedIn shows all of the Recommendations
> you've received, as well as links to the profiles of the people who have
> recommended you (see Figure 8-2). This provides that social validation
> you want by allowing people to see exactly who is endorsing you.
>
> ✔ **In Advanced Search:** One of the options for sorting the results of a LinkedIn
> search is Degrees and Recommendations. This option sorts first by the
> number of degrees or levels a connection is away from you in ascending
> order (for example, your first-degree connections first), and then by the
> number of Recommendations someone has received in descending order
> (for example, those with the most Recommendations first).
>
> ✔ **In the Services section:** The main page displays a list of recent
> Recommendations within your network. Within each category, you can
> choose to view either the most recent Recommendations or the most
> highly recommended service providers within the category. Every
> service provider listed must have at least one Recommendation to be
> included (see Chapter 13 for a more detailed discussion).

Because the number of Recommendations is used as both a sort option for
searching and a display option in the service provider directory, having a
large number of Recommendations has a very real impact on your profile's
searchability, besides just being impressive. More is definitely better.

That said, the quality of the Recommendations matters, as well as who
they're from. Five very specific Recommendations from actual clients talking
about how you helped them solve a problem is probably worth more than 50
Recommendations from business acquaintances saying, "I like Sally — she's
cool," or, "Hector is a great networker." And any Recommendations that heartily
endorse the number of cocktails you had at the last formal event probably need
revision. Check out the later section, "Gracefully Declining a Recommendation
(Or a Request for One)," if you're receiving those kinds of statements.

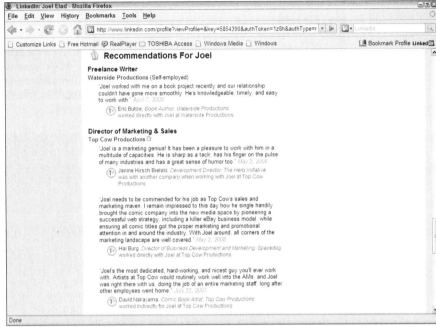

Figure 8-2:
Recom-
mendations
shown on a
profile page.

Writing Recommendations

I suggest you practice making some Recommendations before you start requesting them. Here's the method to my madness: When you know how to write a good Recommendation yourself, you're in a better position to help others write good Recommendations for you. And the easiest way to get Recommendations is to give them. Every time you make a Recommendation and the recipient accepts it, she is prompted to give you a Recommendation. Thanks to the basic desire that most people want to be fair when dealing with their network, many people will go ahead and endorse you in return.

Choose wisely, grasshopper: Deciding who to recommend

Go through your contacts and make a list of the people you want to recommend. As you build your list, consider recommending the following types of contacts:

✔ **People you've worked with:** I'm not going to say that personal references are completely worthless, but standing next to specific Recommendations from colleagues and clients, they tend to ring pretty hollow. Business Recommendations are much stronger in the LinkedIn context. Your Recommendation is rooted in actual side-by-side experience with the other party, you can be specific on the behavior and accomplishments of the other party, and the examples you give are most likely to be appreciated by the professional LinkedIn community at large.

✔ **People you know well:** You may choose to connect with casual acquaintances or even strangers, but reserve your personal Recommendations for people you have an established relationship with (and by that, I mean friends and family). Remember, you're putting your own reputation on the line with that Recommendation. Are you comfortable risking your rep on them?

Only recommend people whose performance you're actually happy with. I can't say it enough: Your reputation is on the line. Recommending a real doofus just to get one Recommendation in return isn't worth it! Here's a great question to ask yourself when deciding whether to recommend someone: Would you feel comfortable recommending this person to a best friend or family member? If you say no, well then, you have your answer.

When you complete your To Be Recommended list, you're probably not going to do them all at once, so I suggest copying and pasting the names into a word-processing document or spreadsheet so that you can keep track as you complete them.

If you copy your contacts directly from your LinkedIn contact list into your spreadsheet or word processor, a link to your contact profiles will be included when you paste the information, making it easier to work from the list.

Look RIGHT here: Making your Recommendation stand out

Here are a few things to keep in mind when trying to make your Recommendation stand out from the rest of the crowd:

✔ **Be specific.** Don't just say the person you're recommending is great — talk about her specific strengths and skills.

✔ **Talk about results.** Adjectives and descriptions are fluff. Clichés are also pretty useless. Tell what the person actually did and the impact it had on you and your business. It's one thing to say, "She has a great eye," and another to say, "The logo she designed for us has been instrumental in building our brand and received numerous positive comments from customers."

✔ **Tell how you know the person.** LinkedIn offers only the very basic categories of colleague, service provider, and business partner. If you've known this person for 10 years, say so. If she's your cousin, say so. If you've never met her in person, say so. Save it for the end, though — open with the positive results this person had provided, or the positive qualities the person exhibited in your interaction, then qualify the type of interaction.

✔ **Reinforce the requestor's major skills or goals.** Look at her profile. How is she trying to position herself now? What can you say in your Recommendation that will support that? That will be far more appreciated by the recipient. For example, if you read her profile and she is really focusing on her project management skills as opposed to her earlier software development skills, your Recommendation should reinforce that message she is trying to convey on her profile.

✔ **Don't gush.** By all means, if you think someone is fantastic, exceptional, extraordinary, or the best at what she does, say so. But don't go on and on about it.

✔ **Be concise.** While LinkedIn has a 3000 character limit on the length of Recommendations, you shouldn't reach that limit. That should be more than enough to get your point across. Make it as long as it needs to be to say what you have to say, and no longer.

Creating a Recommendation

Now you're ready to write your first Recommendation. To create a Recommendation, first you need to pull up the person's profile:

✔ Click the Connections link (part of the Contacts section) from the left navigation menu of any page.

✔ Then select a name from your connections list. This is the person you're recommending.

✔ Your Recommendation goes directly to that person, not prospective employers. If a prospective employer wants a specific reference, they can request it through doing a Reference Check on LinkedIn, which I cover in greater detail in Chapter 12.

✔ Click the Recommend This Person link to the right of their name and photo.

✔ Visit the profile of the person you want to recommend.

Now that you've identified your person to recommend, you can get your recommending groove on. Follow these steps:

1. **Select a category for that person.**

   As soon as you click the Recommend This Person link, you are immediately prompted to choose an option describing how you know this
   person, as shown in Figure 8-3. Your three choices are

   - *Colleague:* You worked together at the same company.

   - *Service Provider:* You hired the person to provide a service to you
     or your company.

   - *Business Partner:* You worked with the person, but not as a client
     or colleague. (The common use of "business partner" is that you
     are partners in a business together, but that isn't what this means.
     In that case, if you work in the same company as the other party,
     choose Colleague, even if you are both owners and not manager or
     employee.)

   Note that, currently, there's no option for a personal relationship, nor
   for you being a service provider to the person. In these cases, I recommend that you select Business Partner.

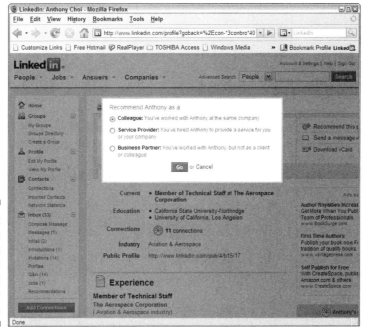

Figure 8-3:
Tell LinkedIn
how you
worked with
the person
you are rec-
ommending.

2. **Click the Go button to proceed. The Create Your Recommendation page appears, as shown in Figure 8-4.**

   In the case of a Service Provider, the page will look different, but I cover that Recommendation in detail in Chapter 13.

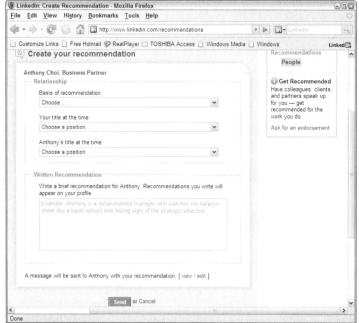

Figure 8-4:
Create your
Recom-
mendation
from this
page on
LinkedIn.

3. **Define your relationship with the person you're recommending by answering a few questions.**

   Each of the three drop-down boxes on-screen ask you to pick an answer from a pre-defined list. Specifically, you will be asked to:

   a. *Define the basis of your relationship.*

      If you are a colleague of the person, LinkedIn wants to know if you managed the person, worked side-by-side with the other party, or if that person was the manager or senior official. If you are a business partner, LinkedIn wants to know if you worked at a different company from the other person or whether the person was a client of yours.

   b. *Define your title at the time.*

      You are asked to identify which position you held when you observed the behavior you are recommending in the other person. This list is generated from the positions you defined in your LinkedIn profile. If your experience overlaps multiple positions, pick the position that best defines your relationship with the other party.

    c. Define their title at the time.

      You have to select at least one position the other party held to associate the Recommendation. You can only enter one Recommendation per position, but you can recommend the other party on multiple positions.

    By answering these questions, this informs anyone reading the Recommendation about how you know the person you're recommending. Perhaps you were the person's manager at one time.

 4. **Write the Recommendation in the Written Recommendation box provided.**

    Remember the tips I mentioned earlier about staying specific, concise, and professional while focusing on results and skills. Keep in mind that Recommendations you write also appear in your own profile in a tab marked Recommendations. Believe it or not, people judge you by the comments you leave about others, not just what they say about you. So, look over your Recommendation before you post it, and watch for obvious spelling or grammatical errors.

 5. **If you want, include a note in the Personalize This Message text box.**

    When you send your Recommendation, you have the option to also attach a personal note. Simply click the View/Edit link next to the line "A message will be sent to X with your Recommendation." If it's someone you're in recent contact with, the note is probably unnecessary — the endorsement should speak for itself. But if it's someone you haven't spoken to in a while, take advantage of the opportunity to reconnect with a brief note (see Figure 8-5). You can keep the boilerplate text, "I've written this Recommendation of your work to share with other LinkedIn users" or you can write your own note, like I did in Figure 8-5.

 6. **Click the Send button.**

    The Recommendation is sent to the recipient.

After you've sent your Recommendation, remember that the other person has to accept it before it's posted. Don't take it personally if she doesn't post it, or at least not right away. It's a gift, freely given. The primary value to *you* is in the gesture to the recipient, not the public visibility of your Recommendation. And if she comes back with requested changes to the Recommendation, by all means accommodate her, so long as it's all true and you feel comfortable with it. It's a service to her, not you.

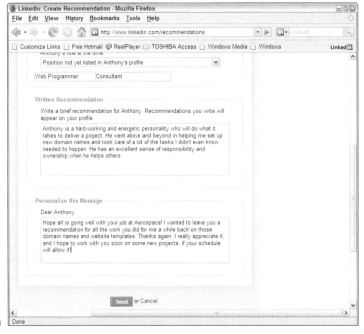

Figure 8-5:
Sending a
personal
note with
a Recom-
mendation
is a good
idea.

Requesting Recommendations

In an ideal world, you'd never request a Recommendation. Everyone who's had a positive experience working with you would just automatically post a raving Recommendation on LinkedIn.

But the reality is that most likely only your raving fans and very heavy LinkedIn users are going to make unsolicited Recommendations. Your mildly happy customers, former bosses whose jokes you laughed at consistently, and co-workers who you haven't seen in five years could all stand a little prompting.

Be prepared, though: Some people feel that Recommendations should only be given freely, and they may be taken aback by receiving a Recommendation request. So it's imperative that you frame your request with a personal message, not just a generic message from LinkedIn.

Choosing who to request Recommendations from

Request Recommendations from the same people whom you might write them for: colleagues, business partners, and service providers. The only difference is that you're looking at it from his point of view.

Relationships aren't all symmetrical. For example, if someone hears me speak at a conference and buys this book, that person is a customer of mine. My customers know my skills and expertise fairly well — perhaps not on the same level as a consulting client, but still enough to make a Recommendation. I, on the other hand, may not know a customer at all. I'm open to getting to know him, and I'm willing to connect, but I can't write a Recommendation for him yet.

Creating a polite Recommendation request

When you identified in your mind the person (or people) you want to write you Recommendations, you're ready to create a Recommendation request. To get started on authoring your request follow these steps:

1. **Click the Profile link from the left navigation menu.**

2. **Scroll down to the position for which you want to request an endorsement and click either the Request Recommendations link (displayed if you don't already have any for that position) or the Manage link (if you already have one or more Recommendations for the position).**

   If you look at Figure 8-6, you can see the link you have to click. If you already have Recommendations, you have to scroll down the page and click the link labeled Request Endorsements from Up to X Connections, where X is the amount of first-level connections you currently have, as shown in Figure 8-7.

3. **Click the Select Connections button and select the person you want to request a Recommendation from. You can send this request to as many as 200 people**

   You will see a new window pop up like in Figure 8-8. Scroll through your list of first-degree connections and click the check box next to each person to whom you would like to send this Recommendation request.

Request Recommendations link

Manage link

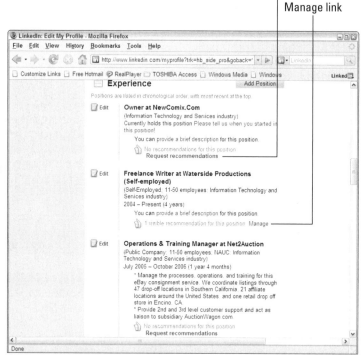

Figure 8-6:
Click the
link next
to the
position
to be
associated
with your
requested
Recom-
mendation.

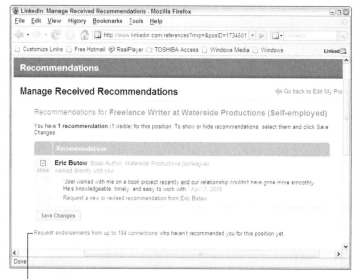

Figure 8-7:
If you
already
have at
least one
Recom-
mendation
for a posi-
tion, you
can request
more.

Request Endorsements link

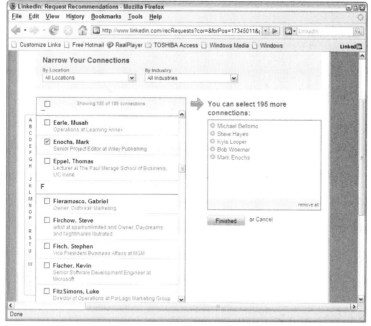

Figure 8-8:
Pick the
person (or
people) to
request
Recom-
mendations
from.

4. **Click the Finished button to close the Connections window and go back to your Request Recommendations screen.**

5. **Create your message by typing in the box provided, as shown in Figure 8-9.**

   The same etiquette is recommended here as in other requests — you should not accept the boilerplate text that LinkedIn fills in, but rather customize it to create a personal note, like I did in Figure 8-9. You can customize not only the body of your message but the subject line as well.

6. **Check your spelling and grammar.**

7. **Click the Send button to send your request.**

   The Recommendation request is sent to the intended recipient.

Giving people some context as to why you're making the request helps motivate them more effectively. Also, even though you should be asking only people that would be comfortable recommending you (you are, aren't you?), you still want to give them a gracious way to decline.

Remember, you're asking a favor. The person you're contacting is in no way obligated, so don't expect anything and you won't be disappointed.

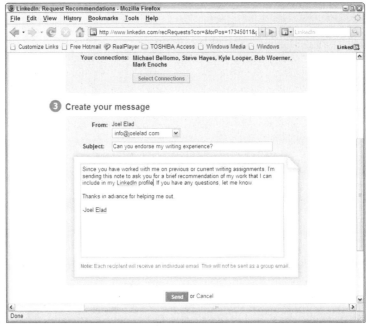

There's really no such thing as too many Recommendations, so long as the quality is good. Even if you have just two or three mediocre ones, people will start to think that a lot of them are fluff. LinkedIn doesn't give you control over the display order either, so you have all the more reason to make sure that the ones displayed are good quality.

Gracefully Declining a Recommendation (Or a Request for One)

Unfortunately, not everyone naturally writes good Recommendations, and all of your LinkedIn connections haven't read this book, so eventually it's bound to happen: Someone will write a Recommendation that you don't want to show on your profile.

No problem. Just politely request a replacement when you receive it. Thank him for thinking of you, and give him the context of what you're trying to accomplish:

Wei:

Thank you so much for your gracious Recommendation. I'd like to ask a small favor, though. I'm really trying to position myself more as a public speaker in the widget industry, rather than as a gadget trainer. Since you've heard me speak on the topic, if you could gear your Recommendation more towards that, I'd greatly appreciate it.

Thanks,

Alexa

If he's sincerely trying to be of service to you, he should have no problem changing it. Just make sure you ask him for something based on your actual experience with him.

You also may receive a request for a Recommendation from someone you don't feel comfortable recommending. If it's because she gave you poor service or was less than competent, you have to consider whether you should even be connected to her at all in LinkedIn, since it *is* a business referral system. I discuss how to remove a connection in Chapter 6.

But it may just be that you don't have sufficient experience with her services to provide her a Recommendation. If that's the case, then just reply to her request with an explanation:

Alicia:

I received your request for a Recommendation. While I'm happy to be connected to you on LinkedIn, and look forward to getting to know you better, or even work together in the future, at this point in time I just don't feel like I have enough basis to give you a really substantive Recommendation.

Once we've actually worked together on something successfully, I'll be more than happy to provide a Recommendation.

Thanks,

Wei

Managing Recommendations

Relationships change over time. Sometimes they get better; occasionally they get worse. And sometimes they just change. Also, as you get more Recommendations, you may decide that you don't want to display them all, or that you would like some of them updated to support your current branding or initiatives.

Fortunately, neither the Recommendation you give nor those you receive are etched in stone (or computer chips, as the case may be). You can edit or remove the Recommendations you've written at any time, and you can hide or request revisions to those you receive.

Editing or deleting Recommendations you've made

To edit or remove a Recommendation you've made, follow these steps:

1. **Click the Profile link from the left navigation menu.**

2. **Click the Recommendations tab in your profile.**

   All of the Recommendations you've made are listed in reverse chrono-logical order, as shown in Figure 8-10. You can narrow the list down by clicking the link for Colleagues, Service Providers, or Business Partners below the header Manage Recommendations You've Made.

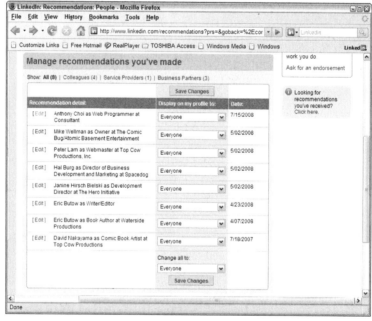

Figure 8-10:
Pick the
Recom-
mendation
you want
to edit or
delete.

3. **Click Edit next to the Recommendation you want to change or remove.**

   You are taken to the Edit Recommendations screen, as shown in Figure 8-11. You can update some of the Relationship choices, like Basis of the Recommendation, or update your Recommendation text.

Withdraw This Recommendation link

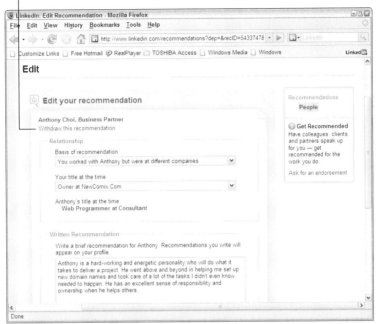

Figure 8-11:
Make
changes
to your
Recom-
mendation
or withdraw
it altogether.

4. **Edit the Recommendation and click Send or click Withdraw This
   Recommendation.**

If you edit a Recommendation, it is submitted to the recipient again for
approval. If you remove it, it comes off immediately, and the recipient (or is
that the *un*recipient?) doesn't receive any notification.

You can change the Basis of the Recommendation field, which describes the
exact relationship, such as whether you worked in the same department,
or one of you was subordinate to the other. However, you can't change the
type of Recommendation, for example, Colleague versus Service Provider
versus Business Partner. If you need to do so, you have to remove the current
Recommendation and write a new one, choosing the appropriate option.

Handling new Recommendations you've received

Every time you receive a Recommendation from someone else, you will see a
message show up in your LinkedIn inbox, as shown in Figure 8-12.

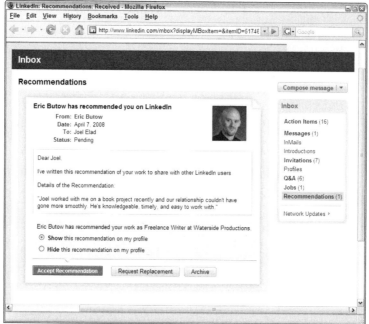

Figure 8-12:
Here is
where you
can accept
an incoming
Recom-
mendation.

When you receive a Recommendation, you have these options:

- ✔ **Accept and show it on your profile.** Make sure the Show this Recommendation on my profile option is selected.

- ✔ **Accept and hide it.** You might choose this option if you don't want to decline the person's Recommendation, but for some reason you don't want to display it (see the following section).

- ✔ **Request replacement.** If you aren't completely happy with his Recommendation, choose this option and you'll be given the opportunity to send him a brief note explaining what you would like changed.

- ✔ **Archive it.** This removes the Recommendation message from your LinkedIn inbox. It is available for later retrieval, just not as easily as if you choose the Hide option. You simply have to click the link "Show archived messages" when looking at your LinkedIn inbox for Recommendations; I cover the inbox in further detail in Chapter 9.

Removing a Recommendation or requesting a revision

To remove a Recommendation you've received or request a revision, here's what you do:

1. **Click the Profile link from the left navigation menu.**

2. **Scroll down to the position the Recommendation is for and click the Manage link.**

   This will take you to the Manage Received Recommendations page, as shown in Figure 8-13.

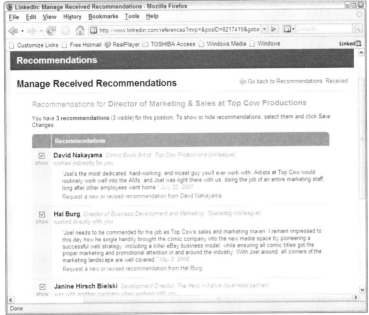

Figure 8-13: Remove a Recommendation or request a revision here.

3. **To hide a Recommendation, deselect the Show check box. Then click the Save Changes button to hide your Recommendation.**

4. **To request a new or revised Recommendation, click the Request a New or Revised Recommendation From link.**

   This takes you back to the Request Recommendation screen (which I cover in the earlier section, "Creating a polite Recommendation request") where you should write a brief note explaining why you're requesting a change.

5. **Click the Send button to send your request.**

Negotiating the social graces around Recommendations may feel a little awkward at first, but it will quickly become comfortable with a little practice. By both giving and receiving good Recommendations, you'll build your public reputation, increase your social capital with your connections and have a good excuse for renewing some of your relationships with people you haven't contacted recently.

Chapter 9

Keeping Track of Your LinkedIn Activities

I talk a lot about the different functions available on LinkedIn for you to use, and hopefully you've started to set aside some time on a regular basis to keep track of various tasks as you build up your profile and network. Because of the growing amount of functions available on LinkedIn, you should take a look around the site to see how you can manage this new set of tasks most effectively.

In this chapter, I detail the different ways you can access the LinkedIn functions, as well as how you can keep track of incoming mail, Invitations, and other messages that require your input or approval. I discuss the functions that you can access from the left navigation menu on the LinkedIn home page. I also take a look into the LinkedIn Inbox, where all your messages, Invitations, answers, and communication are received. Then, I go over some ways you can set up the LinkedIn site to communicate with you through e-mail and keep you informed of communication from other LinkedIn users, whether it refers to Invitations, Introductions, Recommendations, Answers, or other LinkedIn functions.

Using the LinkedIn Home Page as Your Command Console

The LinkedIn home page is, by default, full of information about how you use the site and should be thought of as your command console for working with LinkedIn. You can get to the home page at any time by clicking the LinkedIn logo in the top-left corner of every LinkedIn Web page. When you do so, you see a variety of information, as shown in Figure 9-1. Keep in mind that your home page is unique to your LinkedIn identity and will look different from mine (shown in Figure 9-1) or any other user on LinkedIn. Your page is built based on the first-degree connections in your network, your pending messages in your Inbox, and the level of participation with functions like LinkedIn Answers or Recommendations.

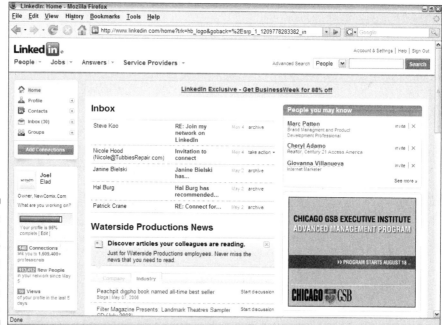

Figure 9-1:
Coordinate all your LinkedIn activities through the home page.

First off, check out the menu in the top-left corner. I refer to this menu as the left navigation menu. This menu has all of the major categories for checking your activities on LinkedIn. By clicking the plus (+) signs next to each function, you can expand the menu to see more options. Figure 9-2 shows a fully expanded menu.

Figure 9-2:
Fully expand
your menu
options!

If you expand these menu options, LinkedIn remembers this and always show you an expanded menu whenever you go back to the Web site.

As you can see from the expanded menu, any unanswered messages or invitations in your Inbox show up as numbers in parentheses next to the corresponding category of the Inbox. You can click any of those categories to go straight to that part of the Inbox to check them. If you look at Figure 9-1 again, notice that you can go to your Inbox by clicking the word Inbox from the middle of the screen (if you have any pending messages), or you can go straight to one of the five most recent messages in your Inbox by clicking the appropriate subject link.

If you scroll down your LinkedIn home page, you see modules of other aspects of LinkedIn, like Answers, Jobs, and Network Updates, as shown in Figure 9-3. Based on your profile, positions, and whether you participate in functions like LinkedIn Answers, the site provides a default configuration for your home page and includes the modules it thinks are most useful to you.

Reading your network updates

One of the ways to stay involved with your LinkedIn network is to stay up to date on how your first-degree connections are using LinkedIn (for more on connection degrees, see Chapter 1). To that end, a section called Network Updates gives you a summary of all the activity within your immediate LinkedIn network.

Figure 9-3 gives you an idea of what this network update can contain. If you are looking at the Network Updates section of your LinkedIn home page, you can scroll down and click the See More Network Updates link to get a full listing of your network updates, as shown in Figure 9-4.

You can customize the network updates you see in your section, so you need to decide which of the following events are worth keeping track of:

✔ Any Photo updates to your connections' profiles

✔ Any Profile updates your connections make to their profiles

✔ Any Recommendations given by a first-degree connection

✔ Any new connections in your extended network (meaning any new connections your first-degree contacts made)

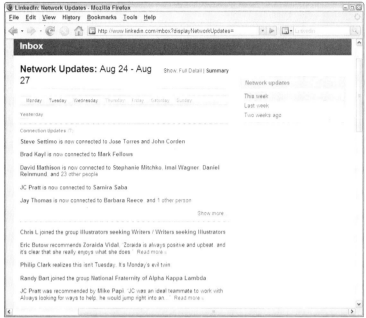

Figure 9-4:
Get the
full story
on your
LinkedIn
Network
Updates.

✔ Any changes in your first-degree connection's status on LinkedIn

✔ Any questions posed by a first-degree connection

✔ Any answers given by a first-degree connection

✔ Any groups a first-degree contact of yours has joined

✔ Any discussions from your company group (if you belong to a company group)

If you'd like to change the criteria of your Network Updates section, just follow these steps:

1. **Click the Account & Settings link in the top-right corner of any LinkedIn page.**

   You arrive at the Account & Settings page.

2. **Scroll down to the Settings header and look for the Home Page Settings section and click the Network Updates link.**

   You see the Network Updates page, as shown in Figure 9-5. By default, all of the criteria shown on this page should be set to Show.

3. **(Optional) If you want to remove any of the criteria from the list, simply click the Hide radio button on the corresponding line to turn off that criteria.**

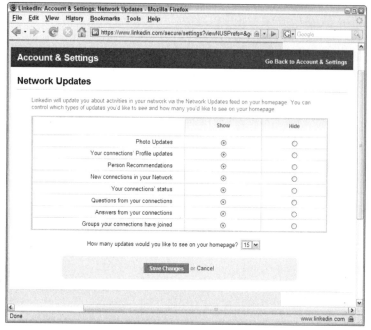

Figure 9-5:
Decide what
network
updates you
want to see.

Additionally, you can change the number of network updates being displayed on your home page by picking a number from the drop-down list near the bottom. (The default is 15; you can choose between 10 and 25.)

4. **When you're ready, click the Save Changes button to save your choices.**

You're taken back to the Account & Settings page.

Having LinkedIn automatically contact you

Sure, you can do all the footwork by going to the LinkedIn home page and looking around to see what messages or changes have occurred. The true power of staying connected, however, is having LinkedIn automatically contact you with the information you need to stay informed.

When you click the Account & Settings link on the home page, you go to the Account & Settings page, which contains information about your account and your LinkedIn settings. Scroll down to the Settings section, as shown in Figure 9-6. This is your hub for controlling how you interact with LinkedIn and how the site will communicate with you.

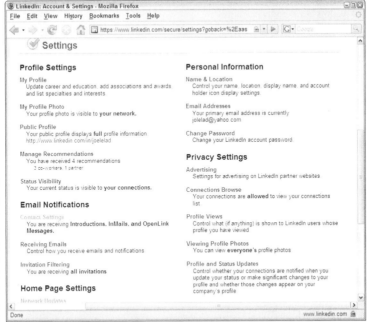

Figure 9-6:
Control your
LinkedIn
settings
from the
Account
& Settings
page.

Start by looking at your e-mail notifications. If you go to the Email Notifications section, you can review your e-mail notifications from LinkedIn by following these steps:

1. **On the Account & Settings page, click the Receiving Messages link in the Email Notifications section.**

   You're taken to the Receiving Messages page, as shown in Figure 9-7.

2. **Review the list of options and decide how you want to receive your e-mails. Select the radio button in one of the three columns:**

   • *Individual Email:* As soon as something occurs in a given category, like Introductions, Invitations, or Job Notifications, LinkedIn will send you an e-mail with that one item in the email.

   • *Digest Email:* Instead of individual e-mails, LinkedIn would group together all the activities in a given category and send you one e-mail per week in a digest format, with a summary at the top of the e-mail and the detailed activities below the summary.

   • *Web Only:* You can turn off e-mail notification by selecting the Web Only option. You can read the message when logged in to the LinkedIn site.

3. **(Optional) Select the Send Me Messages about New Features and Tips check box to sign up for a monthly newsletter from LinkedIn.**

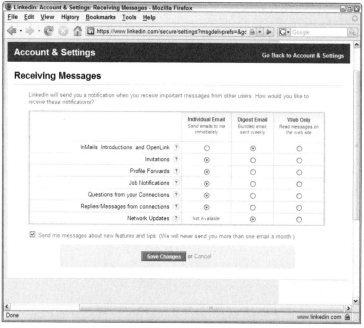

4. Click the Save Changes button to save your work.

You are returned to the Account & Settings page.

Understanding your Inbox

The best hub for your communications is the LinkedIn Inbox. You can get to the Inbox by clicking the Inbox link in the left navigation menu. In most cases, you go to the action items (or new messages that require your attention) in your Inbox, as shown in Figure 9-8. If you have no pending items, you will see a link to display all your archived (old) messages.

Here are some things to keep in mind when navigating your Inbox:

✔ **Using the links on the right:** You can click any of the links along the right side to see your InMail, Introductions, Invitations, Q&A, Jobs, Messages, forwarded Profiles, or Recommendations. Boldface type indicates that you have unread or action items to clear out.

✔ **Archiving:** In some cases, the items in this list have been acted on (In the upcoming Figure 9-9, an InMail from Kay Luo has been accepted), but if you want the item removed as an action item, click the subject link to bring up the message and then click the Archive button from inside the message to remove the item from your Inbox.

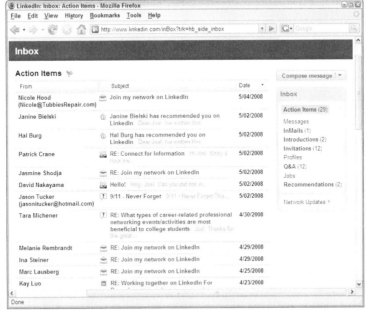

Figure 9-8:
Review the
action items
in your
Inbox.

✔ **Viewing the archive:** If you ever want to view your archived messages, look for a link entitled Show Archived Messages, which appears near the top of any of your Inbox subject pages, like Messages, Introductions, and so on. When you click that link, your archived message appears in the list with all other messages.

✔ **Flagging your message:** If you click the drop-down arrow next to Compose Message (in the top-right corner of your Inbox page) you can choose from several options, like sending an Invitation, Introduction, Recommendation, or Job notification.

Tracking Your InMail and Your Introductions

Although many of your communications with immediate first-degree LinkedIn connections take place through your own e-mail system, communications with people *outside* your network of first-degree connections need to be tracked and responded to using LinkedIn. So take a look at how you can track InMail and Introductions through your LinkedIn Inbox.

You can click either the InMail or Introductions link underneath the Inbox link, in the left navigation menu, to go directly to your list of InMail messages or Introductions. For example, when I click the InMail link, I go to the InMails page shown in Figure 9-9. Note that, even though I've accepted the InMail, the top message shows up as an action item (see the flag next to the person's name) because I haven't yet used LinkedIn to reply to or archive this message. In addition, you can easily switch between received and sent InMails by clicking the Received or Sent links near the top right of the screen.

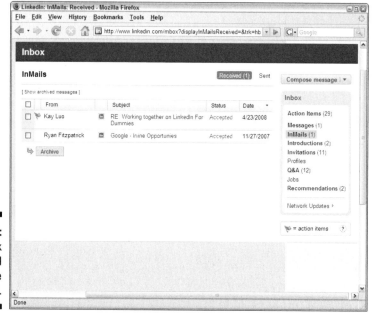

Figure 9-9:
Take a look
at the InMail
you've
received.

If you take a look at your Introductions message list, you see a setup like the one shown in Figure 9-10. You can easily switch between received and sent Introductions by clicking the Received or Sent links near the top right of the screen. Figure 9-10 is set to show received Introductions. The top Introduction in this example, Patrick Crane, has been accepted but is awaiting my reply to Mr. Crane's acceptance. The second Introduction, from David Nakayama, has yet to be acted upon, but both items still retain the action flag indicating a current to-do item.

The process is similar for tracking your answers for any questions you may have posed on LinkedIn Answers and for any Recommendations you may have received. Turn to Chapters 7 if you want to find out about how to respond to Answers, and see Chapter 8 for more info on Recommendations.

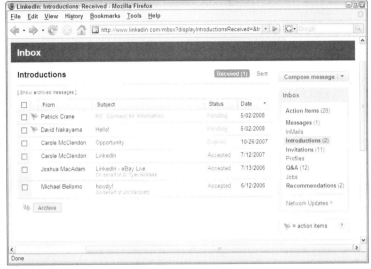

Figure 9-10:
Take a
look at the
Introduction
messages
you've
received.

Tracking Invitations

As you grow your network, keep track of the Invitations you've made to your connections and any incoming Invitations from other people. I cover Invitations in Chapter 2, and I talk about setting up your notifications for receiving e-mail about Invitations in the section "Having LinkedIn automatically contact you" earlier this chapter, but the following sections tell you about monitoring your Invitations on the LinkedIn Web site.

Tracking sent Invitations

The last thing you want to do is send out repeat Invitations to the same person because you didn't monitor your Sent Invitations list. Also, you may want to review your Sent Invitations list because someone hasn't responded yet; you can send that person a follow-up e-mail either through LinkedIn or via your own e-mail account. Thankfully, LinkedIn keeps a running list of all the Invitations you sent out with the current status (Accepted, Doesn't Know, Expired, or Sent) of each Invitation on that page as well.

When you want to track your sent Invitations, follow these steps:

1. Click the Contacts link in the left navigation menu.

This opens up the list of all your current first-degree connections, as shown in Figure 9-11.

Sent Invitations link

Figure 9-11: Click the Sent Invitations link to see all your sent Invitations.

2. **Click the Sent Invitations link to pull up a list of all your sent Invitations.**

You see the Sent Invitations page, as shown in Figure 9-12. The status besides each Invitation shows up as Sent (gray), Accepted (green), or Don't Know (red).

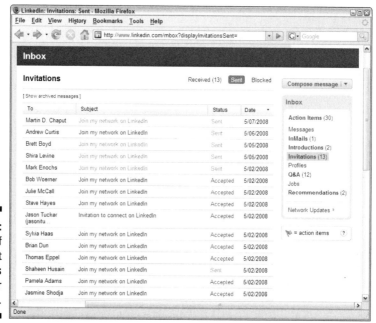

Figure 9-12: See a list of your sent Invitations and their statuses.

3. **You can click any of the column headers (like To, Subject, Status, or Date) to change the sort order of the list.**

   For example, you can group all your Invitations by Status: Just click the Status column header once to sort the list by status. At the top are Accepted messages, then Doesn't Know, Expired, Sent, and finally Withdrawn invitations.

4. **To view an individual Invitation, click the Subject link for that particular Invitation.**

   You see a copy of your Invitation, like the one shown in Figure 9-13. In this particular case, you see the options presented because the recipient has not acted on the Invitation yet.

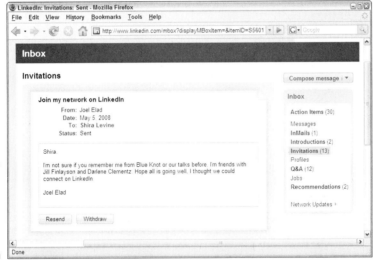

Figure 9-13: Review an Invitation you've sent out.

5. **Click the Resend button to send a reminder to this person; click the Withdraw button to delete your Invitation request.**

   When you withdraw the request, no message is sent to the other person.

Tracking received Invitations

When growing your LinkedIn network, you should be responsive to others who want to add you to their LinkedIn connections lists. To review your received Invitations, follow these steps.

1. **Click the plus sign next to the Inbox link and then click the Invitations link in the list that appears in the left navigation menu.**

   You're taken to a list of your received Invitations, as shown in Figure 9-14. The status of each Invitation is shown in the Status column.

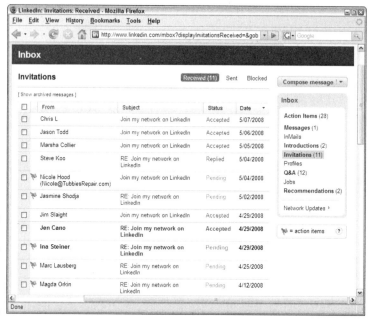

Figure 9-14: Review your received Invitations here.

2. **When you want to review a Pending Invitation, click the Subject link. (It will typically say Join My Network on LinkedIn, but the other party may have customized the text.)**

   You see the Invitation Request. Click either Accept, I Don't Know (this person), or Archive. There are also links you can click to Reply (to get further clarification in case you do not recognize the person) or Flag as Spam. (See Chapter 6 for tips on growing your network.)

   In some cases, you may see an entry with the subject link RE: Join My Network on LinkedIn and the status of Pending. These are replies to invitations you made to a person. When you click the Subject link, you see the reply, along with three buttons, as shown in Figure 9-15, that allow you to View Invitation, Reply, or Archive the message.

3. **To change the status of this message from Pending, either click the Reply button to send this person a response or click the Archive button to remove it from the list.**

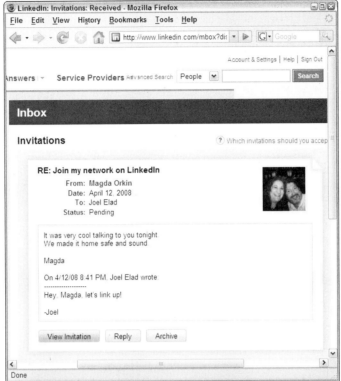

Figure 9-15:
Review
any replies
to your
Invitations.

Chapter 10

Using LinkedIn with Your E-Mail and Browser

*T*his chapter delves into how you can use LinkedIn as a part of your overall presence on the Internet, especially when it comes to communication. Specifically, I focus on two aspects of your Internet experience: your e-mail account and Internet Web browser.

LinkedIn makes it convenient for you to exchange information between your e-mail program and your LinkedIn profile and to enhance your World Wide Web browsing experience with specialized LinkedIn functions. One feature that LinkedIn offers is to enable you to import your contact list from programs such as Microsoft Outlook into LinkedIn. You can also do the reverse — that is, export your LinkedIn contact list to a variety of e-mail programs, including that for your Mac OS X. Another neat feature in LinkedIn is some toolbars that you can easily install to work with your e-mail program and Web browser. For example, the Outlook toolbar allows you to access certain LinkedIn information while writing e-mails in Outlook. I cover all these cool features in this chapter.

I also tell you about a nifty tool that LinkedIn offers to create an e-mail signature block for you that helps you promote your LinkedIn profile.

Importing Contacts into LinkedIn

One of the most popular (and necessary) activities people use the Internet for is e-mail. Your e-mail account contains a wealth of information in the form of lists and memos with everyone you regularly communicate with via e-mail. Therefore, because you've already established this base of communications, LinkedIn offers a way for you to ramp up your network by importing a list of contacts from your e-mail program. After all, if you've already sent or received an e-mail from someone (who's not a spammer, of course), chances are you know that person in some respect and would like to connect with them via LinkedIn if you haven't already. Importing your e-mail contacts into LinkedIn takes the drudge work out of going through your Address Book and copying addresses into LinkedIn. The next sections show you how to generate a list of contacts and import that list into LinkedIn to update your connections.

Importing a Contacts list from Outlook

One of the most popular e-mail programs used today is Microsoft Outlook, especially in corporations that run the Windows operating system. This section shows you how to import your Microsoft Outlook Contacts list into LinkedIn. To do so, follow these steps:

1. **On the main Outlook screen, click Contacts to bring up your Contact List (similar to that shown in Figure 10-1).**

Figure 10-1: Pull up your Outlook Contacts list.

2. **Choose File ➪ Import and Export.**

   The Import and Export window appears.

3. Select the Export to a File option and click the Next button; then, in the Export to a File window, select a file type.

You see a list of options, like Comma Separated Values (DOS), Comma Separated Values (Windows), Microsoft Access, and so on.

4. Select the Comma Separated Values (Windows) option and click the Next button.

The Export to a File window appears, as shown in Figure 10-2. Here, you're asked to pick a folder that you want to export. You need to look for the Contacts window, which contains your list of Contacts through Microsoft Outlook.

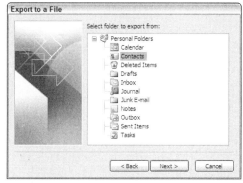

Figure 10-2:
Select your Contacts folder to export.

5. Select the Contacts folder to export and click the Next button.

If you have created categories within your Outlook Contacts list, you can select one of those subcategories under the main Contacts folder and export just those contacts.

6. In the next Export to a File window that appears, click the Browse button to find a suitable folder for this file, create a filename in the box provided, and click the Next button.

In the last box, Outlook displays the action it's about to take as shown in Figure 10-3.

Be sure to remember the filename and location of your exported Contacts file because you'll need this information in a few steps. Pick a memorable name and save the file to a commonly used folder on your computer.

7. Click the Finish button to start the export of your Outlook Contacts file.

Depending on the size of your Contacts list, the export process may take a few minutes. When the export is complete, the message box disappears from your screen and you re ready to go to the next step.

8. Using your Web browser, go to LinkedIn and log in to your profile; then, on the left navigation menu, click Connections to bring up your LinkedIn network.

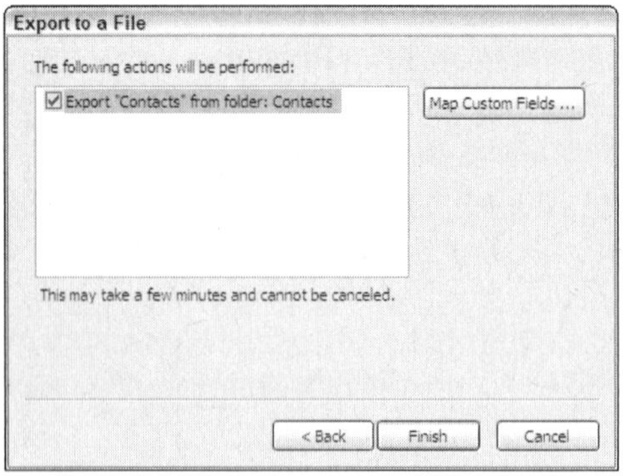

Export to a File

The following actions will be performed:

☑ Export "Contacts" from folder: Contacts   Map Custom Fields ...

This may take a few minutes and cannot be canceled.

< Back   Finish   Cancel

Figure 10-3:
Outlook
verifies
the Export
action.

9. **Click the Add Connections link from the top of the Connections screen and then, click the Import Contacts tab. On the page that appears, click the Other Address Book button.**

   The first page of the Upload Your Contacts File appears, as shown in Figure 10-4.

10. **Click the Browse button to locate the Contacts file you just exported from Microsoft Outlook. When you've located that file, click the Upload Contacts File button to start the process.**

    After LinkedIn has read your entire contacts list, LinkedIn displays a few sample names to make sure it has imported your list correctly, as shown in Figure 10-5.

    When LinkedIn imports the list, they usually drop the middle name from each person's full name when creating the imported contacts. You may need to edit your contacts to add the appropriate information.

11. **Review the sample names and, if correct, click the Finish Upload button to complete the process.**

    If the names aren't correct, you can click the Send to Customer Service button to send this list to LinkedIn Customer Support for help, or you can click the Cancel Upload button to abandon the process.

12. **If you clicked the Finish Upload button, you should see your new contacts in the Imported Contacts screen of your Connections list, similar to that shown in Figure 10-6.**

    You can select the box next to individual contacts, or select the Select All check box, and then click the Invite Selected Contacts button to invite each of these people to your LinkedIn network.

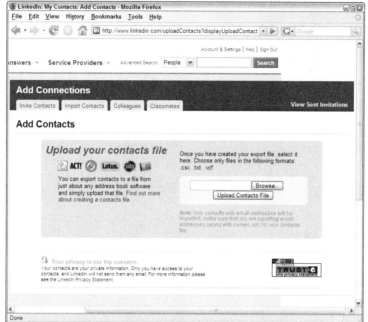

Figure 10-4:
LinkedIn is ready for your Outlook Contacts list.

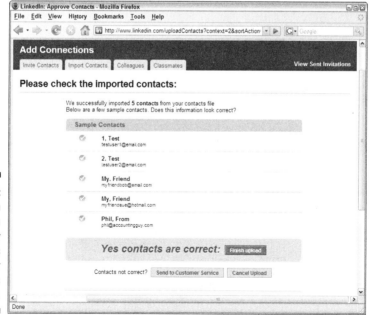

Figure 10-5:
LinkedIn asks you to verify some names on your Contacts list.

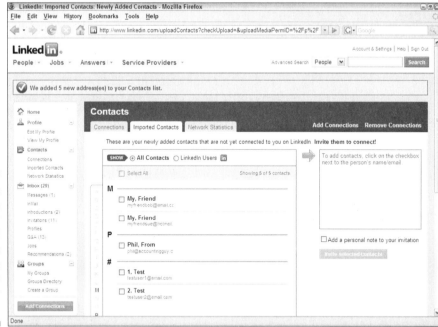

Figure 10-6:
Pick which
of your
imported
contacts
gets an
Invitation
to your
network!

Importing contacts from a Web-based e-mail program

Many people use a program based on the World Wide Web to send and receive e-mail. Gmail (from Google), Yahoo! Mail, and Hotmail are among the most prevalent of this type of program, which is known as *Webmail*. If you use a Webmail program, you can still import your contact list and feed it into LinkedIn to expand your network. For the example in this section, I use Yahoo! Mail, but the other systems work similarly to Yahoo! for importing contacts.

To import your Webmail contact list, just follow these steps:

1. **Using your Web browser, go to LinkedIn and log in to your profile; then, on the left navigation menu, click Connections to bring up your LinkedIn network.**

2. **Click the Add Connections link at the top of the Connections screen and then click the Import Contacts tab.**

   The Check Webmail page appears, as shown in Figure 10-7.

3. **Click the Check Webmail button.**

   After you click this button, LinkedIn asks you to pick your Webmail program from a list presented (Hotmail, Yahoo, Gmail, and AOL) by selecting the appropriate radio button. After you select the service, you will either provide your login information on the same screen or click a button to be taken to the program, as shown in Figure 10-8.

4. **Follow the instructions to access your Webmail account.**

For this example, I clicked the Login to Yahoo! Button, which took me to the Yahoo! login screen. After I logged in to my account, Yahoo! requested my permission to let LinkedIn access my Yahoo! Address Book, as shown in Figure 10-9. You must click the I Agree button if you want LinkedIn to import your contacts. When you do this, LinkedIn automatically goes into the account and starts importing contacts, and you're returned to the LinkedIn Web site.

5. **When you connect your Webmail account to LinkedIn, review the imported contacts and whom you want to invite to your LinkedIn network.**

Select the check box next to each person you want to invite and then click the Invite Selected Contacts button to send the Invitation.

Figure 10-7:
LinkedIn can check your Webmail program for contacts.

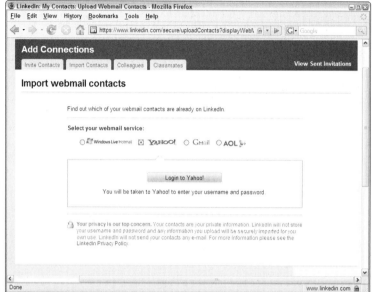

Figure 10-8:
LinkedIn will
go to Yahoo!
to read your
Contacts
list.

Figure 10-9:
You need
to allow
LinkedIn to
read your
Address
Book.

Exporting Contacts from LinkedIn to Your E-Mail Application

As you use LinkedIn and build up your contact network, you may find yourself in the situation of having more contacts "on file" in your LinkedIn network than your e-mail program. As you transfer your communications with LinkedIn members from the LinkedIn message system to your e-mail program, adding people one by one to your address book could take a while. Thankfully, LinkedIn has a function to make this easier.

In essence, your list of LinkedIn connections is similar to a list of names that could be found in an e-mail program's Address Book. Therefore, just as you can import contacts from an e-mail program into LinkedIn, the reverse is also true — you can export your LinkedIn contacts to your e-mail program. Exporting is a simple process that amounts to doing the following:

1. You export your LinkedIn connections into a contacts file.

2. You import the contacts file into your main e-mail program.

You can always pick and choose which contacts to export, and your e-mail program should be able to detect any duplicates — meaning if you try to import any names that already exist. I walk you through the process of exporting your LinkedIn contacts in the next few sections.

Creating your Contacts export file in LinkedIn

First, you need to generate your exported file of contacts from LinkedIn. To do so, follow these steps:

1. **On your LinkedIn profile page, click Connections on the left navigation bar and scroll to the bottom of the page that appears.**

2. **Click the link marked Export Connections.**

   You will be taken to the Export Connections page, as shown in Figure 10-10. Pick the e-mail program you want to export your contacts to from the drop-down list provided. Then, enter the security image text into the box provided.

3. **Click the Export button to generate your Contacts file.**

   The file dialog box appears, asking whether you want to open or save the file. Click Save to save the file to your computer. Give it a custom name, if you like, but remember the filename and location, because you will need that information when you load this file into your e-mail program, which I discuss in the next sections.

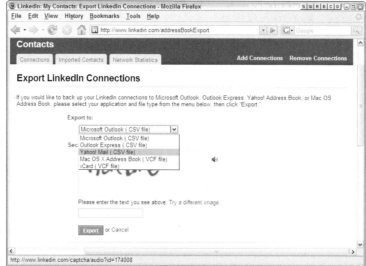

Figure 10-10:
Pick your
e-mail
program
and create
an exported
file of
contacts.

Exporting contacts to Outlook

After you have created your export file and are ready to export your contacts
to Microsoft Outlook, just follow these steps:

1. **On the main Outlook screen, choose File⇨Import and Export.**

   The Import and Export window appears.

2. **Select the Import from Another Program or File option and click the
   Next button.**

3. **When Outlooks asks you to select a file type to import from, select the
   Comma Separated Values (Windows) option and click the Next button.**

4. **When Outlook asks you for the file to import, enter the path and filename of your exported file, or click the Browse button to find the file
   on your computer. Be sure to select the Do Not Import Duplicate Items
   option and then click Next to continue.**

   If you don't select the Do Not Import Duplicate Items option, you risk
   flooding your Outlook account with multiple e-mail addresses and
   names for the same people, which will make your life more difficult and
   flood your connections with unnecessary e-mail messages.

5. **When Outlook asks you to select a destination folder, click the
   Contacts folder and click Next.**

6. **Verify that you're importing your contacts file into Outlook and click
   Finish to start the process.**

Exporting contacts to Outlook Express

Fortunately, even if you prefer Outlook Express to the full Outlook program, you're in luck: Your LinkedIn contacts can go live there just as easily as they can elsewhere. After you've created your export file (as described earlier, in the "Creating your Contacts export file in LinkedIn" section), you can export your connections to Outlook Express by following these steps:

1. **On your main Outlook Express screen, choose File➪Import.**

2. **In the Import window opens up, select the Other Address Book option and click Next.**

3. **When Outlook Express asks you to select a file type to import from, select the option Text File (Comma Separated Values) and click the Import button.**

4. **When Outlook Express asks you for the File to import, enter the path and filename of your exported file, or click the Browse button to find the file on your computer. Click Next to continue.**

5. **Verify the fields that you're importing into Outlook Express (click the Change Mapping button if you want to change how the information is being imported) and then Click Finish to start the process.**

Exporting contacts to Yahoo! Mail

If you're using a Web-based mail program, like Yahoo! Mail, you can follow this basic procedure to export your LinkedIn contacts into your mail program. After you have created your export file (as described earlier, in the "Creating your Contacts export file in LinkedIn" section), you can export your connections to Yahoo! Mail by following these steps:

1. **Using your Web browser, go to Yahoo! Mail and log in and then click the Contacts tab or the Address Book link to go to the Yahoo! Address Book.**

    You will see a page similar to that shown in Figure 10-11. Note that Import/Export Link in the top-right corner.

2. **Click the Import/Export link.**

    The Import and Export screen appears, as shown in Figure 10-12.

3. **In the drop-down list under Choose a Program to Import Contacts From , select Yahoo! (.CSV). In the box under Specify the File to Import, enter the path and filename of your exported file, or click the Browse button to find the file on your computer.**

4. **Click the Import Now button to start the process.**

Import/Export link

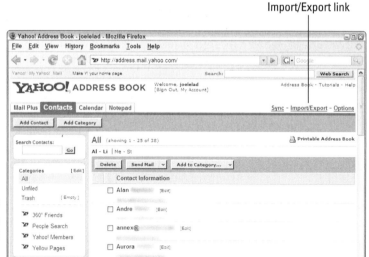

Figure 10-11:
Accessing
your Yahoo!
Address
Book.

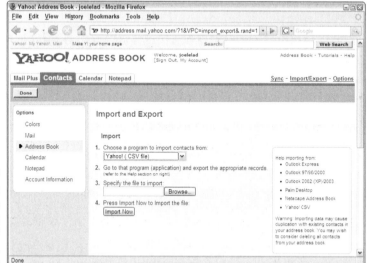

Figure 10-12:
Using the
Yahoo!
Import/
Export tool.

Exporting contacts to Mac OS X Address Book

After you've created your export file (as described earlier, in the "Creating your Contacts export file in LinkedIn" section), you can export your connections to Mac OS X Address Book by following these steps:

1. **Open your Mac OS X Address Book program by clicking it.**

2. **Look for the contacts file you created in the previous section on your computer.**

3. **Drag this file into the Address Book.**

    This should start the importing of contacts from your LinkedIn contacts file.

Using the LinkedIn Outlook Toolbar

If you use Microsoft Outlook for your e-mail and you find yourself constantly switching between Outlook and the LinkedIn Web site to retrieve information, send e-mail to your connections using Outlook, and screen incoming e-mail by jumping to LinkedIn to read their profile, you're in luck! LinkedIn has developed a special toolbar that you can install in your system that automatically ties into its Web site. This toolbar appears as part of your Microsoft Outlook screen and gives you several functions to make the connection between Outlook and LinkedIn smoother.

Understanding the toolbar's requirements and features

To use the LinkedIn Outlook toolbar, you need to have certain levels of software on your computer for the toolbar to work correctly.

- ✔ Your operating system needs to be either Microsoft Windows XP or Vista.

- ✔ Your Microsoft Outlook program should be the XP (or 2002), 2003, or 2007 version.

- ✔ You should have at least 5@nd10MB of free space on your hard drive before installing this program.

Here are the main benefits you can enjoy after installing this toolbar function:

✔ **This toolbar will suggest sending an Invitation to someone to join your network based on the number of times you e-mail that person.** The higher the "e-mail frequency," the more likely you should add them to your LinkedIn network.

✔ **This toolbar allows you to send Invitations with one click, instead of your having to find the person's profile on LinkedIn and clicking through the Invite process.** You can also pull up the LinkedIn Web site with one click using the toolbar.

✔ **This toolbar automatically displays a LinkedIn "mini-profile" of someone when you read an e-mail from that person using Outlook.** This way, you can get more information about the sender, in the form of a pop-up, instantly rather than manually going to LinkedIn to research the person.

✔ **Your Outlook contact information for a LinkedIn connection is automatically updated with that connection's profile information.**

✔ **You can receive e-mail notifications when someone in your LinkedIn network updates his or her profile information.**

✔ **You can access a LinkedIn "dashboard" to get a snapshot of your LinkedIn network and the status of your connections.**

Installing the Outlook Toolbar

To install the Outlook toolbar, just follow these steps:

1. **Go to LinkedIn's home page, scroll to the bottom of the page, and in the section marked Tools, click the link Outlook Toolbar.**

   The Outlook Toolbar screen, shown in Figure 10-13, appears.

2. **Click the Download It Now button and, when the LinkedIn Outlook Toolbar Setup Wizard opens, click the Next button.**

   The page with the License Agreement appears.

3. **Review the License Agreement, select the I Accept. . . check box, and click the Next button.**

4. **In the Choose Install Location screen that appears, accept the default location (recommended) or pick a new directory to install the toolbar program; then, click Install to start the process.**

   LinkedIn installs all the necessary files for the toolbar onto your computer. Allow at least a few minutes for this process to be completed. When the toolbar is installed, a Build Network Wizard window appears.

5. **Click the Start button and follow the steps to have the toolbar scan your Outlook program for contacts.**

   You can send an Invitation to these contacts to join your LinkedIn network.

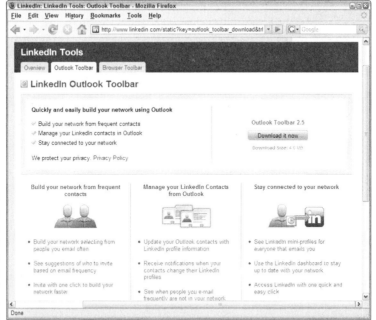

Figure 10-13:
Install the
Microsoft
Outlook
LinkedIn
Toolbar
here.

If you have already imported your Microsoft Outlook Address Book into LinkedIn, going through the Build Network Wizard may not result in a lot of new contacts, but this process can find contacts you have not saved to your Outlook Address Book.

Using the LinkedIn Browser Toolbar

Do you find yourself going back and forth between LinkedIn and other Web sites? Whether you do further research on someone from a general Web search by looking up their LinkedIn profile, or you're actively looking for a job and frequently switch between LinkedIn and other career job sites, LinkedIn has the tool for you!

Regardless of whether you use Microsoft Internet Explorer or Mozilla's Firefox Web browser, LinkedIn offers you a toolbar you can install that shows up as part of your Web browser and provides you with instant access to the LinkedIn Web site. The toolbar also offers integrated functions that give you access to items such as profile information with the click of a mouse.

You can get to the main LinkedIn Browser toolbar page (shown in Figure 10-14) by clicking the Browser Toolbar link from the Tools menu along the bottom of the LinkedIn home page. The following sections tell you how to install the toolbar, depending on your browser.

Figure 10-14:
LinkedIn
offers
two Web
browser
toolbars.

How to install the Internet Explorer toolbar

When you're ready to install the Internet Explorer toolbar, just follow these steps:

1. **Log in to LinkedIn, scroll to the bottom of the page, look for a menu bar labeled Tools, and click the Browser Toolbar link.**

2. **Click the Download It Now button under the IE Toolbar header.**

   A window like the one shown in Figure 10-15 opens, asking whether you want to open this installation file directly from the Internet or to save the installation file to your computer, where you can run it locally. Pick the option best for you and click the appropriate button.

   If you have a fast Internet connection, you can click Open to have the toolbar installed over your Internet connection. Otherwise, I recommend that you save the file to your computer and then run the file from your hard drive.

3. **When the LinkedIn Internet Explorer Toolbar Setup Wizard appears, click the Next button to start the process.**

   Accept the License Agreement and then click the Next button.

4. **On the Choose Install Location screen that appears, click the Install button to accept the default and start the installation of the toolbar.**

   You can also click the Browse button to pick another directory for the toolbar, but the default location should be fine.

Figure 10-15:
Windows
asks you
how to
install the
toolbar.

When the toolbar starts installing, you need to close all Internet Explorer windows. When you see the warning message from LinkedIn, click Yes, and the installation program will close all active windows for you.

5. When a screen appears confirming that LinkedIn has installed the IE Toolbar successfully, select the check box next to Launch Internet Explorer with LinkedIn Toolbar and click Finish.

A new Internet Explorer window opens containing the LinkedIn toolbar, as shown in Figure 10-16.

Figure 10-16:
Your IE
toolbar is
installed
and ready to
be used!

Installing the Firefox Companion toolbar

To install the Firefox Companion toolbar, just follow these steps:

1. Log in to LinkedIn, scroll to the bottom of the page, look for a menu bar labeled Tools, and click the Browser Toolbar link.

2. Click the Download It Now button under the Firefox Toolbar header.

A window like the one in Figure 10-17 appears, asking whether it should install this software.

3. Click the Install Now button.

LinkedIn installs the toolbar onto your computer, and you should see a confirmation message that the toolbar was installed successfully.

Figure 10-17:
Firefox
needs your
permission
to install the
toolbar.

4. **Click the Restart Firefox button to close and restart your Web browser session.**

The LinkedIn button is installed in the top-right area of your browser window, as shown in Figure 10-18. Anytime you need a LinkedIn function, just click the LinkedIn logo in the toolbar to bring up the special menu.

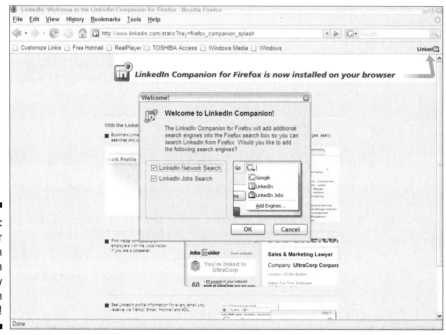

Figure 10-18:
Your
LinkedIn
companion
is ready
for use in
Firefox!

Creating E-Mail Signatures

One of the best ways to communicate your presence on LinkedIn is to add your LinkedIn profile to your e-mail signature, if you've created one. Every time you send an e-mail, you can have text appear automatically at the end of your message similar to a written signature you would put at the end of a letter. Some people just sign their name; others use this space as an opportunity to put their name and some contact information, such as phone numbers, e-mail addresses, physical addresses, and, more recently, Web site addresses. Some LinkedIn members have been including their profile URL, so anyone getting an e-mail from them can take a look at their person profile and learn more about them.

LinkedIn has decided to develop a cool tool that will allow you to build your own advanced e-mail signature using the LinkedIn Web site. You can decide what information you want to include in your signature, and LinkedIn helps you with formatting, graphics — the entire "look and feel" of your signature.

You can find the e-mail signature tool by clicking the Tools Overview link at the bottom of the LinkedIn home page. When you get to the Tools page, skip down below the toolbar sections and look for the Email Signature section (which is shown in Figure 10-19).

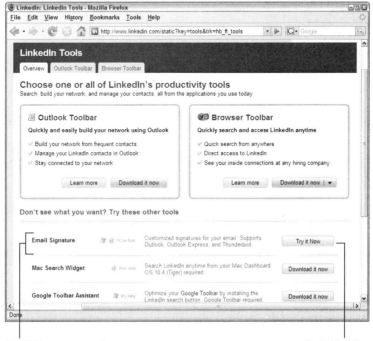

Figure 10-19:
Access
the Email
Signature
tool from the
Tools page.

Email Signature section

Try It Now button

When you're ready to create your e-mail signature, just follow these steps:

1. **Log in to LinkedIn, scroll to the bottom of the page, look for a menu bar labeled Tools, and click the Overview link.**

2. **On the Tools Overview page, scroll down to the section on Email Signature and click the gray Try It Now button.**

   When you click the Try It Now button, LinkedIn takes you to a special Profile page entitled Create Email Signature.

3. **On your Profile page, click the drop-down arrow next to Select Layout to pick which Layout option you want.**

   You have multiple options to select from. Some, such as Ingot or Plastic Curve, add a graphical look, whereas a Simple option lists your information as text, and the Executive layout presents your information in a more professional manner than the simple layouts do.

   Click around and pick a few layouts to see the automatic preview of that layout on your screen. This gives you an idea of which layout and color scheme you want. You may want to revisit this step after you enter all your information so that you know how your finished signature will appear.

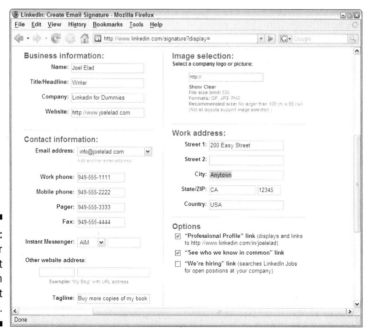

Figure 10-20: Put your contact information in the right boxes.

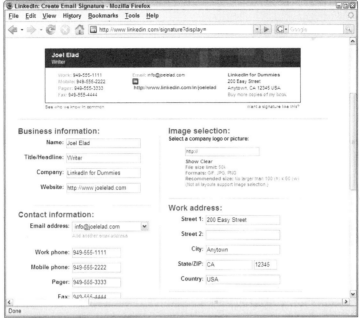

Figure 10-21:
Here's how
your info
looks in your
e-mail
signature!

4. **After you have picked your layout style, you need to enter the contact information you want to appear in your signature.**

   You can input as much or as little as you'd like in the boxes provided (see Figure 10-20), and that information will be reflected in your signature file (see Figure 10-21).

5. **Add a picture to your signature, if you want, by entering the URL of that picture's location in the box provided under Image Selection.**

   If you've already uploaded a picture of yourself for your LinkedIn profile, you can include it here as well.

6. **Decide which of three links can appear as part of your signature by clicking the appropriate check box(es):**

   - *The Professional Profile link* creates a URL link to your LinkedIn Profile page.

   - *The See Who We Know in Common link* creates a link to LinkedIn that, when a LinkedIn member clicks the link, shows other LinkedIn members who are connected to you and that person.

   - *The We're Hiring link* creates a link that takes someone back to LinkedIn and starts a Job Search query for job openings in the company you've listed in your LinkedIn profile.

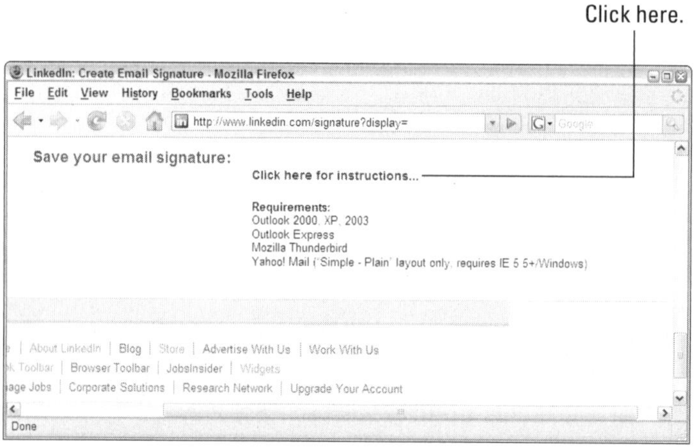

Click here.

Figure 10-22: Click this link to generate your e-mail signature.

I highly recommend turning on the Professional Profile link. The other two links are fine to have as well, especially if you want to promote job listings at your own company.

7. **Click the Click Here for Instructions link under the Save your Email Signature header to create and save your e-mail signature (see Figure 10-22).**

This action results in a pop-up window with your e-mail signature information. If you have a pop-up blocker on your Web browser, you may want to deactivate it temporarily before performing this step, or be ready to temporarily allow pop-ups from LinkedIn.com.

8. **When the page with the pop-up window containing the "code" of your e-mail signature appears, as shown in Figure 10-22, you can simply select all the text in the box and paste it into your favorite e-mail program, or you can scroll down and follow the instructions.**

LinkedIn provides instructions for the most popular e-mail programs, such as Outlook and Yahoo! Mail. Click the drop-down arrow to bring up your e-mail program and instructions will appear at the bottom of the window, as do the instructions for Outlook Express in Figure 10-23.

Figure 10-23:
Your e-mail
signature
is created!
Copy and
paste into
your e-mail
program.

Part IV
Finding Employees, Jobs, and Services

The 5th Wave   By Rich Tennant

"Still trying to create a flock on LinkedIn?"

In this part . . .

I'm a firm believer in the phrase "Good help is hard to find." I'm not sure why that's the case, but it seems to be tougher and tougher to find someone you can trust who can help you out. I could get all philosophical and wax poetic about the good ol' days, when everything cost a nickel and you had to hike up the mountain, covered in two feet of snow, *both ways,* to get a jug of milk. But I digress. . . .

This part of the book talks specifically about how LinkedIn can help you do one of three things: Find a good employee, find a job, or find a qualified service professional, like a graphic designer, an accountant, or even a gardener. I provide detailed instructions on how to access the Jobs portion of LinkedIn, whether you're a job seeker or an employer, and gear all the functions that LinkedIn offers with specific advice on how you accomplish these three tasks.

Chapter 11

Finding Employees

. . . .

In This Chapter

▶ Posting a job listing

▶ Advertising your job listing to your network

▶ Reviewing applicants

▶ Screening any potential applicants using LinkedIn

▶ Doing a reference check on a candidate

▶ Search strategies for finding active or passive job seekers

. . . .

*W*hen you have a handle on the key elements of improving your LinkedIn profile and experience, it's time to look outward towards the LinkedIn network and talk about some of the benefits you can reap from a professional network of tens of millions of people.

Whether you're an entrepreneur looking for your first employee, a growing start-up needing to add a knowledgeable staffer, or a part of a Fortune 500 company filling a recent opening, LinkedIn can provide a very rich and powerful pool of potential applicants and job candidates, including the perfectly skilled person who isn't even looking for a job! One of the benefits of LinkedIn, when it comes to looking for an employee, is that you aren't limited to an applicant's one- or two-page resume and cover letter. Instead, you get the full picture of the applicant's professional history, coupled with recommendations and his knowledge and/or willingness to share information. Even if you find your candidate outside LinkedIn, you can use the site to perform reference checks and get more information about your candidate.

In this chapter, I cover the basics of using LinkedIn to find an employee for your company or startup. I start with the basics of how you can post your job listing on LinkedIn and review your applicants. I then move on to the Reference Check function, where you can use LinkedIn to screen potential candidates, and I finish the chapter with search strategies you should employ to find the right person.

Posting a Job Listing

LinkedIn offers a Hiring page for companies to manage their job listings. Click the drop-down arrow next to the Jobs link on the top navigation bar on the home page, and select Hiring Home to see the Hiring home page, as shown in Figure 11-1. This is where you start the process of creating a job listing, reviewing the applicants you get, and paying LinkedIn to post the listing.

Figure 11-1: LinkedIn offers a Hiring page to manage your job listings

As of this writing, it costs $195 for one standard 30-day job listing on LinkedIn. LinkedIn also offers packs of five or ten Job Credits (one Job Credit allows you to post one job listing) that reduce the per-listing cost by up to 40 percent or so. You can pay for your job listing with a major credit card such as Visa, MasterCard, American Express, or Discover.

If you know that you're going to need multiple or ongoing job postings on LinkedIn, you might want to consider LinkedIn Corporate Solutions to get discounts on multiple credits for job postings and InMail. You can get more information by completing a request at www.linkedin.com/static?key=corporate_inquiry.

You can choose to renew your listing at the end of the 30-day window. Your *date posted* (the date you set up the job listing) will be updated with the renewal date instead of the original posting date, so the listing will appear at the top of search results. The cost for renewing a job listing is the same as the initial job posting cost.

You can advertise only one open position per job listing. If you solicit applications for more than one position within a single job listing, LinkedIn will remove your listing or require you to purchase multiple job credits.

Posting a job listing

To post your job opening, follow these steps:

1. **Click the Jobs drop-down arrow in the top navigation bar, and select Post a Job.**

   You see the Step 1: Compose Job screen, as shown in Figure 11-2.

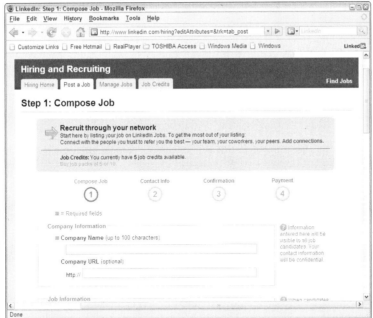

Figure 11-2:
Start composing your job posting here.

2. **Complete the text boxes provided in the Company Information and Job Information sections.**

   Provide your company name, job title, function, industry, type, and experience level. Then, you can compose your job description in the text box provided (see Figure 11-3) or copy the description from another source and paste it into the box. Just make sure any formatting (like spacing, bullet points, font size, and so on) is correct after you paste the text.

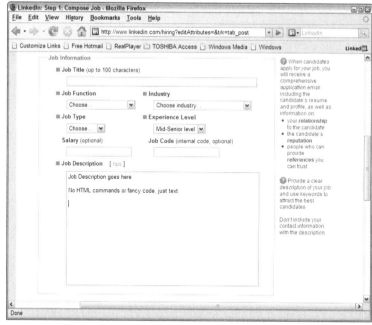

Figure 11-3:
Enter the job
description
in the text
box
provided.

If your company or job title isn't that well known, you should include some details about the company or job title in the Job Description field as well as the responsibilities and duties of the position.

3. Scroll down and fill in the Location Information and Additional Information sections.

LinkedIn automatically fills in your city, country, and postal code in the boxes provided (see Figure 11-4) based on your profile, but you should update them if necessary with the location of the position. You can select the check boxes under Additional Information to add more requirements to the job.

If you're advertising this job only on LinkedIn, select the check box labeled This Job Is Available Exclusively on LinkedIn to get a special star next to your listing, which alerts job seekers that the position can only be found on LinkedIn.

4. Click the Next button to proceed to the Step 2: Contact Information page as shown in Figure 11-5.

You're asked whether to link your profile to the job listing. Select the Yes button to link your profile. Scroll down and identify your hiring role (are you a hiring manager, a human resource representative, a recruiter, or an employee?) and the e-mail address where you want the job applications to be sent.

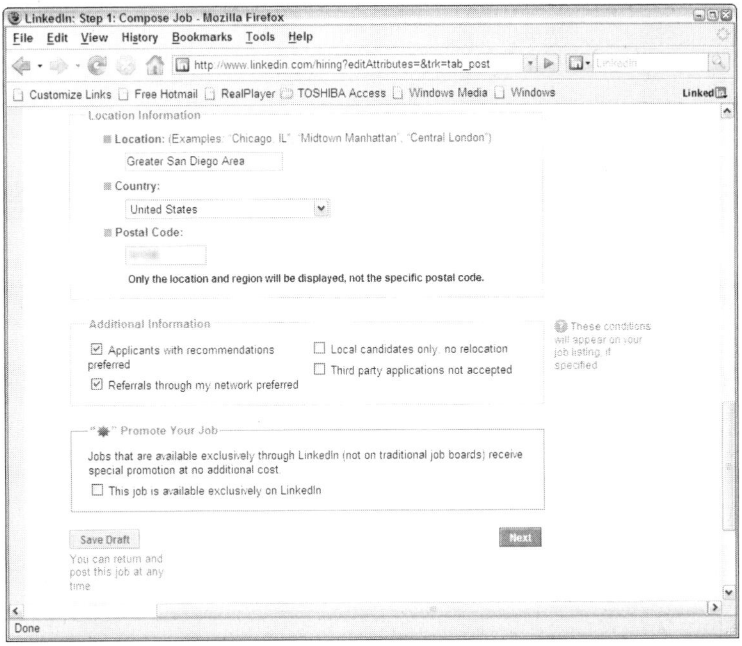

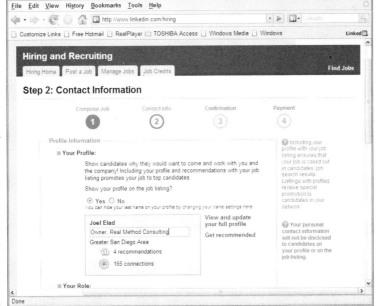

Figure 11-4:
Set your location and additional requirements.

Figure 11-5:
Decide whether to connect your profile with your job listing.

5. **Click the Next button to proceed to the Step 3: Confirmation page as shown in Figure 11-6.**

   Review all the information you entered from Steps 1 and 2 by scrolling through the listing. If you need to make any changes, click the Edit link in the appropriate section to go back and correct that part.

6. **Select your payment method (Visa, MasterCard, American Express, Discover, or a pre-paid Job Credit) and click the Post This Job button.**

   If you haven't already paid for Job Credits, you're taken to Step 4: Payment, where LinkedIn collects and processes your credit card information. After that has been done, your listing will be posted to LinkedIn Jobs.

That's it! You have completed the all-important first step: you posted your job listing. Next up, you should use your LinkedIn network members to spread the word about your job listing and see who they recommend.

Advertising your job listing to your network

When you send your job posting out to the Internet, you're hoping that the extensive database of job seekers will find the posting and the appropriate parties will submit their resumes and cover letters. When you use LinkedIn for a job, however, you have a distinct advantage: *your own network.* You're connected to people who you know and trust, people who you have worked with before so you know their capabilities, and most importantly, people who know you and (hopefully) have a better idea than the average person as to what kind of person you would hire.

LinkedIn allows you to send all or some of the people in your network a message, letting them know about your job opening and asking them if they, or anyone they know, might be interested in this job. When you're ready to advertise your job listing, follow these steps:

1. **Click the drop-down arrow next to Jobs (on the top navigation bar) and then select Manage Jobs.**

   After you've posted your job, you should see the position listed in the Manage Jobs window under Open Jobs. Click on that job title to bring up the Job Status window for that job listing, as shown in Figure 11-7.

2. **Click the Tell Your Network! button to generate a LinkedIn message.**

   LinkedIn automatically generates a response, as shown in Figure 11-8, that you can send out to your network. Feel free to edit the text in the message box to make it sound like it's coming from you, or just leave the default message in place.

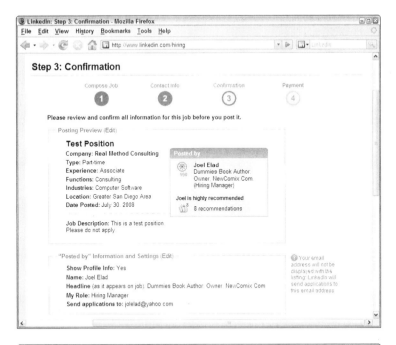

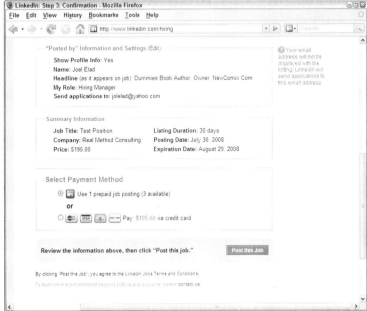

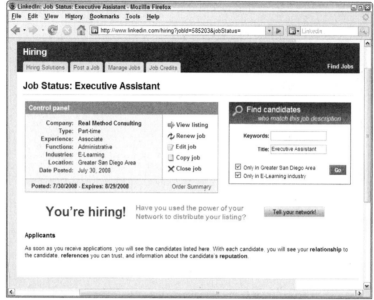

Figure 11-7:
Tell your
network
about your
new job
listing.

3. **Click the Select Connections button to decide who will get this message from you.**

   A window opens up with all your connections, as shown in Figure 11-9. You can use the options under Narrow Your Connections to reduce the list you see in the window.

4. **From your Narrow Your Connections window, select the people you want to send this message to by clicking the check box next to their names, so their names appear in the list on the right.**

   You can also select the check box next to "Showing X of X connections" to automatically select up to 200 connections from your network.

5. **Click the Finished button to return to your message. Look over the text in the window again, make sure you have the right people selected, and when you're ready, click the Send button as shown in Figure 11-10.**

Your LinkedIn connections will receive a message in their LinkedIn inboxes and, depending on their notification settings, an e-mail with this message as well. They can click a link from the message to see the job listing and either apply themselves or forward it to their contacts for consideration.

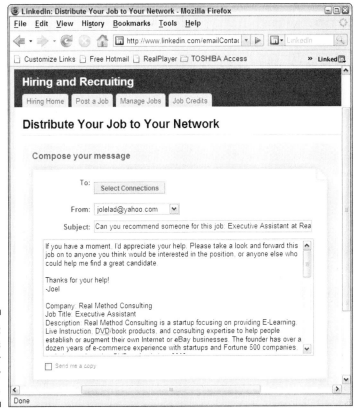

Figure 11-8:
LinkedIn lets you ask your network for help.

This shows how many connections you have to choose from.

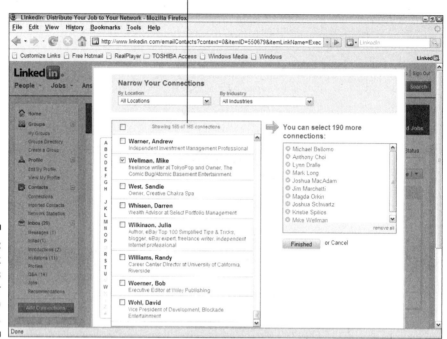

Figure 11-9:
Pick
members
of your
network to
be notified.

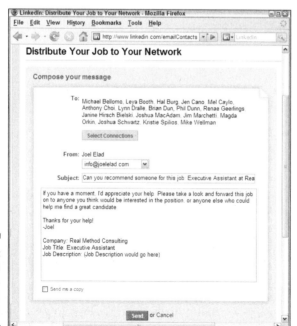

Figure 11-10:
Proofread
your mes-
sage and
send it out!

Reviewing applicants

Once you've posted your job listing on LinkedIn, you should expect to get some applicants for the position. Every time someone applies for that job, you will receive an e-mail from LinkedIn notifying you of their application. In addition, LinkedIn records their application in the Applicants section of the Job Status page.

When you are ready to review the applicants for your job, follow these steps:

1. **Click the drop-down arrow next to Jobs (on the top navigation bar) and then select Manage Jobs.**

   You should be taken to the Manage Jobs: Open Jobs window as shown in Figure 11-11.

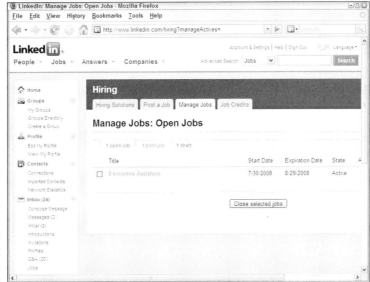

Figure 11-11: Review your open job listings to see who has applied.

2. **Click the Job Title of the job listing you want to review.**

   This brings up the Job Status page for the job listing, as shown in Figure 11-12. You should see the Applicants listed under the Control Panel statistics for the job listing.

3. **Review the LinkedIn profile, resume, and cover letter for each applicant by clicking on the appropriate link in each line of the applicants list.**

   Each applicant's profile, resume, and cover letter are available through clicking the designated link. If you scroll down the page, you can see all the applicants for the job listing, as shown in Figure 11-13.

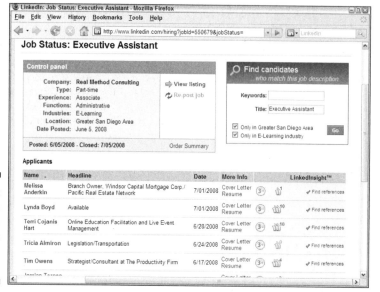

Figure 11-12:
Go through
each
applicant's
resume and
cover letter.

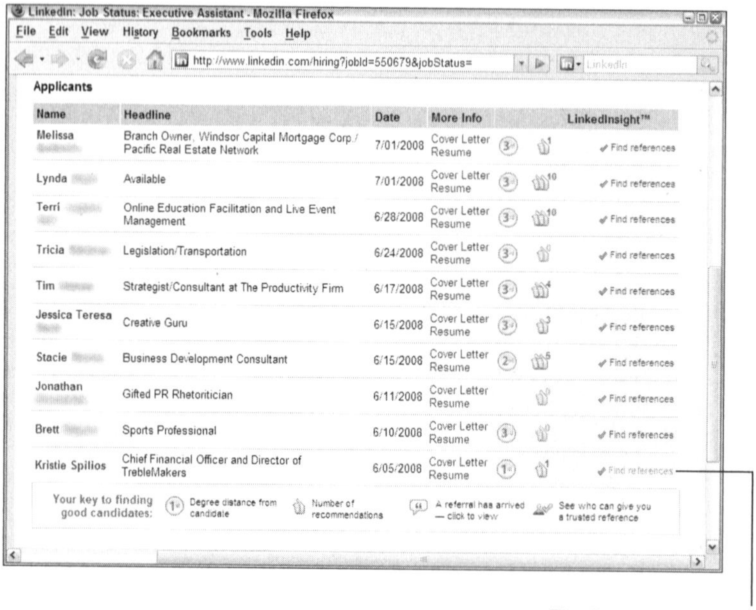

Figure 11-13:
Review
all of your
applicants'
information.

The Find references link

4. **Click the Find references link in an applicant's summary line to do a reference check on that applicant.**

   In this example, I am going to attempt a reference check for one of the applicants, Kristie Spilios. When I click the Find references link, I am taken to a Reference Search Results page, as shown in Figure 11-14. LinkedIn displays all the positions in Ms. Spilios's profile and in the search results, highlights the common position between each result and Ms. Spilios. This will help you determine if the person in the search result worked alongside the applicant or not.

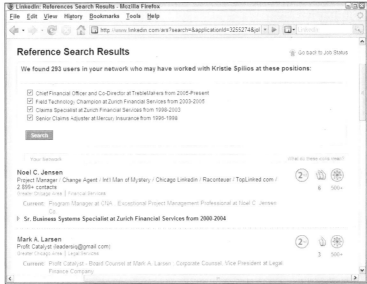

Figure 11-14: See who in the LinkedIn network might have worked with your applicant.

   At this point, you should go through the search results and look for someone you want to request a reference for your applicant. Preferably, you want someone who is only two or three degrees away from you because then you can use a first-degree connection to introduce yourself to this person and that might encourage the other person (who is two or three degrees away) to respond.

5. **Click the name of a potential reference check and ask her for a recommendation of your applicant.**

   When you click the name in the search results, you will bring up the person's profile. You can use InMail or an Introduction to send a message to this person (which I cover in Chapter 5) and you can ask if she has worked with your applicant and whether she's willing to offer her own assessment of the person.

6. **You can ask for additional recommendations by repeating Steps 4 and 5 and identifying other individuals who might be able to help.**

   Since the first person you ask may not respond, you may want to contact additional people in the search results screen, in the hope that one person will respond in the necessary timeframe. See the next section of this book for some specific reference search and screening techniques.

Performing Reference Checks and Screening Candidates with LinkedIn

When you use LinkedIn to post a job request, the screening part of your hiring process clearly benefits from using LinkedIn. Rather than asking for references from the applicant and ordering a background check from a services company, you can use LinkedIn to verify a lot of the information in your applicant's resume and application at any stage of the process, without paying a dime!

Here are some reference search strategies to keep in mind:

- **Start by checking for the applicant's LinkedIn profile.** If the applicant has a common name, use additional information from her resume or application (such as past jobs, location, or education) to narrow down your search. When you find her profile, compare it with her resume or application. Is she consistent in how she presents her experience?

- **Read through the applicant's recommendations and follow up.** If your candidate has received recommendations, go through them and see whether it's applicable towards your open position. Pay attention to recommendations from former bosses or co-workers. If necessary, ask your candidate whether you can contact the recommender through InMail and use that person as a reference.

- **See whether you're connected to your candidate.** When you pull up your candidate's profile, you will see whether she is a second- or third-degree network member, which would mean there are one or two people who connect you with the candidate. If so, contact that person (or ask for an Introduction to reach the correct party) and ask for more information about the candidate. Chances are good that you might get a more honest assessment from someone you know rather than the recommendations provided by the candidate.

- **Evaluate the candidate's total picture.** If your candidate mentions any Web sites, blogs, or other Web presences on her LinkedIn profile, click the links and see how they're involved. Take a look at the listed interests and group affiliations and see whether they add to (or detract from) your picture of the job candidate.

Because most LinkedIn users have already defined each company where they worked and the years of employment, LinkedIn offers an interesting and helpful application called Reference Search. It works like this: Say you're evaluating a candidate who says he worked at Microsoft from 2000 to 2005. You'd like to find out whether you know anyone in your immediate or extended network who might have worked with your candidate. LinkedIn scans everyone's profile and looks for matches in the company name and years employed, and it shows you who is a possible match. You can then follow up and hopefully will get a much more honest, unbiased opinion of the candidate than someone the candidate has pre-selected to deliver a glowing recommendation. Beware, though, in case you get the ex-employee with an axe to grind.

There is one catch: you have to have a paid account in order to perform a reference search. (I discuss the benefits of paid accounts in Chapter 1.) You can start your search using a free account, but you will only see a summary of the results, and not the full set of results to actually find a reference.

Performing a reference check is easy; just follow these steps:

1. **Click the drop-down arrow next to People (on the top navigation bar) to expand your choices. Click Reference Search to bring up the window shown in Figure 11-15.**

Figure 11-15:
Do a
reference
search to
see whether
you can find
someone
who knows
the candi-
date.

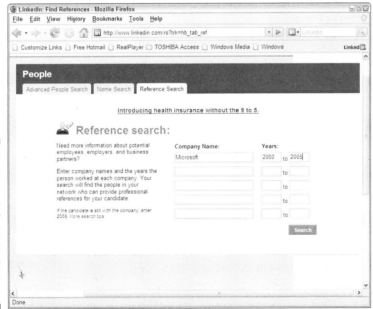

2. **Enter the company name and years of employment in the text boxes provided.**

   If the candidate is currently working at the company, enter the current year in the second year box. You can enter more than one company in the boxes provided, and your result list will contain anyone who matches at least one of the companies provided.

3. **Click the Search button to start the reference search.**

   You see a results screen, as shown in Figure 11-16, where your search results are sorted by the number of degrees away from you. Therefore, first-level contacts show up first, followed by second-level contacts, and so on.

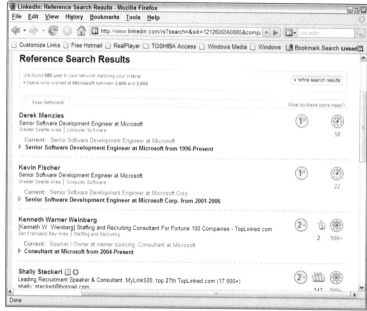

Figure 11-16: See who you know might've worked with your candidate.

4. **Evaluate each profile in your results list to see whether the applicant worked in the same division, and if so, contact the person in your results list for a reference.**

   Obviously, for a big company, like Microsoft in my example, you may have to search multiple people to find the right division.

If you add a division name right after the company name (for example, you put Microsoft Excel instead of Microsoft), you're severely limiting your search to people who have defined their position in that exact word order.

Search Strategies for Finding Active or Passive Job Seekers

One of the powers of LinkedIn is the ability not just to find the active job seeker, but the passive job seeker or someone who didn't even realize she wanted a new job! You can tap an extensive network of professionals who have already identified their past experiences, skill set, interests, educational backgrounds, and group affiliations. Also, through LinkedIn Answers, you can even find out about their thoughts and knowledge.

The best piece of advice, in my opinion, for this type of search comes from Harvey Mackay and the book he wrote back in 1999, whose title is:

> *"Dig your well before you're thirsty."*

You should be building up a healthy network and keeping your eyes on potential candidates before you have a job opening to fill. The earlier you start, and the more consistent you are with the time you spend on a weekly or monthly basis expanding your network, the easier it is to identify and then recruit a potential candidate to fill your opening.

There are specific steps you should take to make your strategy a reality. Whether you start this process in advance or just need to fill a position as soon as possible, here are some tactics to consider:

- ✔ **Perform detailed advanced searches.** If you want the perfect candidate, search for that candidate. Put multiple keywords in the advanced search form, look for a big skill set, narrow your search to a specific industry, and maybe even limit your range to people who already live close to you. If you come up with zero results, remove the least necessary keyword and repeat the search, and keep doing that until you come up with some potentials.

- ✔ **Focus on your industry.** If you know that you're probably going to need software developers, start getting to know potential candidates on the site and stay in touch with them. Look for people to connect with, whether they share a group affiliation with you or respond to LinkedIn Answers, and actively network with these people. Even if they say no to a future job opportunity, chances are good that someone in their networks will be more responsive than the average connection. While Software Developer A may say no, that person probably has several software developers in their network who could respond favorably.

✔ **Read the LinkedIn Answers section.** If you're looking for outgoing people who love sharing their knowledge and want to see a sample of how they approach a problem, take a look at the Answers section. Search for questions that involve something in your industry and read all the answers to find potential candidates who impress you.

✔ **Ask your own questions in the LinkedIn Answers section.** After you've read through the questions, ask one yourself! Pose a question that you would ask in an interview to potential candidates, and see who responds. Better yet, you'll see *how* the people respond, and you'll be able to decide from their answers who to focus on for a follow-up. You'll be able to see the public profiles of the people who provide answers and send those people who respond messages.

Chapter 12

Finding a Job

*O*ne of the most important ways that LinkedIn has benefitted people's lives is how it helps to improve their job search experience. Before LinkedIn, everyone remembers what was involved when you had a job search — making lots of phone calls and visits (and some e-mails) to people you knew, asking them whether they knew anybody who was hiring, asking whether they knew somebody at Company X who might talk to you, or asking something else related to your search. It was a tedious and inefficient process, but now LinkedIn has improved it. Understand, however, that LinkedIn hasn't replaced the entire process. You still need to do some face-to-face meetings and phone calls, but LinkedIn can help you find the right person before you pick up the phone.

In this chapter, I discuss some of the ways that you can use LinkedIn to help find a job, whether you're an active job seeker (I need a job right now!) or a passive job seeker (I don't mind where I'm at, but if the right opportunity comes along, I'm listening) on the market. I start by talking about LinkedIn's job board and how you can search for openings. Then I move into more strategic options like improving your profile, devising specific strategies, searching your network for specific people, and incorporating functions like LinkedIn's JobsInsider tool when surfing the Internet.

Searching for a Job by Using LinkedIn

LinkedIn offers lots of tools that can help you look for a job. The most direct way is to search for open positions on LinkedIn's job board, which I cover in the following section. There are other things to keep in mind when looking for a job, which I cover in the later sections, like improving your visibility and optimizing your profile. Part of the success of finding a job is to have an appealing LinkedIn identity so hiring managers can find you and want to contact you with an opening. After all, the best search is when someone comes to you with an opportunity without you sweating the details.

Searching for an open position

The most obvious way to look for a job is to look through LinkedIn's advertised job openings. After all, someone is getting hired when a company runs a job listing, so why can't that candidate be you? When you search for a job on LinkedIn, you can see what skills and positions companies are hiring, which you can keep in mind as you refine your job search and LinkedIn profile.

When you're ready to search for a job opening, just follow these steps:

1. **Click the Jobs drop-down arrow from the top navigation bar, and select Advanced Job Search.**

   The Advanced Job Search page appears, as shown in Figure 12-1.

2. **Enter keywords describing the job you want in the Search For text box provided.**

   To be more precise in your search, you can enter additional criteria in the sections below the Search For text box, such as location, specific job title or company, or job function or industry.

3. **When you're done entering criteria, click the Search button.**

   You're taken to a LinkedIn Jobs results screen like the one shown in Figure 12-2, where you see the basic components of the job listings, like Title, Company, and Location. What's unique to LinkedIn (compared to other job listing sites like Monster.com) is the last column: Posted By. This column shows you who within that company posted the job, and it provides a link to view that person's LinkedIn profile. Furthermore, if the job poster is in your extended network, you see her name and degree of connection to you, and she is automatically sorted to the top of the list.

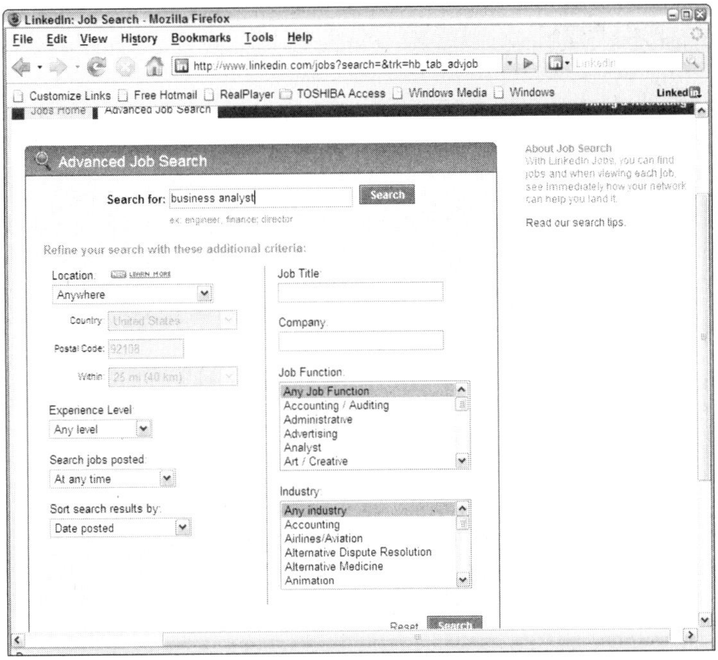

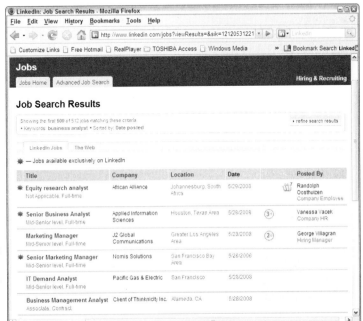

Figure 12-1:
Look for
a job on
LinkedIn.

Figure 12-2:
See your
job search
results!

If you want to expand your job results, click the tab labeled The Web next to the LinkedIn Jobs tab above the table of job titles, companies, and so on, in Figure 12-2. This shows you the results of searching all job listings that have been aggregated from all over the Internet through a company called SimplyHired.

4. **Click an individual job title to see the details of that job posting.**

   You see the detailed write-up on the next screen as shown in Figure 12-3, where you can find out more about the job and the job poster. If the person who posted the job is in your network and has opted to show her name, you can click the See Who Connects You link to find out how to use LinkedIn to reach that person.

Figure 12-3:
Find out more about a specific job listing.

5. **When you see a job you want to apply for, click the Apply Now button.**

   In most cases, LinkedIn takes you to the job application form, as shown in Figure 12-4. (In some cases, you're taken to the company's specific applicant tracking system — for instance, any job from Google does this. In those cases, simply follow the instructions displayed to apply for that job.)

6. **Write a cover letter (or cut and paste one from your word processing program) in the text box provided.**

You should write a brief summary of why you feel you are qualified for the job in the text box provided. If you like, you can update and reuse an older cover letter you've used to apply to a similar job: Simply open a word processing program (such as Microsoft Word), find the letter, copy the contents, and paste it into the text box here on LinkedIn.

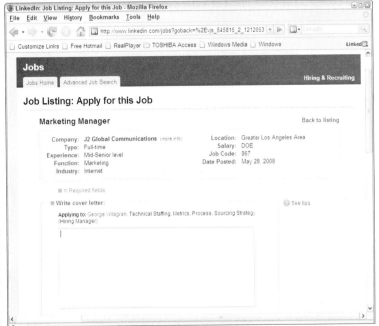

Figure 12-4:
Start
applying
for a job on
LinkedIn.

If the job poster is in your extended network, I recommend that you read her profile first, see what common interests you have, and incorporate that information into your cover letter. If you have the time, approach that person first with an Introduction or InMail to get some more information about the job posting before you apply.

7. **Scroll down and enter your contact information in the text boxes provided as shown in Figure 12-5.**

8. **Click the Browse button to find a copy of your resume on your computer to be uploaded into the job application.**

9. **Scroll down and click the Next button to review your application. Then click the Submit Application button.**

   You see all the details you entered as shown in Figure 12-6, so make sure they're all correct before you submit the application.

Congratulations! You've applied for a job. Repeat the preceding Steps 2–9 to keep looking and apply for future jobs.

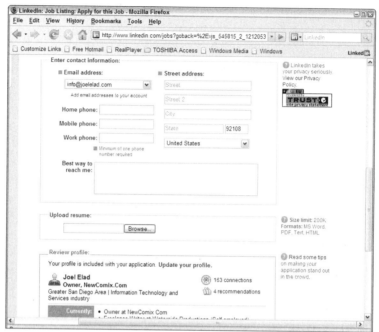

Figure 12-5:
Provide your
contact info
and resume
for this job
application.

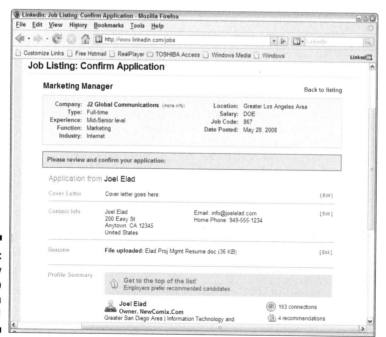

Figure 12-6:
Verify
your job
application
details!

Improving your visibility and attractiveness

When you're looking for a job, the manual acts of scanning job listings and sending in resumes are only part of the process. You also have to prepare your job-seeking strategies. The most obvious examples of these are your resume (or CV) and your cover letter. When you include LinkedIn in your job search, you need to prepare your total LinkedIn profile and network in order to get the optimal job search experience.

Although no strategy can 100-percent positively guarantee the job of your dreams, these strategies can improve your odds of getting that right contact person, interview, or extra consideration for your job application that's in a stack of potential candidates.

Here are some strategies to keep in mind:

- ✔ **Connect with former managers, co-workers, and partners.** This may seem like an obvious strategy, but let me elaborate. Part of getting the job is communicating (to your future employer) your ability to do the job. Nobody knows your skills, your potential, your work attitude and capability, better than people who have worked with you and observed you in action.

  Therefore, make sure that you have connected with your former managers, co-workers, and so on. When these people are part of your network, the Introductions they can facilitate will carry extra weight because they can share their experience with the person you want to meet. You can encourage them to provide recommendations for you to express to the entire community your capability and work ethic.

- ✔ **Look at colleague's LinkedIn profiles.** Using the search functions or your first-degree connections in your network, try to find people with goals and work experience similar to yours. When you see how they describe their work experience on their profiles, you might get some good ideas on how to augment your profile.

- ✔ **Get referrals from past bosses and co-workers.** After you've added your past bosses and co-workers to your network, keep in contact with them, let them know your current job search goals, and ask for an appropriate referral or Introduction. They can use their knowledge of your work history and their expanded networks to make more powerful Introductions or requests than just a friend asking another friend, 'Hey, can you hire my friend Joel?'

Don't be afraid to provide extra information to your past bosses or co-workers to help them make an effective referral. Before the Internet, when job seekers asked a past boss or co-worker to write a letter of recommendation, it was acceptable to include some bullet points of stories or points you hoped they would cover in their letters. The same is true in the LinkedIn world. Guide your contact to emphasize a work quality or anecdote that would be effective in the referral or Introduction.

✔ **Collect your Recommendations.** Nothing communicates a vote of confidence from your network quite like a Recommendation. When anyone reads your LinkedIn profile, he can see exactly what other people have said about you. Because he knows that you can't alter a Recommendation, he's more likely to trust the content and believe you're the right person for the job. (See Chapter 8 for more information on how to get more Recommendations.)

✔ **Use LinkedIn Answers to demonstrate your experience and knowledge.** Your network of connections has an idea of your knowledge and capabilities, but what about everybody else out there? If someone is evaluating you for a job, she'll probably access your LinkedIn profile to learn more about you, so the more your profile can say about you at any given point in time, the better. One way you can improve your overall presence is to participate in LinkedIn Answers. You can share knowledge you've gained by answering other LinkedIn member's questions and providing advice. All of your replies to questions posted on LinkedIn Answers are available from your profile. (See Chapter 7 for more information on how to use LinkedIn Answers.)

Optimizing your LinkedIn profile

The core of your LinkedIn presence is your profile, which is included with every job application you make on LinkedIn. Odds are good that prospective employers are going to check your LinkedIn profile when evaluating you for a job, so you want to make sure your profile is optimized to make you as appealing as possible to your prospective employer. Here are some things to keep in mind when bulking up your profile for a job search:

✔ **Complete all the sections in your profile with as much accurate information as possible.** It's easy to put up a skeleton of your employment history and never get around to fully completing your profile. Unlike a resume (where you could feel confined in terms of page length), you can be as expansive as you want with your LinkedIn profile. You never know what part of your profile will get you included in someone's search result, but the more information you provide, the better chance someone will find you.

Auditioning with Answers

There are several benefits to actively using LinkedIn Answers. Not only can people see examples of your knowledge or experience by reading your answers, they get an idea of how helpful or enthusiastic you are in a professional environment. After all, most employers want to know that you will be a healthy addition to a team and that you'll communicate well with co-workers and think about the big picture. Your active involvement in LinkedIn Answers shows an employer that you're willing to help others to achieve their goals. They also get a glimpse into your communication and written skills, which are important in many jobs today. When you give with LinkedIn Answers, you receive as well.

- ✔ **Focus on accomplishments rather than duties.** I've seen a lot of people prepare their LinkedIn profiles in the same way they do their resumes, focusing solely on the duties they performed at each job. Although you want to give people an idea of what you did, hiring managers want to know the *results* of what you did, and the more concrete the example, the better. Saying you "organized procurement processes in your division" may demonstrate a skill, but saying that you "cut procurement costs by 16% in your first year" carries a bigger impact. Go back and talk to past co-workers or bosses, if necessary, to get whatever specifics they can provide on your performance.

- ✔ **Add all relevant job search keywords, skill sets, and buzzwords to your profile.** When prospective employers are searching for someone to hire, they may simply search for a core set of skills to see who can fill the position. Therefore, just stating your job titles is not enough. If your profile says "Software Developer," prospective hiring managers could assume that you're qualified, but the only way you'd be considered is if these managers did a search for "Software Developer." What happens if a hiring manager does a search for the programming languages C++, Java, Perl, and Python? If all of those keywords are not somewhere in your profile, you won't show up in the list to be considered at all.

- ✔ **See how other people position themselves.** Imagine if you could get a book of thousands of resumes from current employees that you could then use as models to position yourself. Do a search for people with a job, education, or skill set similar to yours and see how they've worded their profiles or how they put their experiences in context. Use that insight to adapt your profile to make it clearer to others.

- ✔ **List all of your job experiences on your profile, not just full-time positions.** Did you do any short-term or contract jobs? Were you an advisor to another company? Perhaps you're a board member for a local non-profit group or religious organization. Your LinkedIn profile is designed to reflect all of your job experiences, which is *not* limited to a full-time job that provided a W2 slip. Document any work experience that adds to your overall profile, whether you were paid for that job/experience or not.

Make sure that every experience you list on your profiles helps contribute to your overall career goals. After all, employers may not care that you were a pastry chef one summer and will question why you thought it was so important that you listed it on your profile.

Job Search Strategies Using LinkedIn

When you're looking for a job, there are a lot of potential ways you can include LinkedIn as part of your overall job search, beyond the direct task of searching their jobs database listings and e-mailing a job request to your immediate network. In this section, I discuss various job search strategies you can implement that involve LinkedIn to some degree and can help add information, contacts, interviews, and hopefully some offers to your job search. Use one or use them all, but pick the methods you feel most comfortable with implementing.

Remember that a job search should be treated as a full-time job. Some of these strategies involve a long-term commitment and might not instantly result in multiple offers.

Leveraging your connections

One of the biggest benefits of LinkedIn is being able to answer the question, "Who do my contacts know?" It's important to think of LinkedIn as not only the sum of your first-degree immediate connections, but your extended network of second- and third-degree network members that your colleagues can help connect you with for information, referrals, and hopefully, a new career.

Therefore, it's important to keep these second- and third-degree network members in mind so you can best leverage your connections to get progress. Keep these points in mind when you're working on your job search using LinkedIn:

- ✔ **Change the Sorted By option to Degrees Away from You, or Degrees and Recommendations.** When searching for the right contacts, like recruiters, headhunters, or company or job specialists, be sure to change the Sorted By option from Keyword Relevance to another option based on Degrees. This allows you to see which members of your extended network should be at the top of your list.

- ✔ **Ask for referrals whenever possible.** Exchange information first and then work your way up to request a referral.

- ✔ **Get your friends involved.** Let your immediate network know about your goals so they can recommend the right people for you to talk to, and hopefully they'll generate the right Introductions for you as well.

Same title, different place

If you're looking for a specific job, one way to approach your job search is to ask this question: Who is going to know that job better than other people doing the same job? This means one source of help should be people with the same (or very similar) job title or responsibilities. Although these people may not have hiring authority, they can help give you the right perspective, share the right insider tips about what the job truly entails, and let you know what skills or background the hiring manager considered when they were hired.

Because these people are already employed and not your direct competition, they're more likely to offer help and advice. They have practical knowledge of what it takes to do that job and what qualities will best help someone succeed in that position. When you're ready to implement this strategy, just keep these points in mind:

✔ Perform an advanced search for people with a similar job title as the one you're applying for. Put the job title in either the keywords section or the title section.

✔ Narrow and clarify your search by industry. For example, Project Manager of Software Development is much different than Project Manager for the Construction industry. Pick multiple industries if they are similar enough.

✔ When you find someone who has the job title you'd like to have, see whether she's interested in meeting for an informational interview. Asking outright for a job lead will most likely not result in anything positive.

All about the alma mater

Typically, people who share a school in common have an ongoing affinity, whether the school is an undergraduate or graduate college, or even a high school. You can rapidly increase the chance of someone considering your request if you and that person attended the same school. Therefore, take advantage of your alumni status and try to connect and work with people who went to one of the same schools as you. Here are some tips to help further this type of search by using LinkedIn:

✔ **Search for Alumni Association Groups of any school you attended by clicking the Groups Directory from the expanded left navigation menu and join those groups.** This gives you access to the member list of that group, so you can see other alumni, regardless of graduation year, and communicate with them.

✔ **Connect as a former classmate and ask for information first, referral second.** Your shared alumni status will help open the door, but don't expect a golden handout right away. Be ready to offer one of your contacts in exchange for the former classmate's help or consideration.

✔ **Use the Finding Former Classmates function available in Add Connections to look for classmates from the schools in your profile.** (I discuss how to use this function back in Chapter 6.) You should expand your range of graduation years to include some years before and after your graduation date. This allows you to find classmates you may have met who were in different grades or levels in their study but may have shared classes or study time with you.

✔ **Check the connection list of any of your contacts who attended school with you.** This is a good safety check to see whether there are any classmates on your contacts' lists that you might not have initially considered.

✔ **Try doing an advanced search with the school name as a keyword, and if necessary, try different variations of the school name.** For example, try the school name with and without acronyms. When I look for classmates from the University of California, Irvine, I search for the term UCI, as well as University California Irvine. (I talk more about doing advanced searches in Chapter 4.)

✔ **If your school has changed or updated its name, search for both the old and new names.** For example, because my department name at UCI has changed from the Graduate School of Management, or GSM, to the Paul Merage School of Business, I will search for both the old and new search terms, because my classmates may have defined their educational listings differently.

Finding target company referrals

Sometimes, your job search involves a specific company and not necessarily a job title. Suppose you know you want to work at one of the top computer database software companies. Now, you can use LinkedIn to help you find the right people at those companies that can help you. Here are some points to consider:

✔ **Make a list of the ten companies you'd like to work for and do an advanced search for each one.** Put the company name in the Company field and select the check box labeled Current Companies Only. For larger companies, you need to search for a specific department or industry area to find the right contact. See who you know that works in those companies by sorting by Degrees Away from You. Ask these people you've identified for referrals to someone in your target organization like a hiring manager.

You can even skip a step by changing the Interested In field from the default option of All Users to the Hiring Managers option. This way, your search produces only hiring managers in your extended network.

✔ **If you can't find someone who currently works at your target company, look for people who used to work there and see what advice they can give you.** You do this through an advanced search where you deselect the check box labeled Current Companies Only. Many times, past employees still maintain contacts at their old company, and they can definitely attest to the work environment and corporate culture.

✔ **Get some information from the person you're replacing.** Find the person at the company whose job you're taking and ask her for her opinion of it, information about the hiring manager, company, and so on. If you can't find the person you're replacing, try looking for people with a past position like the one you're interviewing for. I got this tip from Garage.com founder Guy Kawasaki in his blog post entitled "How to Change the World: Ten Ways to use LinkedIn," which resides on `http://blog.guykawasaki.com`.

Using the LinkedIn JobsInsider

As more and more people were using LinkedIn to get the inside track on their job searches, LinkedIn saw the value in providing a tool that gave searchers easy access to the right information that would aid the job search. So the folks at LinkedIn developed a tool called JobsInsider that works with the major job search engines by scanning a job listing for the employer's name and then providing a summary of statistics of employees that work at that company and how they're connected to a given LinkedIn user.

After the people at LinkedIn developed the JobsInsider tool, they decided to incorporate it into their browser toolbars so it became an automatic benefit. After all, you can't search a job site like Monster.com without a Web browser, right? The toolbars are designed to augment a Web search with LinkedIn information, and so is JobsInsider, which makes it a logical addition to the toolbar.

JobsInsider benefits

Your job search is a job unto itself, so any tool that can help you do your "job" is definitely an asset. JobsInsider helps expand your regular job search by giving you the insight of your LinkedIn network and job database to make you a better and more effective job applicant.

Some of the benefits of the JobsInsider tool are

✔ **It's automatic.** After you install the browser toolbar, the JobsInsider tool activates itself automatically anytime you use your Web browser to navigate to any major job site, like Monster.com, CareerBuilder.com, HotJobs, craigslist, SimplyHired, Dice, or Vault.

✔ **It's informative.** You get several pieces of valuable information that update automatically depending on the job listing you're seeing. You see how many people work at the target company that are in your extended network, how many people are friends of your connections (which means they're second-degree connections) and how many people live in your region, (like the San Francisco Bay area or the Greater San Diego area). Clicking any of those links opens a window to LinkedIn with a search result showing you their profile summaries.

✔ **It's free.** No monthly cost, no registration cost, no setup fee. Regardless of the status of your LinkedIn account, this tool is free to install and use.

✔ **It's timesaving.** As you search for a job, instead of stopping your search from a job site to go to LinkedIn to find a contact or more information, you can access that information concurrently through new panes or windows opening.

Using JobsInsider

If you're interested in using JobsInsider, you need to download one of the LinkedIn Browser toolbars and install it on your computer because JobsInsider is available only as part of a Browser toolbar. I cover installing the Internet Explorer and Firefox Companion toolbars in Chapter 10.

After you install the toolbar, whenever you go to one of the main job search sites (like Monster.com, CareerBuilder.com, or Dice) a side pane or new window opens, where you can basically start a LinkedIn job search.

For example, suppose that you're on Monster.com looking for a project manager position. After you start a search and come up with a results screen (as shown Figure 12-7), you see the JobsInsider function come up.

More importantly, however, when you click an individual job posting, you see the JobsInsider pane fill in with information on who you know at the hiring company and how many people you're connected to who can help.

If you can't easily identify the employer from the job listing, or if the company's name is withheld or confidential, no information shows up in the JobsInsider pane.

Suppose I click a Web developer position at eBay. My JobsInsider pane shows me precise connection information, as shown in Figure 12-8. I can click on any of the numbers to bring up a people search of hiring managers who can help me apply for this job.

JobsInsider can also be used to search for people, like the hiring manager for a job you find on another job site, so you can research that person and write a better cover letter or get an Introduction.

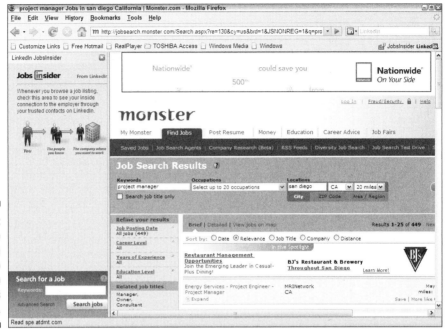

Figure 12-7:
Do a job
search
online to
bring up
Jobs
Insider . . .

Figure 12-8:
. . . and for
every open
position,
see which
LinkedIn
connections
can help
you apply.

Chapter 13

Finding Professional Services

In This Chapter

▶ Searching for a service provider

▶ Writing an excellent recommendation

▶ Recommending a service provider

*T*wo of the main reasons people search the LinkedIn network are to find a job or new employee. And now there's an up-and-coming tool that takes advantage of the millions of self-employed people who use LinkedIn to promote not only themselves, but their services.

LinkedIn now has a Service Provider section, where LinkedIn members can write recommendations for service providers they have personally used that are also members of the LinkedIn network. Because recommendations are one of the top reasons someone picks one service provider over another, and because many of these service providers are on LinkedIn already to increase their contact base and professional network, it makes sense to allow members to recommend each other based on services, not just shared employment.

In this chapter, I cover how to use LinkedIn to search for a recommended service provider. I also cover how you can file a recommendation for a service provider and get him or her listed in the directory.

Searching for a Service Provider

When you need to hire someone to do a specific job, you probably open up the Yellow Pages and search for a provider. Sometimes, you call family members or friends and ask them to refer you to somebody qualified. Now, LinkedIn has a way for you to search your network of first-, second-, and third-degree contacts, or the greater LinkedIn network, to find qualified professionals referred by other LinkedIn members.

To search for a service provider, just follow these steps:

1. **Click the drop-down arrow next to Companies from the top navigation bar, then click the Service Providers link.**

2. **The Service Provider Recommendations home page appears, as shown in Figure 13-1.**

   LinkedIn automatically picks providers based on recent recommendations. If you scroll down the page, you see some of the Top people in different categories, like Top Real Estate Agents and Top Child Care Providers. ("Top" is defined as providers that have received the most recommendations from other LinkedIn users so far.)

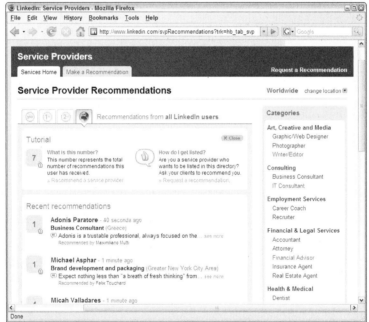

Figure 13-1: Start your Service Provider search here.

3. **In the Categories pane, click the category that matches the type of service provider for your search.**

   For this example, I'm searching for a Writer/Editor, so I click Writer/Editor. You should see the recommendations page for Writer/Editor, as shown in Figure 13-2.

Now that you've reached a page loaded with recommended service providers, you might want to use some of the following tricks to navigate it and find the one that's just right for you:

✔ **Sorting based on date or top results:** By default, the list that's returned is sorted based on the date of the most recent recommendation. You can change the sort by clicking the Top Results link, to find a list of Writers/ Editors with the most recommendations, as shown in Figure 13-3.

✔ **Sorting by recommendations from your network:** Click the icon marked 1st or 2nd to get a list of service provider recommendations based on the first- or second-degree connections in your network.

You see something like what's shown in Figure 13-4. The list of results shows who made the most recent recommendation.

✔ **Sorting based on location:** Click the Change Location link to get a targeted search list close to where you live.

When you click the Change Location link, you're asked to input your country and postal code. After you do so, you are returned to the search results page, but with a target list now sorted by the proximity to your new location setting. After all, if you are looking for a dentist or gardener, you probably want one close to home.

✔ **Reading all of a provider's recommendations:** Click any provider's name to read all of that provider's recommendations.

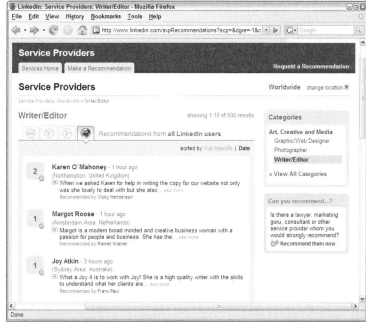

Figure 13-2: See a list of recommended service providers based on date of recommendation . . .

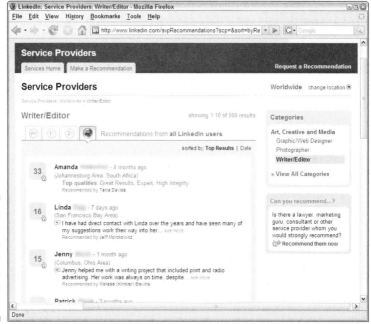

Figure 13-3:
. . . or
sorted by
the number
of recom-
mendations
received.

2nd Degree icon

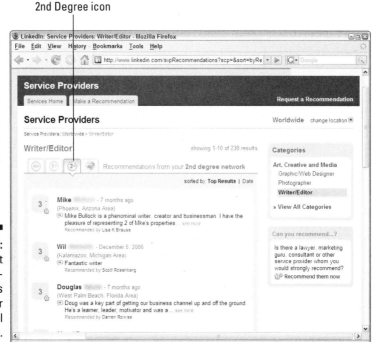

Figure 13-4:
See a list
of recom-
mendations
from your
personal
network.

Recommending a Service Provider

The flip side of looking for a good service provider is sharing your experiences and recommending somebody you've hired or worked with. The success of the LinkedIn database depends on sharing this expertise, which simply makes a better network for you to enjoy and benefit from. Before you enter that recommendation, however, you need to keep a few things in mind to make that write-up stand out.

Planning a good recommendation

When you've received excellent service, it's time to consider how you'll recommend someone. For your recommendation to have some weight and give prospective customers a good idea of what this provider can accomplish, you need to think about the type of recommendation you plan to leave and make sure that you cover or emphasize the appropriate things. You have a 3,000 character count limit, but you also don't want to provide a long thesis of why provider X is the best on Earth.

Instead, you want to provide a concise, factual testimonial that conveys your recommendation in a way that will make sense to the reader and validate the provider's abilities. Here are some things to keep in mind:

- ✔ **Stick to the basics:** Although you may want to gush and go on and on about why this provider is the best, anybody reading this will lose interest and stop reading, which hurts the provider's chance of getting new business and makes you, the recommender, look unprofessional. Provide summaries of your experience, highlighting the most important aspects.

- ✔ **Lead with the most important info:** Most people don't read beyond the first sentence. Therefore, you want your introductory sentence to give a complete picture of the person you're recommending. This way, you hook your reader into finding out why this person is so qualified and deserves his or her business.

- ✔ **Give examples/accomplishments:** Saying someone is a hard worker or very intelligent is nice, but if that's all you say, someone reading your recommendation might wonder whether this is just your opinion or fact. When you give specific examples of the provider's accomplishments, you provide a measurable aspect that readers can relate to and help prove the quality of that provider. Who would you hire: someone whose recommendation says, "Great accountant," or someone whose recommendation says, "Paul balanced my business receipts and records in 3–4 hours and found me $4,000 in extra deductions for last year's tax returns"?

✔ **Be a little personal:** In the end, no matter how qualified somebody is, people typically hire someone they enjoy working with on a project. Therefore, after you mention a person's great capabilities and accomplishments, be sure to include some personal experiences on what working with this person was like. "I have been Alex's client for the past 5 years, and I am consistently pleased and amazed at the service he has provided."

Posting a recommendation

When you have your recommendation planned out, it's time to show it to the world. To leave a recommendation, just follow these steps:

1. **Click the drop-down arrow next to Companies from the top navigation bar, then click the Service Providers link.**

2. **On the Service Providers page that appears, click the Make a Recommendation tab.**

   You're taken to the first step in the process (see Figure 13-5), where you have to decide who you want to recommend.

3. **Enter the first name, last name, and e-mail address in the box provided, or click the Select from Your Connections List link to find someone in your network.**

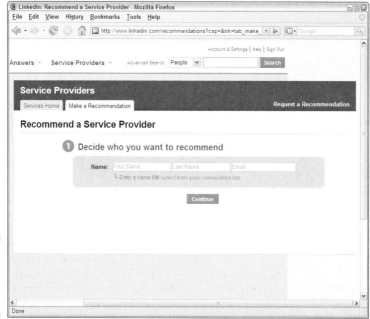

Figure 13-5:
Decide who you want to recommend.

4. **After you've entered the contact info, click the Continue button to proceed.**

   You're taken to the Create Your Recommendation page (see Figure 13-6).

5. **From the first drop-down list, select the position this service provider had when you hired him.**

6. **Select an option from the Service Category drop-down list; then select the year you first hired or worked with him from the Year First Hired drop-down list.**

7. **If you've worked with this person more than once, select the check box next to the Year First Hired drop-down list.**

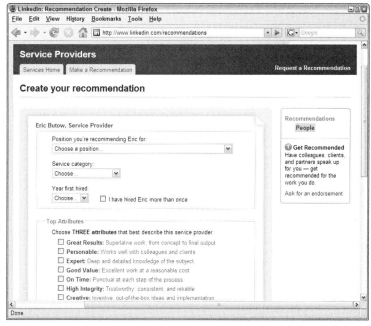

Figure 13-6:
Create your
Service
Provider
Recommen-
dation.

8. **Scroll down and pick the top three attributes that best describe the service provider.**

   You can select up to three check boxes from the list provided. Remember, you will have a chance for a Written Recommendation in the next step.

9. **Scroll down and write your written recommendation in the text box provided.**

This is the space where you can talk about your provider's accomplishments, qualities, and your experience working with him. (See the previous section for what to focus on in your written recommendation.) You simply enter this recommendation in the box provided (see Figure 13-7).

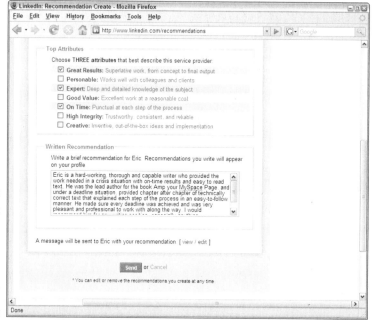

Figure 13-7:
Provide your written recommendation in the box provided.

10. **Click the Send button to enter your recommendation into the system.**

    You see a confirmation message that your service provider recommendation has been created.

If you've already left a personal recommendation for this person, you now have two recommendations on this person's profile, with the only visible difference being the Top Qualities line in the Service Provider recommendation. You may want to delete your old personal recommendation if it overlaps with your new one.

Part V
Using LinkedIn for Everyday Business

The 5th Wave   By Rich Tennant

"So that's why he wouldn't introduce me to his connections. Well, I feel a lot better now.

In this part . . .

Have you ever tried to pound the square peg into the round hole, thinking that there might be a purpose for the square peg that no one thought of? Some see that as stubborn, but others see that as curious. It's good to wonder how to use something beyond its stated or obvious purpose, because you might create something new or beneficial for the world.

This part covers some of the specific applications of the LinkedIn Web site that may not be the obvious, but are definitely useful. I apply the LinkedIn Web site to situations that matter to some of you, and I try to tell you all about how LinkedIn can help you increase your sales, how you can use LinkedIn to market yourself, how LinkedIn can help you close a big deal, and why that square peg won't fit. Okay, I can't help you with that last problem, but the rest are good to go. I mix advice with some examples, so find the parts that apply to you and enjoy!

Chapter 14

Getting Connected with LinkedIn Groups

*W*hen it comes to the reasons that people get to know each other, there's more to a professional's life than his or her colleagues and classmates. People have always been drawn to groups based on a common interests, backgrounds, or goals, and this natural tendency to join together can be seen from the sports teams to Boy/Girl Scouts, from social action organizations to non-profit charity groups. Naturally, LinkedIn also offers a way for people to connect with each other as a group, and it's called LinkedIn Groups.

In this chapter, I discuss the overall idea and structure of LinkedIn Groups and what you can expect to find. I then talk about how to search for existing groups on LinkedIn, and I walk you through the steps necessary to join that group. Finally, if you see that there should be a group for something on LinkedIn but it doesn't already exist, I discuss how to start your own LinkedIn group and how to invite others to join it.

LinkedIn Groups — What They Are and What They Aren't

When people who are familiar with other social networking tools are first exposed to LinkedIn Groups, they're often in for a bit of a surprise. They aren't like Yahoo! Groups or groups on most other social networking sites, because there's no group interaction — no mailing list, no discussion forum, and so on. Being a member of a LinkedIn group has some benefits over other networking sites:

- **Connections:** Fellow group members are a special sort of connection. Although you don't have access to their extended networks for Introductions, you're considered directly connected to them, such that you can see their full profiles and they can appear in your search results, even if you aren't within three degrees of everyone in the group. If you sort search results by degrees of separation from you, fellow group members appear between your first and second degree contacts.

- **Visibility:** By joining several groups — particularly large, open ones — you can increase your visibility in the LinkedIn network without having to add thousands of contacts.

- **Group logos:** The logos of the groups you're in are displayed on your profile and in search results. This is a sort of visual branding, reinforcing your association with those groups without a lot of words. For example, Figure 14-1 shows how a LinkedIn member who belongs to several groups might appear in a search result.

Figure 14-1: Group logos displayed on a profile.

Some LinkedIn Groups are extensions of existing organizations, whereas others are created on LinkedIn by an individual as a way to identify and network with people who share a common interest. In either case, they're useful tools for growing your network and leveraging your existing affiliations.

Types of LinkedIn Groups

Because there are lots of reasons to create a group, LinkedIn has established the following six primary categories of groups:

- ✔ **Alumni:** These groups are alumni associations created by schools or teaching institutions as a means to keep in touch with past graduates. Graduates can also keep in touch with each other through an alumni group. As you develop your career, you can tap into the alumni network of like-minded, qualified individuals. Loyalty to your alma mater makes you, and everyone else in the group, more likely to help out a schoolmate than a complete stranger.

- ✔ **Corporate:** Because every company has its own unique culture, who better to understand that culture than current and past employees? Corporate groups allow employees from a single employer to stay in touch.

- ✔ **Conference:** As conference attendees plan to attend a particular conference, using a conference group to network with attendees before, during, and after the conference can be advantageous.

  Before the conference, you can relay important information, such as subject matter and agenda, and any events, lectures, seminars, parties, or other info that matters to the attendees. Perhaps there are last-minute changes or announcements that need to get disseminated quickly. During the event, you can quickly relay announcements, as well as news being generated at the conference and any on-site changes. After the conference, these conference groups allow attendees to stay in contact and help the conference organizers and presenters to see how the subject matter and industries have changed or progressed.

  Also, as the conference becomes a yearly event, the conference group becomes a constant area of discussion and planning.

- ✔ **Networking:** A common interest is all that's needed to come together and meet similarly minded people. Networking groups are organized around concepts like women's networks, angel investors in new companies, or even Rotary Clubs. These LinkedIn groups allow you to stay involved in your interests and meet people with similar or complementary goals to your own.

✔ **Non-profit:** After talking business all day, it's comforting to have a group where you can talk and plan any upcoming events that benefit your favorite non-profit organization. These LinkedIn groups allow far-flung volunteers to organize, plan, and execute projects and events relating to their charity without being in the same room — which is especially convenient if everybody has a busy schedule. These groups also allow any non-profit organizers to bring new members up to speed and answer their questions quickly so more people become involved.

✔ **Professional:** Finally, who knows your career issues better than others in your industry and/or job title? Professional groups allow you to network with people in the same type of work who are probably experiencing the same issues, problems, and potential solutions as you. Whether it's an organization of CFOs, workers in the wireless industry, or SAP Certified Consultants, these groups can be invaluable to further your career and give you an avenue to evaluate job tips and industry news.

Joining a Group

When you look at the LinkedIn groups out there, one of the most important things to keep in mind is that you should join only groups that are relevant to you. Although you might think it to be fun to join another alumni association group besides your alma mater, it won't really help you in the long run.

As you use LinkedIn more and decide that you want to get involved by joining a LinkedIn group, you have a couple of options for getting started:

✔ You can click the Group logo found on the profile of one of your first-degree connections in order to join the group yourself.

✔ You can search the LinkedIn Groups directory to find a group that interests you; then click the logo to join the group.

The first option may come about when you're browsing your first-degree connections list and you see a group that you're interested in joining. After you click the logo, you simply have to click a Join this Group button on the next page that you see, and you have completed the process.

When you're more proactive and plan to seek out a group to join, just follow these steps:

1. **From the left navigation menu, expand the Groups option and click the Groups Directory link.**

   You're taken to the Groups Directory page on LinkedIn, as shown in Figure 14-2.

Search Groups

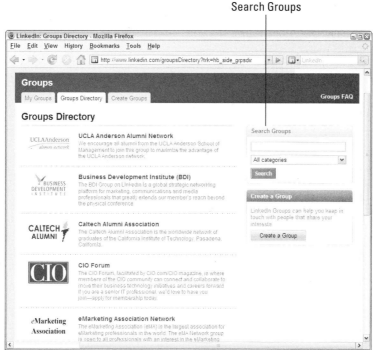

Figure 14-2:
You can
look for
specific
LinkedIn
Groups.

2. **When you see the Groups Directory page, enter some keywords in the text box underneath Search Groups.**

   In the text box, enter keywords that would describe the group that interests you. Say for example that I'm looking to join a group that promotes or encourages public speaking. I would enter **public speaking** into the text box.

3. **Click the Search button to see a list of groups that match your keywords.**

   Go through the results list, as shown in Figure 14-3, and read the descriptions of each group on the list. If you need more information about the group, click the Owner's name to see his profile and send him a message about the group.

4. **When you see a Group that you want to join, click the Title of the Group (or the Join This Group link after the group description).**

   When you click either link, you're taken to the Group summary page, as shown in Figure 14-4. You see the summary of the group, number of members (in the top-right corner), and you need to decide whether to join the group.

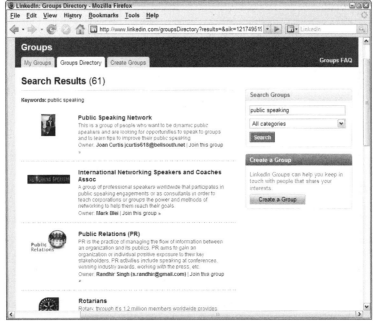

Figure 14-3:
Look
through a
list of
potential
groups you
could join.

Figure 14-4:
Read the
summary
of your
LinkedIn
group
before you
join.

5. Click the Join this group button to join the LinkedIn group.

That's it! You see a confirmation message, and you're taken back to the My Groups page with your newly added group on the list. Depending on the requirements for membership, your request will either be immediately approved or sent to the group manager for manual approval.

Case study: CalTech gets connected

Caltech Alumni Association launched an official alumni group on LinkedIn in 2006. Out of some 20,000 contactable alumni, it now has approximately 2,000 members in the LinkedIn group — about 10 percent. Andrew Shaindlin, Executive Director of the association, is one of the early adopters of using third-party social networking sites to help alumni stay connected.

With more than a year of experience running the group, Shaindlin noticed some cool things that his alumni members were doing with this new LinkedIn group, including the following:

✔ Alumni group members saw higher search engine placements for their member's names and more page views for CalTech in general.

✔ Graduates were making connections between their alumni network members and their non-alumni network members when they were networking.

✔ The CalTech Alumni Web site saw an increase of traffic from members clicking through from LinkedIn via the LinkedIn group Web site URL link.

✔ The CalTech Alumni Association has more graduates' e-mail address on file, attributed partially to their LinkedIn group.

✔ Most importantly, there are success stories about CalTech alumni finding jobs, employees, and investors through their LinkedIn Group.

Searching a Group

After you've joined a group, you'll probably want to see who's in the group and how the group members are connected to you! After all, the point of these groups is to stay in touch with like-minded individuals and have them be part of your extended network.

To search a group, follow these steps:

1. **From the left navigation menu, click the Groups link.**

   This brings up your My Groups page.

2. **Click the View Members link under the logo and name for your group.**

   This brings up a list of members in the group, sorted by how many degrees they are away from you in your LinkedIn network.

3. **(Optional) Click the Refine Search Results link and add other search criteria to get a more targeted results list.**

   This brings up an advanced search page, as shown in Figure 14-5. You can see that the search is automatically limited to members of your group. Now you can add more search requirements such as names, companies, user types, locations, and so on.

4. **Click the Search button, and your search is carried out according to the refined search criteria you entered.**

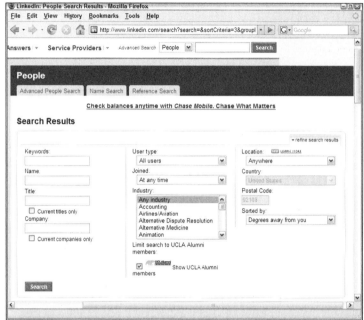

Figure 14-5:
Search your
Group to
find specific
subsets of
people.

Creating a Group

When you're ready to create your own group, just follow these steps:

1. **Click the Groups link in the left navigation menu.**

   You see the Groups page, with three tabs along the top: My Groups, Groups Directory, and Create Groups.

2. **Click the Create Groups tab.**

   This step brings you to the Create a Group page, as shown in Figure 14-6. This is where you input all the information about your newly requested group.

3. **Upload the logos for your group.**

   LinkedIn requires two logos: one sized at 100 x 50 pixels and one sized at 60 x 30 pixels. The larger logo is used on the Groups home page, and the smaller logo shows up in the group members' profile pages. Click the Browse buttons next to each logo box and, in the Choose File dialog box, locate the logo file on your computer so LinkedIn can upload it; then click Open.

Figure 14-6:
Enter your
new group
information
here!

"But where do I get a logo?" you might ask. Well, you can design your own logo at sites like www.logoyes.com or www.logoworks.com. If a logo already exists, like an alumni association, ask one of the administrators for a high resolution copy of the logo, or save a copy of the logo from the group's personal Web site.

Each logo can be only 100 kilobytes in size, so watch that file size as you create your logos.

4. **Provide your group information, including group name, description, type, Web site URL, manager e-mail, and whether you want your group visible on your member's profile pages (refer to Figure 14-7).**

You have only 300 characters in your group description, so choose your words wisely.

If you're wondering what to write for your group description, first click the Groups Directory tab near the top of the page (before writing anything) and read through similar groups in your group type. Then, go back to the Create Groups page and enter your description. (If you check the Groups Directory while writing your description, you'll lose whatever you've typed.)

5. **If your group is located in one geographic region, click the appropriate check box.**

6. **Read through the Terms and Conditions and click that check box when you have reviewed it.**

   At this point, your page should look something like Figure 14-7, where your logos and information are uploaded and ready for review.

7. **When you've entered all your information, click the Submit Group for Review button to send your request to LinkedIn.**

   You're taken back to the My Groups page and your request has been submitted.

   You should see your newly created group on your page, with the note `Pending approval` underneath, as shown in Figure 14-8. Allow some time for LinkedIn to review your request, and once it is approved, your new group is ready for members!

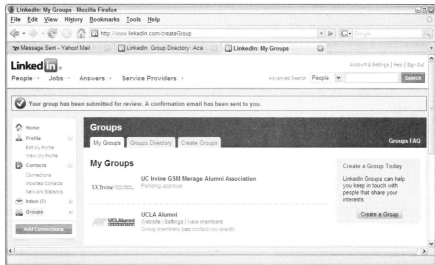

Figure 14-8:
Your group
request has
been
submitted!

Inviting Members

After you get your confirmation from LinkedIn that your new group has been
created, your next step is to invite members to be a part of this group! The
way this is handled with LinkedIn is actually a multi-part process:

1. You have to define a list of pre-approved members of your group, which
   you will upload to LinkedIn. You should do this *before* you send out any
   Invitations.

2. You're allowed to e-mail your prospective members with an Invitation to
   join your new group. LinkedIn provides you with a customized link that
   you can use as your Invitation.

3. When a new member clicks that link, LinkedIn checks to see whether
   that member is on your Pre-Approved list. If so, she automatically
   becomes a member. If not, you (the group manager) will see a member
   request in the Manage section of your group entry, which you will
   have to manually approve so the user can officially join the group. The
   user's status will show up as Pending on their My Groups page until you
   approve her membership request.

Building your member list

The easiest way to build your list of members is to use a spreadsheet program like Microsoft Excel and create something called a Comma Separated Values file (.csv file) which is simply a text file of members and their e-mail addresses. You should definitely have your member list in front of you before starting this process.

If many of the members are already connected to you in LinkedIn, you can simply export your connections to start building your member list. See Chapter 6 for more information on how to do this.

When you're ready to build your list of members, just follow these steps:

1. **Open a spreadsheet program, such as Microsoft Excel. Select File⇨New from the top Excel menu to create a new blank document.**

2. **In the first row, create these entries, which will be the three column headers:**

   • First Name

   • Last Name

   • E-mail Address

3. **Starting in the second row, fill in the members' names and e-mail addresses.**

   As you fill in your list, it should begin to look like Figure 14-9.

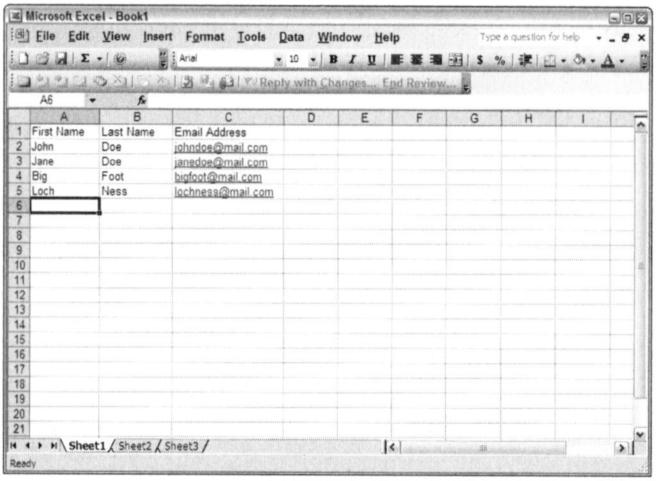

	A	B	C
1	First Name	Last Name	Email Address
2	John	Doe	johndoe@mail.com
3	Jane	Doe	janedoe@mail.com
4	Big	Foot	bigfoot@mail.com
5	Loch	Ness	lochness@mail.com

Figure 14-9: Use Excel to build your Group member list!

4. **Choose File⇨Save As.**

   The Save As window pops up, as shown in Figure 14-10.

5. **Make sure that the Save as Type option is set to CSV (Comma delimited) and click OK when prompted.**

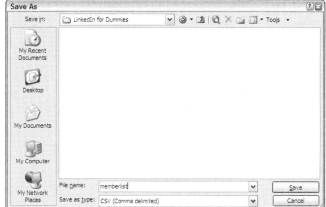

Figure 14-10:
Don't forget
to save your
file as CSV
(Comma
delimited).

6. **Go to your LinkedIn account and click the Groups link in the left navigation menu to bring up your My Groups page.**

7. **From the My Groups page, click the Manage link underneath the name of your group.**

   This brings up the Current Members page of your group (as part of your My Groups tab), as shown in Figure 14-11. At first, you're the only current member of this new group.

8. **Click the Invite Members link from the Manage This Group pane on the right.**

   This brings up the Invite Members page, as shown in Figure 14-12. For right now, you're interested in the bottom part of the page, where you can upload your newly created list.

9. **Click the Browse button to find the CSV file on your computer.**

10. **After you've indicated the list of members, click the Upload File button to upload the list of members into your group.**

    The next page indicates whether the file was uploaded correctly. You should see your member list uploaded correctly, as shown in Figure 14-13. Here, you have two options.

    • *Upload and Replace:* If you want to replace an existing list of members with the list you are uploading, click the Upload and Replace button.

    • *Upload and Add:* If you want to add a list of members to a pre-existing list, click the Upload and Add button.

    If you're doing this for the first time, just click Upload and Add.

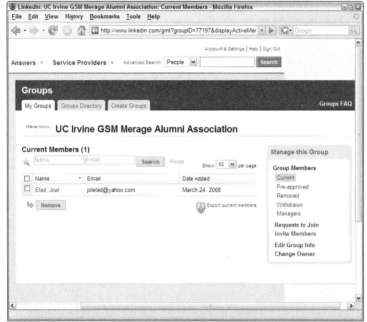

Figure 14-11:
The Members page is where you manage all the members of your new group.

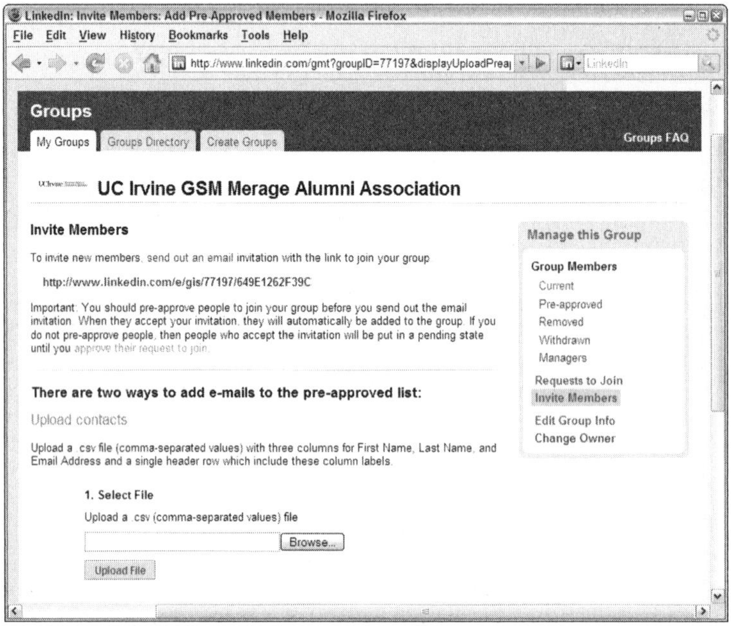

Figure 14-12:
Import your list of members here.

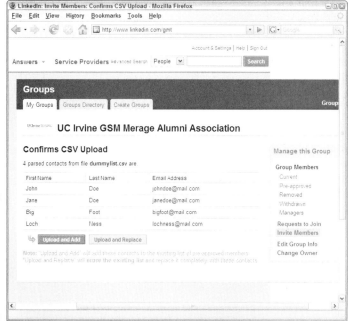

Figure 14-13:
Look through your list and add members to your group.

You're done! Your new members will appear on the Pre-Approved list for this group.

You can always click the Invite Members link and use the form to manually add additional names at any time.

If the e-mail address of a member's LinkedIn profile is different from the e-mail address you put in the Pre-Approved list, this member won't be automatically approved when he clicks the link. You have to manually approve him by clicking the Requests to Join link from the Groups page.

You might have noticed in Step 7, when you clicked the Invite Members link, the top of the page had a special Web URL. This is the exact Web address URL link that you need to e-mail to your prospective members. When they click it, they are added to the group! This will be useful in the next section, "Crafting your Invitation e-mail."

Crafting your Invitation e-mail

LinkedIn doesn't send group Invitations, because the folks at LinkedIn feel that the Invitations should come from the group owner — namely you! Therefore, here are some do's and don'ts to keep in mind as you craft the Invitation:

✔ **Do relate the purpose and benefits of the group.** People are busy and need to understand why they should join this group. Explain the benefits of being connected to other people and what you hope to accomplish with this group. Remember, you're sending this to LinkedIn members, so don't worry about explaining LinkedIn — just explain your group.

✔ **Do make it easy to join.** Make that link easy to find by placing it on its own line, so it's visible and ready to click. Don't bury the link within a paragraph; make sure it stands out. Apply bold or italics the link if you want to give it additional attention.

✔ **Don't go on forever.** One to two paragraphs is the maximum this Invitation should be. Introduce yourself, introduce the group name, give people the benefits of joining, present the link, encourage them to join, and sign off. No one will read a long diatribe or laundry list of reasons to join. Use bullet points and short sentences whenever possible.

✔ **Don't put other offers in the e-mail.** Some people use this as an opportunity not only to encourage one group Invitation, but perhaps a second group Invitation, or another link to the group's non-LinkedIn Web site. The moment you start presenting multiple options for people, you lose their attention and they won't sign up.

You can use any e-mail program to create an Invitation to your group, and your Invitation can look as simple as this:

Hello,

You are hereby invited to join the new UC Irvine GSM/Merage Alumni Group on LinkedIn. Joining this group will allow you to find and contact other alumni, so you can stay in touch, gain referrals, and view other alumnis' LinkedIn profiles.

Here is the link to join:

www.linkedin.com/e/gis/12345/67890ABCDEFG (link from Invite Members screen)

Hope to see you in the group!

—Joel Elad, Class of 2002

After you've sent out the Invitations, as members respond they're moved from the Pre-Approved list to the Current list of your group, and the small group logo appears on their profiles.

Approving members to your group

As more and more people find out about your new LinkedIn group, and as members start joining, you may find that some of the people who have clicked the link to join aren't on your pre-approved list. Perhaps they are people you didn't realize were on LinkedIn, perhaps you didn't realize they were valid group members, or perhaps they clicked the wrong link and/or they don't belong in your group.

Regardless of the situation, you need to go into LinkedIn and either approve or reject people's membership requests so they can be members (or non-members) of your LinkedIn group. When you need to do that, just follow these steps:

1. **From the left navigation menu, click the Groups link to bring up your list of My Groups.**

   You see the My Groups page.

2. **Scroll down until you see the name and logo of the group you are maintaining, as shown in Figure 14-14.**

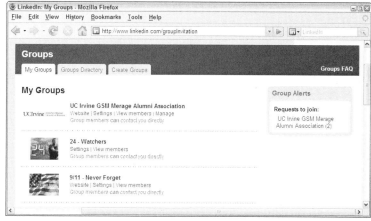

Figure 14-14: You can manage your LinkedIn group membership.

3. **Click the Manage link below the name of your group to bring up the Current Members page. From the right pane, click the link Requests to Join.**

   This step brings up the list of people who are waiting to be approved for your group, like in Figure 14-15.

4. **To accept people, first select the check box next to each person you want to approve to join your LinkedIn group. Then click the Approve button.**

   You can approve people individually or all at once if you want. You can always select the person's name on the list to read his LinkedIn profile and decide whether he belongs in the group or send him a message through his profile.

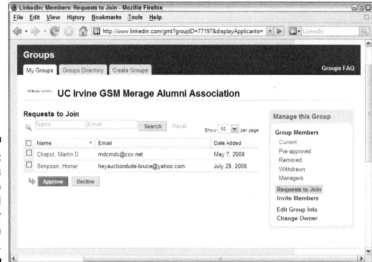

Figure 14-15:
See who is
waiting to
be approved
to your
LinkedIn
group.

5. **To refuse membership, first select the check box next to each person you want to decline membership to the group, and then click the Decline button.**

Similar to the approval process, you can decline people one at a time, or all at once. In either case (approval or decline) the user's name disappears from the Request to Join page.

Chapter 15

Marketing Yourself and Your Business

In This Chapter

▶ Exploring marketing strategies for yourself and your business

▶ Getting yourself listed in the Service Providers directory

▶ Locating marketing partners and doing market research

*I*n this final part of the book, you find out how to start applying everything the previous parts cover about how to use the site for specific situations and needs. After all, every great invention needs to fulfill some sort of purpose, and LinkedIn is no exception. Its value is not just in how it allows you to network and build your brand, but also in how you can use LinkedIn to handle other tasks easier and more effectively.

I start with the age-old discipline of marketing. In this chapter, I discuss how to go about generating sales and how LinkedIn can affect your entire sales cycle. LinkedIn can help you "spread the gospel" of your business mission by serving as a vehicle for positive and rich marketing messages about both you and your business, whether it's a startup or a Fortune 500 company. Part of the power of LinkedIn comes from involving others in your marketing initiatives, so I cover some ways for you to do that as well.

Marketing Yourself through LinkedIn

When it comes to LinkedIn, you are your biggest advocate. Although your network of connections is instrumental in helping you grow, much of your marketing happens without your being involved; that is, after you create your profile, that and any other LinkedIn activity of yours is read and judged by the community at large — on the other members' own time and for their own purposes. Therefore, you want to make sure that you're creating a favorable impression of yourself by marketing the best traits, abilities, and features of you and your business. Because of the nature of LinkedIn, this marketing occurs continually — 24/7. So, you should look at

LinkedIn as something to check and update on a continual basis, like a blog. It doesn't mean you have to spend hours and hours each day, but a little bit of time on a consistent basis can go a long way towards a favorable and marketable LinkedIn identity.

The following sections look at the different ways you interact with LinkedIn, and what you can do to create the most polished, effective LinkedIn identity possible to further your marketing message.

Optimizing your profile

In Chapter 3, I discuss building your professional profile on LinkedIn, which is the centerpiece of your LinkedIn identity and your personal brand. I refer to your profile throughout this book, but here, I focus on ways for you to update or enhance your profile with the specific goal in mind of marketing yourself better or more consistently. As always, not every tip or suggestion will work for everyone, and you may have already put some of these into action, but it's always good to revisit your profile to make sure it's organized the way you intended.

To make sure your profile is delivering the best marketing message for you, consider these tips:

✓ **Use the Professional headline wisely.** Your professional headline is what other LinkedIn users see below your name even when they're not looking at your full profile. I've seen some users stuff a lot of text into this field, so you should have enough space to communicate the most important things about yourself. Simply put, if you have one, or even two, key phrases you want associated with your name, they should be a part of your headline.

A standard headline reads something like, "Software Development Manager at XYZ Communications," but you can write entire sentences full of great keywords for your headline. My friend Anderee Berengian's headline reads: "Growth-Stage, Results-Oriented Internet & Digital Media Professional, Advisor, and Investor." Think about how many people would want to connect with him!

✓ **Make sure you use keyword phrases that match popular keywords for you or your business.** The first step, as I just mentioned, is to put these phrases in your headline. The second step is to make sure these phrases are reflected in your Summary, Experiences, and Interests.

Be careful not to overuse your main keyword phrases. The search engines call this practice "stuffing," which refers to trying to stuff as many instances of a phrase in hopes of achieving a higher ranking. If the search engines detect this, you will actually experience lower ranking results.

✔ **If you're available for freelance work, make sure that at least one of your current positions is labeled Freelance.** Remember, people aren't mind readers (Karnac excluded), so you need to let people know that you're a freelance writer, Web site designer, dog walker, or whatever. If you look at Leya Booth's profile in Figure 15-1, you can see that she's self-employed as owner of Genius Office Services, which offers book editing, transcription, and tutoring services, along with other specialties.

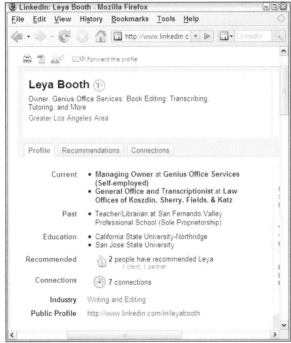

Figure 15-1:
Make sure
a current
position is
labeled self-
employed or
freelance.

✔ **Use the additional fields in your profile to include any relevant information that reinforces your marketing message.** For example, if you want to be seen as an expert in a given field, include references to any articles or books you've written, articles you've been quoted in, focus or advisory groups you belong to, and any speaking engagements or discussions you've participated in.

✔ **Make sure your profile links to your Web sites, blogs, and any other part of your online identity.** Don't just accept the standard "My Company" text; instead, select the option Other: and put your own words in the box entitled Website title, such as "Joel Elad's E-Commerce Education Web site." (See Chapter 3 for more information on linking from your profile to other Web sites.)

For an example of effectively linking your profile to other areas of your online presence, take a look at Ben Hanna's profile, shown in Figure 15-2. His three Web site links replace the bland "My Company," "My Blog," and "My Website" with his own text— Business.com, B2B Search Market Strategy, and My Business How-To Guides. Not only does this give more information to some-one reading his profile, it gives the search engines a better idea of what those links represent.

Figure 15-2:
Give your
Web site
links mean-
ingful
names.

Website links

Marketing yourself to your network

Optimizing your profile in the ways described in the previous section is one of the best ways to market yourself effectively using LinkedIn. Another is to be alert to how well you're communicating with your LinkedIn connections. Whether it's automatic (like when you update your profile and LinkedIn auto-matically notifies your network through a Network Update) or self-generated (when you use LinkedIn InMail or Introductions to send a note to someone else, which I cover in Chapter 5), this communication becomes your ongoing message to the members of your network and keeps you in their minds and (you hope!) plans.

The most effective marketing occurs when people don't realize you're marketing to them. After all, the average American sees approximately 4,000 marketing messages per day. Your goal is to communicate often but not be overbearing about it so your message subtly sinks into people's minds. If you do that, people will think you're GRRRRRR-EAT! (Hmm, why am I hungry for cereal?)

So when you're contemplating how to effectively communicate with your network connections, keep these points in mind:

✔ **Update your profile when appropriate.** Updating your profile means that you're sending an update of your newest projects to your network so that your connections know whether they might want to consider involving you in their own current or future projects. I do not recommend that you update your profile as often as you update a blog, but you certainly don't want to leave your profile untouched for months on end, either. Useful times to update your profile include

- Getting a new job or promotion

- Starting a new freelance or contract job

- Launching a new company or venture

- Adding a missing piece of your Experiences section, like adding a new position, updating the description of an existing job, or clarifying the role of a group or interest on your profile

- Taking on new responsibilities or duties in any of your endeavors

✔ **Take advantage of the "What are you working on?" feature.** When you specify your current endeavors, several things happen. Your profile reflects what you enter here, your network connections see what you enter here when they read their Network Updates about you (see Chapter 9 for more on Network Updates), and over time, you start to build your own "micro-blog," in a sense, because people can follow your natural progression. A similar example of this is the micro-blogging service called Twitter. As you update your Twitter profile with 240-character messages, other people can follow your activities and even subscribe to these updates.

Some people use the status feature to let people know that, "Joel is getting ready for his week-long vacation" or "Joel is finishing up his first draft of *LinkedIn For Dummies*." Other people use the messages to show progression of a certain task, like "Joel is currently interviewing for an Executive Assistant position," then "Joel is narrowing down his choices for Executive Assistant to two finalists," and then "Joel has made an offer to his top choice for Executive Assistant." See Chapter 9 for more on how to use this feature.

✔ **Search for, and join, any relevant LinkedIn Groups that can help you reach your target audience.** It's a good idea to participate in these groups, but whatever you do, don't immediately download a list of all group members and spam them with LinkedIn messages. When you join the group, you're indicating your interest in that group because your profile now carries that group logo. Membership in such groups gives you access to like-minded people you should be communicating with and adding to your network. Spend some time every week or every month checking out LinkedIn Groups and networking with group members to grow your network.

✔ **Ask appropriate questions of selected people rather than the whole network.** When you use LinkedIn Answers (see Chapter 7) to ask a question or gain more knowledge about something, rather than blast your entire network with your request, send a personalized invitation to only those members in your network who seem the most likely to have the knowledge you need.

Don't ask questions to the same people all the time. Change the focus of your questions at regular intervals so that you reach out to more of your network over the year. For example, you may ask some questions on software development for a few months, then change and focus on project management for a while. On the other hand, when you know of a question that could interest your entire network, don't hesitate to let everyone know. Do that too often, however, and people will feel annoyed by it.

✔ **Participate on a regular and consistent basis.** The easiest way to ensure a steady stream of contact with as many people as you can handle is to dedicate a small but fixed amount of time to interacting with the LinkedIn community. Some members spend 15 to 30 minutes per day, sending messages to their connections, reading through the Questions and Answers pages, or finding one to two new people to add to their network. Others spend an hour a week, or as long as it takes to create what they've set as their set number of recommendations, invite their set number of new contacts, or reconnect with their set number of existing connections. You just need to establish a routine that works for your own schedule.

Marketing Your Business through LinkedIn

Currently, LinkedIn offers you two types of business promotion, one for small businesses and another for large ones. For small businesses, owners and managers rely on their own profile pages (which, as mentioned earlier, can contain links to company and other types of Web sites). For large companies, LinkedIn has created Company Profile pages (for free) through an agreement with Capital IQ and BusinessWeek that covers 160,000 companies that these companies gathered information about and supplied to LinkedIn.

If you have a problem with the content of your Capital IQ/BusinessWeek–generated Company Profile page, click the Feedback link on the Company Profile page. If you're a verified employee of the company, you can update the Company Profile page yourself. If you're still stuck, send an e-mail to `linkedinissues@capitaliq.com`.

Online marketing tactics using LinkedIn

Marketing your business on LinkedIn involves working through your own network, employing both your current list of contacts as well as potential contacts in the greater LinkedIn community. Your efforts should also include making use of links from your online activities to your LinkedIn profile and promoting your business online from your LinkedIn identity. Here are some things to keep in mind as you develop your LinkedIn marketing strategy:

- ✔ **Encourage every employee to have a LinkedIn profile and to link to each other.** Extending your network in this way increases your exposure outside your company. And if anybody in your organization is nervous about preparing her profile, just tell her that even Bill Gates has a LinkedIn profile. That should do the trick! (And then buy her a copy of this book to get the profile created.)

- ✔ **Make sure your business Web sites and blogs are linked to your LinkedIn profile.** By offering your Web site visitors a direct view to your LinkedIn profile, you're allowing them to verify you as an employee of the company because they can see your experiences and your recommendations from other people. They may also realize that they share a bond with you and your business that they never would have realized without LinkedIn.

- ✔ **Make sure your LinkedIn profile links back to your business Web site and blog.** Yes, you want your visitors and potential customers to be able to verify who you are, as noted in the previous bullet in this list, but you also want them to go back to your Web site and do some business with you! Make sure that you, and every employee of your company who's on LinkedIn, includes a link to your business's Web site and, if there is one, the company blog.

   If you have a search engine expert working for you, that person may complain about something called a *two-way link,* which is a link from your LinkedIn profile to your Web site and a link from your Web site to your LinkedIn profile. This practice, known as *reciprocal linking,* hurts your search engine ranking. If so, have that person identify which of the two links is more important and implement only that links.

- ✔ **Make sure that your most popular keyword phrases are in your company or personal profile.** Use sites such as `wordtracker.com` or `goodkeywords.com` to find the hottest keyword phrases in your field. If your business is doing any online ad campaigns, make sure those keyword phrases are the same as the ones in your profile. Presenting a consistent image to any potential customer makes you and your company look more professional.

✔ **Develop relationships with key business partners or media contacts.**
When you search for someone on LinkedIn, you can be very precise
about who you want to reach. So, for example, if you know that your
business needs to expand into the smartphone market, you can start
targeting and reaching out to smartphone companies such as Apple,
Research In Motion (maker of the Blackberry), and Palm (maker of the
Treo). If you want to increase your visibility, start reaching out to media
members who cover your industry.

Getting a Services Listing through a recommendation

Now, you may ask, "What if I am my business?" Anyone who provides a
professional service, such as consulting or freelance writing (to name just
a couple), will want to be sure to take advantage of the LinkedIn Service
Provider directory. This directory consists of categories and subcategories
that range from computer-related consultants to attorneys, accountants,
and real estate agents. If you click the drop-down arrow next to the word
Companies in the top navigation bar and then click the Services Provider
link, you can see the list of categories along the right side of the screen.

The tricky part about appearing in this directory is that you can't simply list
yourself in this directory; instead, LinkedIn requires you to obtain a recommendation from another LinkedIn member. The reason for this requirement
is simple: LinkedIn wants a directory of only providers that have at least one
person willing to publicly validate their work.

The moment you receive a recommendation from a LinkedIn member about
your services, your profile is included in the Service Providers directory. To
request a recommendation from someone, just follow these steps:

1. **Click the drop-down arrow next to the word Companies in the top
   navigation bar; then select Service Providers.**

   You should be taken to the Service Providers home page, as shown in
   Figure 15-3. Note the Request a Recommendation link at the top-right
   corner.

2. **Click the link Request a Recommendation to bring up the recommendation page, which is shown in Figure 15-4.**

Request a Recommendation link

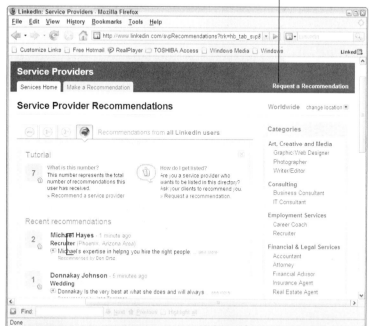

Figure 15-3:
Start at the
Service
Providers
home page.

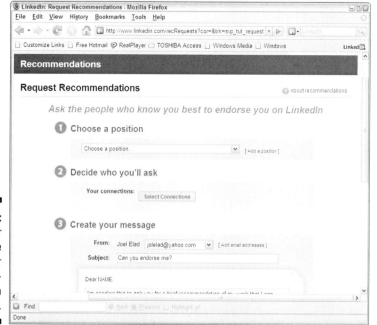

Figure 15-4:
Start your
Service
Provider
Recom-
mendation
request.

3. **Under Choose a Position, click the arrow for the drop-down list to find the position you want someone to recommend you for.**

   If you want your Services recommendation to be tied to a specific role, pick one of your positions that indicates that service, such as Freelance Writer or Website Designer position. If you don't see an appropriate position in your list, click the [Add a Position] link to add a new position to your Experience section of your profile. (For more information on how to update your profile, see Chapter 3.)

4. **Click the gray Select Connections button to pick the people you want to ask for a recommendation.**

   A new window opens.

5. **Click the check box to add people to your list of requests. When you're done, click the Finished button to close that window and return to the Request Recommendations page.**

6. **In the box under "Create Your Message," write a note that will go out to each person you have selected, similar to the example shown in Figure 15-5.**

   Although LinkedIn will fill in this box with canned text, I recommend that you change this text to make it sound as though it's coming from you. Make sure the Subject line is appropriate, too, because doing so helps your chances of getting your intended requesters to actually open the e-mail and respond.

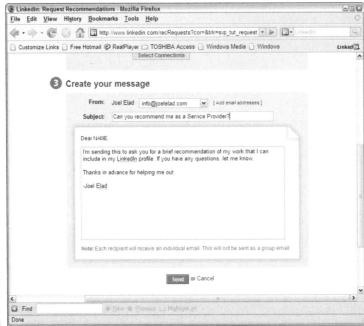

Figure 15-5:
Ask your
network
connections
for a recom-
mendation.

7. Click the Send button.

Your request is sent and your selected connections receive a message from LinkedIn, asking them to come to the site and complete a Recommendation for you.

That's it! If you need information on how to complete a Recommendation for someone who requests one from you, for example, check out Chapter 8.

Finding Marketing Partners through LinkedIn

When it comes to marketing on LinkedIn, your strategy will typically involve more than just you and your business. Part of the success of marketing through LinkedIn is finding the right marketing partners to help you with your goals and take you to the next level. After all, you're connecting with like-minded professionals who have skills similar or complementary to yours, which helps you and them achieve your goals. In some cases, finding the right partner can make a big difference in the growth of your business, as I found out by interviewing Kristie Spilios. See the sidebar "No trouble starting TrebleMakers (with the help of a LinkedIn contact)," located in this chapter.

Your first order of business is to use the LinkedIn Service Providers directory to start identifying potential partners. (See Chapter 13 on how to use the Service Providers directory.) You can look for service providers that may be two or three degrees away from you, or you can target people you want to meet at specific companies by seeing who in your network can arrange an introduction. Ideas to keep mind during your search include

✔ **Pay attention to people's titles.** In the past, you may have told somebody, "I need to talk to someone who works at advertising sales for a major radio network." Today, with LinkedIn, you can look for an Advertising Sales Manager at Clear Channel Communications. Search for who you need to know, specifically, and LinkedIn will show you whether that person is connected to you by one, two, or three degrees.

✔ **Join the LinkedIn groups that would appeal to your business.** One of the quickest ways to signal your interest and find like-minded businesspeople is to join a LinkedIn group that's relevant to your industry or niche. You can then search group members to find potential partners. Also, because your groups are listed on your profile, joining a group means that you'll have a lasting reference on your profile that will let people know that you identify with this group.

✔ **Search LinkedIn Answers for people with similar situations as yours.**
You might find someone at a similar company who looked for an SEO expert and asked the community for help. The people who respond may give you insight on whom to choose and to add to your network.

Odds are, you won't have all the answers when it comes to your strategic plan, marketing plan, or maybe even your business direction. Thankfully, when you're using LinkedIn, you are definitely not alone. LinkedIn allows you to tap the collective knowledge of its community, enabling you to performing market research on a variety of topics and get real- time answers without involving think tanks or putting out thousands of dollars in fees.

The key is to be honest, transparent, and — as odd as this may sound — grateful. You are asking people's advice and thoughts, so don't expect them to write out a 30-page market analysis for you for free. Share your goals and intentions, get people discussing the idea and each other's comments, and be ready to listen. The best research results from the community's exchange of ideas, with a bunch of voices chiming in to validate or discount the theorem of the moment.

✔ **Ask targeted questions on LinkedIn Answers and follow up with people who left the best answers.** As discussed in Chapter 7, LinkedIn Answers provides an excellent and free way to tap the knowledge base of the community, in an abundance of categories. Although you can post a general "Where do we go from here?" question, you can also ask a targeted or focused question concerning one element of your research and then gauge the response. Don't forget to start a dialog with your most enthusiastic responders, because they have already demonstrated interest and knowledge.

✔ **Watch your Question thread closely (through the My Q&A tab) and provide clarification or responses whenever needed.** Some people just throw out a question on LinkedIn Answers and then sit back and wait for the genius to flow in. More often, however, the discussion that ensues on the Answer thread may veer off from your intended topic, or the responses completely miss the mark because they don't interpret your question accurately. You can add clarification to the original question, or add your own reply in when needed. If nothing else, reply with a thank you for a very good answer and encourage others to keep that answer in mind. For more details on how to accomplish this, turn to Chapter 7 and find the section on clarifying your question.

After you've received at least five to ten responses, I recommend that you pick a best answer and some good answers by selecting the appropriate check boxes next to each person's answer. Not only does this reward people who gave you a lot of great information, it indicates to the community which responses best fit, in case someone finds this question in a search later on.

✔ **Keep the conversation open and continuous.** Try to leave part of your question open-ended so that the people answering it can discuss their theories and you will have a more natural reason for follow-up with them individually. Sometimes, keeping the door open is as easy as ending your post with something like "If you think you can help with this situation, let me know."

✔ **Set up a LinkedIn Group that speaks to your target audience and your company's (or your) capabilities.** For example, to cite my tried-and-true example, say that you're trying to reach accountants for financial services companies. To get the ball rolling, you could start the Financial Services Accountants Group, spread the word to your target audience, and stay in touch with that audience via this group whenever you want to know more about your target audience.

No trouble starting TrebleMakers (with the help of a LinkedIn contact)

Several years ago, Kristie Spilios co-founded a company called TrebleMakers, which teaches music enrichment classes to young children.

When she was building her marketing plan with her business partner, she and her partner realized that an important piece was the

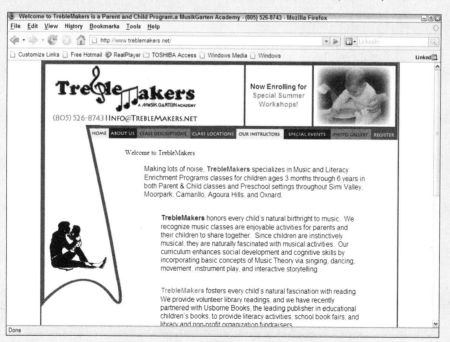

(continued)

(continued)

Web site and logo design they would be using. Given their limited preliminary budget, they were completely unable to find anyone who would address their needs. And then came salvation.

"When all hope seemed lost, I received a LinkedIn e-mail update that announced the connection of one of my contacts with an old, mutual friend from our high school days," relates Spilios. "This shared companion had just opened a consulting business and was enthusiastically eager to work with us despite our start-up woes."

Three months later, TrebleMakers received its "spectacular" Web site and "dazzling" logo for a reasonable fee that fell within their price range. The consultant even included some complementary business cards and letterhead stationery as appreciation for TrebleMakers' belief in him and his latest endeavor. Today, TrebleMakers is thriving and growing, and Spilios credits much of that success to having an informative Web site and prominent logo, saying that "We receive almost as many words of praise on our Web site and logo as we do on the music classes themselves!"

"Without LinkedIn and its awesome networking, my company would most likely still be searching for a cost-efficient marketing solution. But, instead of singing the blues, my business partner and I both have happy harmony, all thanks to LinkedIn!"

Chapter 16

Using LinkedIn to Increase Your Sales

*W*hen it comes to "making the sale," every edge you can gain over the competition is important. LinkedIn provides several ways to help you to get more competitive, close the sale, and even help deliver the winning solution. There are ways throughout the entire sales cycle that a well-connected network and detailed profile can help you narrow the gap, identify with your potential lead, gain some trust, and make that sale.

In this chapter, I tell you about some of the ways that LinkedIn can help you in the area of sales. You find out about prospecting, or generating leads, to not only find potential clients but also narrow them down to the decision maker — the person who's in the position to decide to buy your product or services. After you've identified your target, you can research your prospects using LinkedIn and, when you have succeeded in setting up a meeting with your prospect, you can use LinkedIn to prepare for that crucial meeting. Finally, this chapter covers how LinkedIn can help you deliver the winning solution after you have made the sale, and how you can report a positive experience with your customer, thereby leading to even more sales!

Mining for Your Clients

It's a big world out there, and in terms of clients, you need to ask yourself, Who are you looking for? Is everyone a potential client, or do you have a specific demographic in mind? A specific skill set? Maybe you've written the greatest plug-in tool for accountants who work in the financial services industry and you want to sell this tool directly to your likely users. With LinkedIn, you can conduct a search to find people who match your criteria. After you locate those people, it's up to you to approach them and close the sale, which I talk about in "Closing the Deal," later in this chapter.

Before you start your search, ask yourself a few questions that can help you with generating your leads:

- ✔ Are you looking for people with a specific title or in a particular industry?

- ✔ Are you looking for decision makers within a company, or are you seeking a general audience? (That is, are you trying to sell into a company, or directly to people?)

- ✔ Besides your main target industry, can you approach related industries, and if so, what are they?

- ✔ Does the location of your potential contact matter? Does making the sale require an in-person visit (which means that the contact needs to live near you or you have to be willing to travel to this person)?

With your answers to these questions in mind, you're ready to start searching LinkedIn for your leads.

Generating leads with Advanced People Search

When you're ready to start looking for leads, I recommend jumping right in with the LinkedIn Advanced People Search feature, which allows you to search the database consisting of tens of millions of LinkedIn members based on the criteria you've established for the leads you want to generate.

To start a search, make sure the drop-down list option People is selected in the top-right corner, and click the Advanced Search link next to that drop-down option. Say, for example, that you need accountants who work in the Financial Services industry. To start such a search, you would fill in the Title and Industry fields of Advanced People Search, as shown in Figure 16-1, and click Search.

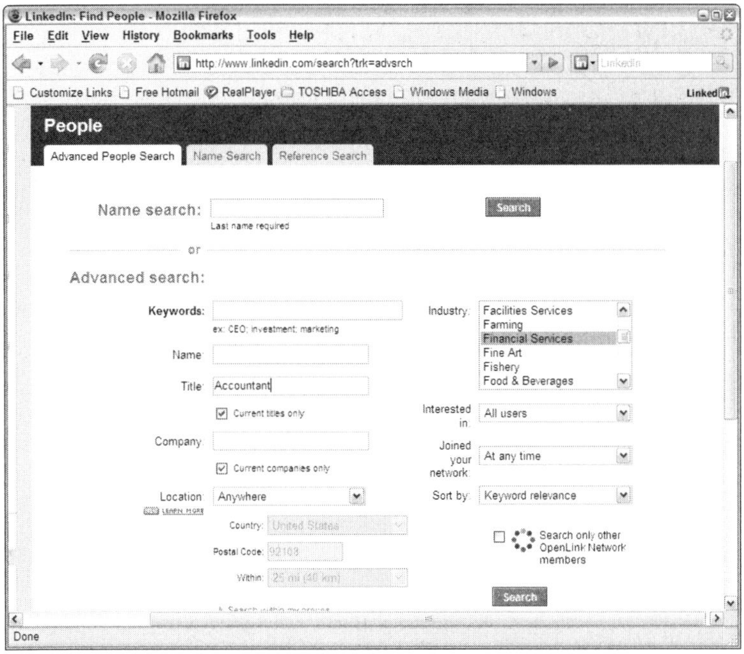

Figure 16-1:
Use
Advanced
Search to
find your
potential
clients.

When you begin your search of the LinkedIn database, your own network can help you identify your *best leads* (people only two or three degrees away from you who you can reach through a first-degree connection introducing you) if you change the Sort By option, shown at the bottom-right corner of Figure 16-1, to Degrees Away from You. (The default option is Keyword Relevance, as shown in the figure.) When you see your search results, as shown in Figure 16-2, you first see which results are closely connected with you via your connections. You can click each person's name to read his or her full LinkedIn profile, see how you are connected to that person, and decide whether you've got a potential lead. (This method provides much more information to you than a simple Google search, which would provide only a LinkedIn member's public profile, instead of their full profile.)

Another way to get different search results is to click the LinkedIn Network tab from the search results screen, which appears next to the Your Network tab above the search result names. This search generates general leads that are neither directly nor indirectly connected to you. Here, you can see the lead's title and company, but not his or her name, as Figure 16-3 shows. You can find out some details from reading their LinkedIn profile, but you will have to use LinkedIn tools like InMail to communicate with these people to pursue the lead.

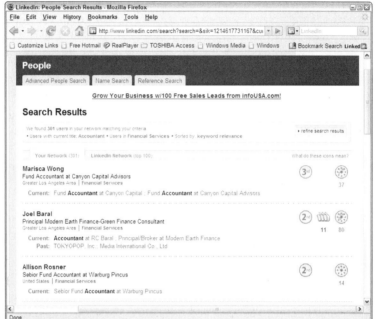

Figure 16-2:
See how you're connected to your potential clients.

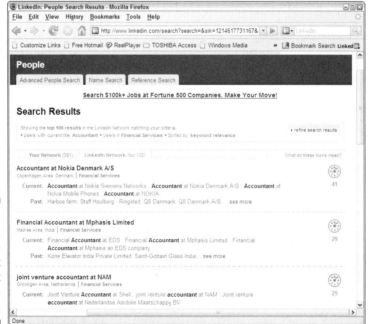

Figure 16-3:
See who in the LinkedIn network at large best matches your search.

When you are doing general prospecting, surveying the market for that "perfect lead" or, at least, a lead in the right direction, try to keep these ideas in mind while filling in the appropriate fields for each strategy:

- **Generalize your search:** If you're looking for your ideal contacts independently of the company they work for, focus primarily on the Title and Industry fields to find your leads.

- **Narrow your search:** Use the Keywords field to narrow your results list when you need to reach people within a certain niche of an industry or job.

- **Target specific people:** Use either the Company or Keywords field, plus the Title field, to help you find specific employees in your target companies.

- **Refine your search by areas of knowledge:** Click on Answers from the top navigation bar and look for people who answered questions in your target area to see whether you spot a potential contact there. (See Chapter 7 for more information on using LinkedIn Answers.)

- **Help your product sell itself:** Search for the customers of your customers. Why would you do such a thing? You want to get those people excited about your product so that they'll demand it from *your* customers, of course! This strategy is also known as *pull marketing*. (See Chapter 15 for more information about how to use LinkedIn for marketing purposes.)

- **Reach out through service professionals:** Search for consultants who are hired by your potential customers by using the Title and Industry fields, or by choosing "Consultants/contractors" from the Interested In drop-down list. You can ask those consultants for help in reaching your potential customers.

Finding the decision maker

Although generating a list of potential leads is a great first step in marketing your product, effective salesmanship often comes down to finding that "right person" whom you can present with an offer to buy something. This person is known as the *decision maker* (or the *final authority,* or even just *the boss*). You can talk to as many administrative assistants and receptionists as you'd like, but without the exact name or contact info of the person who makes the purchasing decisions, your sales effort is stalled.

LinkedIn can help you reach that decision maker in the following ways:

✔ **When you perform an advanced search, include words like Account Manager, Director, or Vice President in the Search For field.** If your results show someone who's in your extended network, now you have a specific name to mention when you call the company. I recommend that you approach that person via LinkedIn and your mutual connections first, thereby making your first contact with him or her more of a "warm call" than a cold one.

✔ **Use the LinkedIn Company Profile pages to find out specific information about your target company.** If you're trying to reach someone within a company you want to target, see whether that person has a Company Profile page. To do so, click the drop-down list next to the word Companies on the top navigation bar and click the Company Search link to search through LinkedIn's company pages. Say, for example, that you need to reach someone within LinkedIn. When you bring up LinkedIn's company profile page, as shown in Figure 16-4, you get some specific information right away.

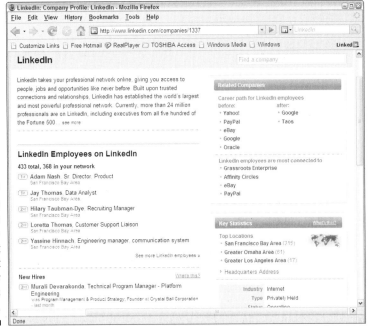

Figure 16-4: Get specific information about your target company through its profile.

You will immediately see who in your network works for this company, so you know whom to approach to pass along your request to the decision maker, or to tell you who that decision maker is. Be sure to scroll down the rest of the page, too, to see other useful information, such as new hires, recent promotions and changes, and open job listings for the company. (See Figure 16-5.)

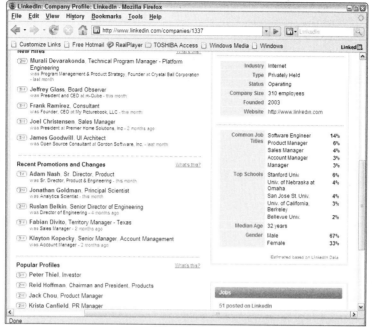

Figure 16-5:
Use a
company's
LinkedIn
Company
page to find
out more
about your
target
company.

✔ **Use your existing network to ask for an Introduction or to point you in the right direction.** Using your network in this manner was basically the original intent of LinkedIn: You contact someone who works at your target company and ask that contact to introduce you to the decision maker. The decision maker is much more likely to receive an Introduction than a cold call. Your network connection might also serve as a recommendation of you to the decision maker, which will carry some weight when you try to close the deal.

✔ **Use InMail to contact people close to the decision maker.** You may find that, in some cases, the decision maker may not be on LinkedIn yet, or his or her profile is closed to Introductions and InMail. In such a case, you can use LinkedIn to find the closest person to the decision maker and ask that person for help, a connection, or information to help you reach the next level.

✔ **Use InMail to contact the decision maker, if he or she is on LinkedIn.** You may not have the time or opportunity to get introduced to your decision maker, and if you're using InMail to approach the decision maker, why not just go for the gusto and make your introduction directly? This is a faster option than waiting or asking for an Introduction, but there is the chance the decision maker will ignore your message. You have to decide what's best for your situation.

Closing the Deal

Establishing a connection to the right person (the one who makes the purchasing decisions) is half the battle of getting your product sold. However, you still have to convince the person and close the deal, of course. In this section, I give you some pointers on how to put LinkedIn to work for you for the final phase of a sales effort: completing it successfully!

The key to getting the most out of LinkedIn for closing the deal is knowing that LinkedIn has more than just names — it has information in the form of detailed profiles of its tens of millions of users, and in the form of knowledge sharing through LinkedIn Answers, associations made through LinkedIn Groups, and corporate information through LinkedIn Company Profiles.

Researching prospects

When you have identified your prospects, spend some time familiarizing yourself with them before you contact them. Gleaning some insight about your potential buyers can go a long way toward getting the person to respond, taking the time to listen to your pitch, and buying your product. Following are some tips concerning specific ways to research your prospective clients:

- **Read the prospect's *full* profile to discover all you can about his or her interests, likes, dislikes, and so on.** You can do far more than simply scan a person's profile looking for past jobs and maybe their education to see whether they share an alma mater with you. A person's LinkedIn profile can be or lead to a gold mine of information about that person. For instance, people may include links to their own Web sites, blogs, or company Web sites. Follow those links, especially to blogs or personal Web sites, and see what you can find out. In the prospect's profile, look over the Interests section and the Additional Information section. And don't forget the Contact Settings section — here's where you can find out under what circumstances this person wants to be contacted. Be sure to respect those wishes.

- **Read your prospect's recommendations for other people.** You can gain a lot of insight by seeing what qualities a person likes to praise in other people, especially if your prospect has left multiple recommendations. In this way, you also gain insight into the people they trust, so check those people who received a recommendation to see whether you have a connection to any of *them.* If so, ask that person first for an Introduction to your prospect.

✔ **Read any questions or answers your prospect wrote for LinkedIn Answers.** If you pull up someone's profile, look for a tab entitled Q&A (shown in Figure 16-6) and click that tab. The page that opens contains all the questions and answers this person has contributed to LinkedIn. When you read these contributions, you might gain some insight into this person's preferences and "hot button issues" — what motivates or annoys him or her.

Figure 16-6: Read through any questions or answers your prospect has contributed to LinkedIn.

Preparing for the client meeting

Say that your initial conversations with your prospects have gone well and you have been granted a meeting with a potential client to make your pitch. Whereas you may have already used LinkedIn to gain more information about the specific person, you can now turn to discovering details about the specific industry, the company, and the company's potential response to your business pitch. Here are ways to go about gathering information about the company:

✔ **Try to get an informational interview with someone at the target company, preferably with someone you know.** Check your LinkedIn network to see whether you have a first- or second-degree contact at the company you're planning to pitch to. Ask that person to spend some time with you for the purpose of gathering information about the company, and try to get some insights into company priorities and culture. Also see what you can learn about the company's top motivation in purchasing decisions — what priorities or issues the company considers before buying something from a vendor.

✔ **Visit the LinkedIn Company Profile page to review all the recent company activities.** As mentioned earlier in this chapter in the "Finding the decision maker" section, when you look at the Company Profile page, you see sections such as Recent Updates and Changes. Peruse these sections before your meeting with your potential buyer to find out who has been promoted or hired, the key statistics of that company, open job listings at the company, and even the most popular profiles of employees at that company. By doing so, you'll have more background information and therefore more confidence; also, this type of knowledge helps you identify interests or commonalities to enhance your sense of connection with your buyer (and his or hers with you).

✔ **Use LinkedIn Answers to get advice from the community at large or your network.** Search LinkedIn Answers to see whether other people have already asked questions about your target company, or to find out how to approach companies in your industry. If you don't find anything directly related to what you're searching for, you can pose a question yourself and see what recommendations you get from other LinkedIn members.

When all else fails, ask for help!

Michael Goodman is a sales professional from Phoenix, Arizona, with more than 30 years of sales experience. But even he admits that with all the new technologies out there, he was a bit lost when trying to figure out exactly how to use LinkedIn and other Web 2.0 technologies to help him make that next sale. So, he went to LinkedIn Answers and posed the following question:

"With all the social media available, including LinkedIn, blogs, Twitter, Plaxo, Second Life, et al., what is the best way to utilize all this stuff, stay ahead of the techno-bleeding edge, and really just find another customer to tell my story to?

I can't keep up with all the social media, Web 2.0 marketing movement. Really, all I want to do is find the next customer. I am hoping someone has figured out the magical answer to taking advantage of technology and simply finding new people interested in what I have to offer. Anyone?"

Goodman received more than 25 responses, some of which were detailed, multiparagraph essays that helped point him in the right direction on how to use LinkedIn. The answers included links to articles about using LinkedIn and references to LinkedIn experts who could fully answer his question.

All these efforts are meant only to prepare you and get you closer to your prospect or target company so that you can make your pitch. Obviously, to complete the sale, you still need to have a compelling product, pitch, and offer for this company. Have all of that ready *before* you approach your prospect.

Using LinkedIn to Help You Complete the Sale

At this stage you have, to borrow a famous phrase, "gotten to yes," meaning that you've contacted your prospect and he or she has agreed to buy your product or service. Congratulations! You've made the sale, and now it's time to deliver. Your membership in LinkedIn can continue to provide value by giving you some resources to help you deliver what you promised and ensure future sales success.

Getting help to deliver the solution

After you've made the sale, go back to your company with the contract in hand and determine the resources and personnel necessary to deliver on your contract. In some cases, you may not have everything you need to deliver the order. As it can in earlier stages of the sales process, LinkedIn can assist you in this stage as well. Here are some of those ways:

- **Find partners to create the winning team.** You've done the hard part: You've gotten the contract. The customer trusts you to deliver on that contract, so it's your job to build the winning team, and your company may not employ full-time all the people you need or you may have agreed to additional items to make the sale that require something where your business has to speed up development. In such a case, you can use your LinkedIn connections to find people who have the missing skill sets you need. (See Chapter 11 for tips on finding an employee.) You can also perform an Advanced People Search or Service Providers search for a consultant or part-time employee who has the skills you need to build your products or consult on your service offering.

- **Get some direction from the LinkedIn community.** You can create a question in LinkedIn Answers that polls your network and the greater LinkedIn community in the problem area you've been hired to solve. Get an idea of how other people would tackle this problem, and use the answers to identify potential partners or contacts you can use to deliver your solution. For example, polling the community about a part of your service offering (a part that isn't client-specific) may result in a LinkedIn member providing a new way of approaching the problem.

✔ **Search LinkedIn Answers for past responses that can help you.** Odds are, the solution you were hired to deliver is not the very first time since the world began that someone had to solve that problem. Therefore, you should try your luck and search through past answers in LinkedIn Answers; you're likely to get lots of ideas by seeing how other people handled similar situations.

✔ **Hire the skills you need.** If you can't find a part-time person or tap the skills you're seeking from someone in your LinkedIn network, it's time to post a job listing on LinkedIn Jobs. See Chapter 11 for the steps on how to post a job listing.

Reporting a positive sale

Reporting the completion of a sale is my favorite part of the business sales process. You've made the sale, developed the solution, and delivered it to the customer. At this point, many people think, "Whew, I'm done. Nothing to do now but enjoy the happy hour!" This is a common and natural response, but as a member of the LinkedIn world, your job isn't really done. You want to demonstrate your growth (and your company's growth) that resulted from handling this project to encourage future contracts to come your way. Here are some actions to consider after you've completed the sale and delivered the solution:

✔ **Invite your customer to your network.** You've worked hard to earn this customer's trust and to meet (or exceed) the customer's expectations by completing the sale. As a result, you should feel comfortable enough to send that person an Invitation to join your network. Doing so could keep you in contact with this customer for future opportunities. Studies have shown that it's six times cheaper to sell to an existing customer than to acquire a new customer.

✔ **Leave your customer a recommendation.** After you've added a customer to your network, post a recommendation for him or her on the system if you feel it's deserved. Doing so gives your customer a sense of "reward" for being a positive contributor, but more important, it informs the community that you did a project for this person, which can help you in the future. Also, the customer may reciprocate by leaving you a recommendation, which strengthens your profile and makes you more appealing to future prospects.

✔ **Stay in touch with your customer.** You can keep track of your customer's activities by monitoring your Network Updates (if he or she is a part of your network). Routinely keep in touch about the solution you delivered, perhaps to open the conversation for selling additional products or services or maintenance contract work.

✔ **Update your profile with the skills you acquired or demonstrated through this sale.** To be ready for future prospects who search the LinkedIn database, it's important to have the right keywords and skill sets on your profile so that these prospects can identify you as someone who can provide a similar solution. If you are a consultant or freelance worker, you can add the project you just completed as experience on your profile as well. (See Chapter 3 on how to update your profile.)

✔ **Tap the customer's network by asking him or her for referrals.** After you've connected with your customer, keep an eye on his or her network. If you think you see a future prospect, consider asking your customer for an Introduction or a Recommendation. Usually, if you provided a quality solution, the customer will readily oblige your request.

Chapter 17

Venture Capital and Angel Funding

. . . .

In This Chapter

▶ Finding investors

▶ Asking the right questions

▶ Building up your management team

▶ Using LinkedIn to get an investor

▶ Searching for investments

▶ Evaluating your potential investments

. . . .

*W*hen you put bunches of Internet-savvy, knowledgeable profession-als who like to network on a growing social networking site like LinkedIn, you're bound to have a community of people who are involved and interested in Venture Capital (VC), where specific firms provide millions (or tens of millions) of dollars in funding as well as support and board mem-bers for emerging companies who want to grow, Or you might run across professionals involved in angel funding, where wealthy investors invest up to a few million dollars of their own money in exchange for ownership per-centages of emerging companies. You could say that LinkedIn has VC at its roots. LinkedIn founder Reid Hoffman is an angel investor who has invested in over 60 companies besides LinkedIn, including such famous companies as Facebook, Digg, Flickr, Technorati, Tagged, and Ning.

LinkedIn has become an important tool for everyone involved in the VC or angel funding industry, from the casual observer to the hyper-extended deal-maker, for many reasons:

✔ LinkedIn can help entrepreneurs figure out how to connect with a Venture Capital firm.

✔ Entrepreneurs can use LinkedIn to build up their management team before a proposal is made.

✔ Business owners can test out their business ideas on fellow first degree connections.

✔ LinkedIn Answers can help entrepreneurs fill in the blanks on their proposals.

✔ VC firms can monitor LinkedIn Answers to get a perspective on up-and-coming trends.

✔ Experienced business veterans can use LinkedIn Answers to give advice, encouragement, and a new perspective to first-timers.

In this chapter, I talk about how you can benefit from using LinkedIn when it comes to Venture Capital or angel funding, regardless of your role or position in the process. I cover different cases and stories on how entrepreneurs have benefited from LinkedIn, as well as how VC firms or angel networks have used LinkedIn to find, evaluate, or advance their deals.

Finding Potential Investors

So, you have a great idea for a company, you want to be the next great thing in your industry, and all you need is a blank check to make your dreams come true, right? Although LinkedIn can't guarantee that you'll find the right funding partner, get the money you need, and build your business with a great return on investment, the site can help you improve your chances of success when dealing with the funding and growth of your business.

No matter what stage your business is in, whether you just thought of a new business idea or invention, you're building a prototype, you earned your first dollar of revenue, or you just hit $1 million in sales, LinkedIn can be an invaluable resource for reaching the next step and beyond. The following sections take a look at some of the ways LinkedIn can assist you in the quest for an investor.

Asking questions and getting LinkedIn Answers

Although you may be an expert in your field, you could probably use some good advice from existing venture capitalists, angel investors, or successful entrepreneurs when it comes to obtaining financing. Thankfully, LinkedIn Answers allows you to tap a vast network of knowledgeable folk who are experts in that field and gladly give general and specific tips. (See Chapter 7 for more information about how to use LinkedIn Answers.) While LinkedIn Answers has a special category for Startups and Small Businesses, I focus on the areas of Venture Capital and angel funding here. If you are not ready for that big investment, definitely check out the Startups and Small Business category for advice.

When you're ready to use LinkedIn Answers to get answers to your specific questions regarding Venture Capital or angel funding, just follow these steps:

1. **Click the Answers link from the top navigation bar to go to LinkedIn Answers. Then, click the link for Finance and Accounting, and find a subsection called Financing.**

2. **Select Financing, which expands the view to reveal the Venture Capital and Private Equity category.**

   When you go to that category, as shown in Figure 17-1, you see a targeted list of questions for this area.

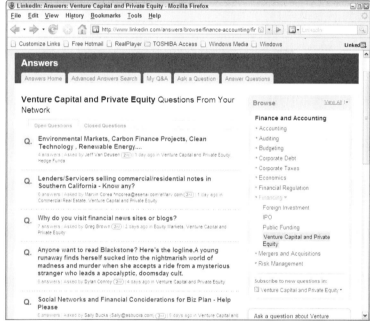

Figure 17-1: See what questions and answers LinkedIn has for VC and equity.

You can pose a question from a very general perspective or target a highly specific topic. Some of the questions people have asked include

✔ What's the difference between a venture capitalist and an angel investor?

✔ What are some good venture capitalist Web sites?

✔ Who should I go to for non-traditional funding of a startup?

✔ Who are the Venture Capitalists who invest in scalable open source ventures?

✔ What is the best way to seek interim funding during a period of heavy VC negotiations?

✔ How do VCs view venture debt prior to a Series A and post angel rounds?

LinkedIn members have used the Answers section to get critiques or reviews of their executive summaries, directly ask for a VC or angel investor to consider their venture, or ask other entrepreneurs how their experience was with a particular VC or angel investor. Most questions, pleas for help, and advice solicitation have received multiple responses, from the one- or two-sentence reply to the pages-long exposition of precise advice and list of accompanying Web sites or contact information.

If you're thinking of using LinkedIn Answers, here are some of the best ways to do so:

✔ **Before you post, search the database.** Believe it or not, you may not be the first person with your particular question to approach the LinkedIn community. Take the time to search LinkedIn Answers to see whether someone has asked your question or a variation of it. If you find your question, look over the answers given and see whether you get the information you needed. If the answers aren't specific enough, rewrite the question in your own words and post it yourself.

✔ **Get the information you're missing.** If you're writing your business plan to get funding and you need some more information to supplement one of your sections, ask the LinkedIn community for the facts. Perhaps you need to know the size of a potential customer market or the top Web sites used by consumers to perform price comparison searches.

✔ **When asking for advice, be as specific as possible.** Your question can gauge people's experiences and ask for advice, instead of a fact or figure. When asking for advice, though, help your audience by being as specific with your request as possible. Asking for help is one thing, but asking for three ways to strengthen your proposal will probably generate more replies. If you're in the middle of a situation, spell out the scenario, terms and all, as much as you are legally allowed to do.

Build your dream team

When you're looking for funding, of any amount, one of the top things that any investor will want to see is your management team. No matter how great your idea is, the execution of that idea will determine your success. Investors see one way to mitigate the risk of their investment by rewarding strong management teams that have the skill to weather unexpected turns. If your management team is lacking in at least one key area, consider LinkedIn as a source to find that missing person.

Here are some things to keep in mind when doing a search on LinkedIn for your next team member:

- ✔ **Experience is key.** Although desire, motivation, and interest are important, the way to improve your chances of getting funding is to have experienced personnel. This means that, when searching for potential candidates, you should study each person's profile to gauge her documented experience at past positions first; then see whether her interests match your company's interests.

- ✔ **Pick complements, not carbon copies.** It's very tempting for an entrepreneur to seek out like-minded individuals with similar backgrounds to build a business. However, companies with the strongest growth had a diverse management team that could handle different situations because the team's skills complemented each other. Put your business needs ahead of your personal preference. Look for LinkedIn members whose profiles indicate strengths that aren't yet represented in your startup.

- ✔ **Gauge the strength of the candidate's network.** Any time you look to add someone to your organization, you should be asking what value the person could bring through his existing network. (After all, who you know can make the difference.) When you connect with someone, see who's a part of his network, if possible. See what groups and affiliations, Web sites, and Q&A are on the candidate's profile, because that indicates his overall reach into the greater network.

Putting it all together

Suppose that you've got your business plan, management team, market analysis, prototype or working model, and you've built up a customer set. You've done some research and are ready to start shopping around and looking for investment. You've perfected your 30-second elevator pitch so you can quickly and accurately describe your business to anyone who's interested, and you can quote the facts and figures you need for any presentation. It's time to seek out a funding partner.

Although this is not the exhaustive list of what you can do, here are some tips that can help you find that partner using LinkedIn:

- ✔ **Gather leads.** Use LinkedIn Answers to post a question to either your network or the general community about the best firms or investors to consider. (You can find out more about LinkedIn Answers in Chapter 7.)

- ✔ **Do research on your leads.** Look up potential investors on LinkedIn and read their profiles. See what interests they have, what group affiliations they maintain, and what information they share or gather using LinkedIn Answers. Follow through on any Web sites, blogs, or profiles they link to from their profiles. See what you have in common or which benefit of your company might interest them the most.

✔ **Work your network and get them working.** Do advanced searches to see how your network can connect you with the right person. Maybe someone in your network knows a VC or someone at the same firm as a VC or angel investor. Perhaps someone in one of your groups has the right connection in one of her other groups. Let your network know what you're looking for and ask, respectfully, for help, advice, or a push in the right direction.

✔ **Get introduced or reach out yourself.** If you have a second- or third-degree connection to a potential investor, use LinkedIn Introductions to ask your contacts to introduce you. If you have no direct connections, consider using InMail to make your own Introduction. (Chapter 5 has more on Introductions and InMail.)

✔ **Do your homework before any meeting.** Use LinkedIn to prepare before you meet any potential investor. Study her profile and check the LinkedIn Company Profiles for information about her company. If she's in your extended network, ask your connections (who know her) for advice and information on your potential investor. See what companies they have invested in and research those companies as well.

Finding Potential Investments

Maybe someone in your VC firm needs to connect with someone in a particular industry, or perhaps your organization wants to invest in an emerging market or new technology. LinkedIn is a great place for you as a potential investor to look for your next investment.

It's all in the network

One of the benefits of a good investor is the network he brings with him to the investment. Though some VCs recommend their own executive and/or board structure to their investments, other investors simply offer advice as to any new hires or support personnel a new company may need in its growth phase. Sometimes, the right investor is someone who knows a new company's customer base well and can help this new company land a key account. This is all possible through a strong network. Therefore, LinkedIn is one of the best ways an investor can grow and strengthen his network. Here are some ways LinkedIn can help:

✔ **Monitor your Network Updates.** Your network is always working, and this point is clearly demonstrated in your Network Updates. Spend some time every day or week to look through your Network Updates to see which contacts of yours have moved companies, started new projects, or participated in questions you may find relevant. (See Chapter 9 for more information on Network Updates.)

✔ **Monitor LinkedIn Answers.** See what questions people are asking in your particular industry, and what answers are being posted by other people. Pay attention to question categories like Starting Up, Venture Capital and Private Equity, and Business Plans. (Chapter 7 has much more on LinkedIn Answers, in case you're dying of curiosity.)

✔ **Identify thought leaders.** As you watch your network, LinkedIn Answers, and any relevant LinkedIn Groups, pay attention if certain names keep popping up over and over again. These people could be thought leaders in your intended industry, people that everyone respects as the authority in their given subject matter, and they are worth connecting to in order to stay ahead and scope out the best opportunities. Reach out to these parties through Introductions or InMail (see Chapter 5) to see whether you can create a meaningful connection now and in the future.

✔ **Strengthen your network.** Build good contacts in your field through regular networking, and avenues like LinkedIn Answers. Identify people in your network who are a part of your desired industry and expand into their networks by getting to know their connections.

Do your due diligence

As new proposals for investments come across your way, or you meet an entrepreneur in one of your industries who could come to you later with an investment proposal, you have to evaluate these proposals and decide how to proceed. Here are some ways that LinkedIn can help you filter all this incoming information:

✔ **Evaluate your entrepreneurs.** When you're evaluating a proposal, do some research by seeing whether the requester has a LinkedIn profile. Compare notes between his business plan and his actual profile. See how he contributes to LinkedIn through Q&A. Evaluate the entire management team.

✔ **Ask for endorsements.** If you're evaluating a proposal or contemplating adding someone to your network, see who in your network knows this person (or company). If you find a connection, ask your connection whether she would endorse or recommend this person.

✔ **Get a sense for your intended market.** Ask questions about the intended market on LinkedIn Answers. Search previous questions to see whether the requesting company has been mentioned or profiled. If so, take a close look at the information.

Chapter 18

Miscellaneous Creative Uses of LinkedIn

*W*hen you think of business networking site such as LinkedIn, the most obvious applications of them spring to mind: finding a job, finding an employee, getting to meet new people, building a new business, getting funding and partners for that new business, and so on. But LinkedIn has acquired even more uses than the obvious ones. The power of the Internet and tens of millions of LinkedIn members has encouraged people to use this large community to accomplish other goals, both close to home and reaching around the world.

In this chapter, I give you a look at the some of the "creative" uses that people have found on LinkedIn. Some people use LinkedIn in combination with other services, such as Google News Alerts. Other people use LinkedIn as a gathering place to find recruits to help mold a new venture. Yet others have been using LinkedIn to meet each other in person! I describe these endeavors as well as provide several case studies with some points to keep in mind if you feel like doing something similar.

Mashing LinkedIn with Other Services

One of the hotter trends on the Internet in recent years has been the creation of mashups. No, I'm not talking potatoes here. A *mashup* is created when somebody takes data from more than one application and puts that data together into one new and useful application. For example, say that you combined real estate sales data from a database application with the Google Maps application, enabling a search result of the real estate data to be mapped onto a satellite image on Google. The satellite image represents a mash-up because it's a new, distinct service that neither application provided on its own.

Something similar to the concept of mashups occurs with creative uses of LinkedIn. As LinkedIn continues to evolve and its members use more and more of LinkedIn's functionality, new uses for LinkedIn continue to emerge, especially as part of a user's Internet exploits. The following sections describe a few smattering of these mashups.

LinkedIn and Google News Alerts

LinkedIn + Google News Alerts = Better-informed communication

I got this tip from Liz Ryan, a workplace expert, author, and speaker, as one of her top ten ways of using LinkedIn. It has to do with using both sites as a business tool when you're trying to reach out to an important potential business contact who you do not know. It works like this:

1. **Click the drop-down arrow next to People in the top navigation bar and then click the Advanced People Search link.**

2. **Fill in the appropriate fields to search for the name of a person at a company who is relevant to your situation, and with whom you would like to connect.**

3. **Armed with the name that turned up in the results, set up a Google News Alert with the person's name and the company name so that Google will notify you when that person is quoted or in the news.**

   When you receive a notice from Google News Alerts, you will have a much better idea of what the person is working on, as well as his or her impact at the company. This knowledge gives you an icebreaker by which to strike up a conversation. Rather than send a random connection request, you can reference the person's speech at the last XYZ Summit or agree with his or her last blog post.

   Don't overuse all this information you get when you contact the person, or, as Liz warns, he or she may think you're a business stalker.

LinkedIn Answers and RSS feeds

LinkedIn Answers + RSS feeds = Searchable targeted information

Millions of people are asking, answering, and reading information through LinkedIn Answers, and sometimes you may want one thread containing every mention of a certain company, person, or concept, instead of having to search through Answers all the time. Well, now you can subscribe to a live RSS feed and get automatic updates when someone asks or answers a question around a given keyword or category. To benefit from this feature, just do the following:

1. **Go to Edgehunt's mashup site at `www.edgehunt.com/mashup/linkedin/answers` and look over the RSS feeds offered. (See Figure 18-1.)**

   Imagine if you were able to subscribe to a file that contained only the newest updates to a Web page, instead of seeing every version of the Web page without knowing what was changed. An RSS feed is simply a file that only contains the changes that have made to a file, like a Web page. Think of it as getting a stream of updates instead of hearing every version of the same story.

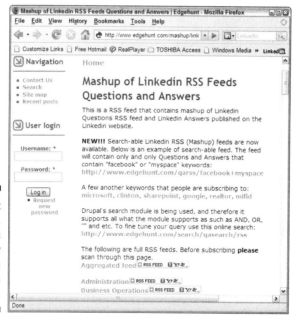

Figure 18-1:
Edgehunt.
com offers
many
LinkedIn
Answers
RSS feeds.

2. **Subscribe to the feed(s) that most interest you.**

   Click the RSS Feed button next to the feed file that most interests you. You would then see a page where you are asked to pick the feed reader you want to use, which is basically the software program that will receive your RSS feed file and display it to you so you can read it.

3. **Set up a news reader to handle the RSS feed(s) so that you can read all this information as it gets fed to you.**

   A popular RSS reader is Google Reader, which you can set up by going to `http://reader.google.com` and following the instructions there.

If you just want an RSS feed of any Answers category, you can now use LinkedIn's RSS feeds for each category. When you're looking at a LinkedIn Answers category, click the orange RSS icon to pull up a menu of links to add that category's RSS feed to your feed reader.

LinkedIn and the Xobni e-mail plug-in

LinkedIn + Xobni e-mail plug-in = More precise sender information

If you use Microsoft Outlook for your e-mail and you're constantly being deluged with e-mail from people you might or might not remember well, Xobni may be the tool for you. Xobni is an Outlook plug-in tool that gives you a window of summary information for each sender of an e-mail you receive. Say that you got an e-mail from Adam Smith, but you can't remember exactly what Adam does, when and how often Adam e-mails you, and so on. With Xobni, the plug-in window shows you who Adam is and how you interact with him. Figure 18-2 shows an example of how Xobni displays information.

Xobni has now integrated LinkedIn information into their plug-in window, so now when someone's summary window is displayed, Xobni will display that person's employer, job title, and profile photo, as well as offer a link directly to the person's complete profile on LinkedIn. If you'd like to add this functionality to your Microsoft Outlook program, just follow these steps:

1. **Go to Xobni's site at `www.xobni.com/download` and download its newest plug-in application setup file.**

   The download window should start up automatically when you go to the site's download page, shown in Figure 18-3.

2. **Run the downloaded file and follow the set-up wizard that opens to install Xobni on your system.**

   The next time you run Microsoft Outlook, you should see the Xobni plug-in on the right side of your Outlook window.

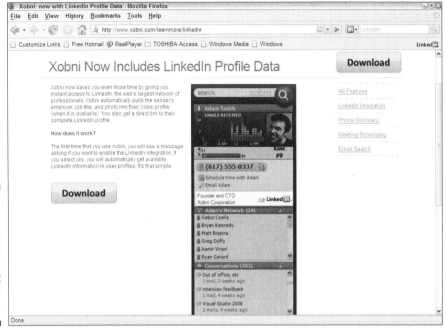

Figure 18-2:
Xobni
displays
precise
informa-
tion about
an e-mail
sender.

Figure 18-3:
Download
the Xobni
application.

Building Your Focus Group

In other chapters, I've told you about the potential for finding qualified partners and customers using LinkedIn, and how LinkedIn Answers can help you
perform market research and gauge reactions to a new product. Here I want
to take these ideas one step further and discuss how LinkedIn can help you
build a focus group for your new or next project.

Who's ready to play DISC?

Cynthia (Cindy) Beale heard about LinkedIn
the way most people do: She got an invitation
from an old contact — a former high school
classmate, in her case. After she joined, Beale
at first used the site for typical purposes, but
eventually she took her use of LinkedIn to the
next level after co-founding her consultancy
business, Stecin Leadership Solutions.

Beale and her co-founder, Steve Settimo, started
Stecin as a consulting and training company
focused on management and leadership training.

The business partners spent two years develop-
ing an exclusive curriculum that can be customized for any size company. Recently, they created
a brand-new board game called DISCFunctional
to demonstrate the power of understanding the
DISC Quadrant behavior system (see the following figure for the layout). This game became a
popular training tool, and Stecin's co-founders
decided to use the power of their LinkedIn networks to help advance the game.

Beale explains, "Suddenly, we had a way to communicate information about our training and consulting business to a group of people that we already identified as knowing." They added the game to their profiles and included a Web site link in each of their profiles so that potential customers could actually order the game. They updated their network with progress reports on how the game was doing, and then they created a special DISCFunctional group on LinkedIn for contacts who wanted to learn more.

This LinkedIn group became a focus group for Stecin Leadership Solutions, as they invited first-degree connections who expressed interest and potential customers who learned about the product elsewhere. Beale and Settimo were very careful about how they invited people to this focus group, doing research on each potential invitee, asking for Introductions through their own personal LinkedIn networks whenever possible, and crafting a polished invitation.

Stecin has built a growing community that has been very influential in the game's development. Beale is happy to report that their first training contract came from a LinkedIn connection! She concludes by saying, "We are always looking for more ways to utilize LinkedIn to reach people who will benefit from our business offerings."

Here are some ideas to keep in mind if you want to build your own focus group using LinkedIn:

- ✔ **Start by building your network.** Your best participants in this group are first-degree connections of yours (or of another employee of your company) because those people are most likely to join based on your recommendation and how well they fit your group's purpose. Try to network and invite potential candidates right away.

- ✔ **Build your accompanying Web site before building the group.** Your focus group participants will want to see something before deciding to join and participate, so make sure you've spent some time building an informational Web page, e-mail, FAQ, or other system that is available for viewing before you start to build your group.

- ✔ **Use your first-degree connections to expand your network.** After you've rustled up some involvement there, expand your group by asking for referrals or Introductions to potential second- and third-degree network members or general LinkedIn members who might get some value and add some insight to your process.

- ✔ **Continually send out updates.** You always should be sending out some form of update, whether you do so by filling out the "I'm working on" option, using LinkedIn Messages, or going through your own e-mail system. (See Chapter 9 for more information about these options.) Don't deluge people with messages — but also don't ask them to sign up and then be silent for weeks or months at a time. Keep your group members informed and ask for input when needed.

> ✔ **Ask for recommendations.** As group members get introduced to your product, ask them for a recommendation on your profile if they liked or approve of the product. Getting their feedback or recommendations will help to build future involvement when your product is live and ready for the mass market.

Location-Based LinkedIn Ideas

It's easy to forget the importance of location when you have easy access to such a resource-rich community as LinkedIn. After all, you can communicate with your contacts through LinkedIn Messages, send Recommendation requests or post questions, or grow your network without leaving your computer. When you're done using your computer, however, you need to interact in the real world, whether your interaction amounts to shoveling snow or catching a plane to a far-flung convention. When it comes to what I call "location-based" situations, meaning that the problem or situation is tied to a physical spot, you can discover solutions through involving LinkedIn.

The best use of LinkedIn for location-based problems is this: Your network is typically spread out across the country and across the world. Therefore, not only can you tap someone's professional experience, you can also tap their knowledge or presence in a specific geographical area to help you solve a problem. Let's take a look at three different location-based situations.

Building your network before moving to a new city

These days, when you have to move to a new city, you can do a lot of planning for it on the Internet. You can research the neighborhoods, look into the school systems, and shop for homes online. You can take this one step further if you plan to move to a different country, and you need information on local customs, cultures, and practices. But what about the questions you can't seem to answer through a Web browser? What about the "local knowledge" of where to go and where to avoid? Thankfully, LinkedIn can help.

Every LinkedIn user has defined his or her location, so you can do a search and figure out which LinkedIn users live in your target area. If nobody in your network is from your target area, start networking and expand that network to include people who reside (or used to reside) in that area who can help.

Here are some specific actions you can take through LinkedIn to help you with the big move:

Hello? Any opportunities out east?

Chuck Hester had a problem. He had to relocate his family from California to Raleigh, North Carolina, and he didn't have a job for himself when he would arrive. In fact, he didn't know anyone in Raleigh! But what he did have was a rich LinkedIn network. Hester quickly saw the value of LinkedIn and started contacting people and building relationships, driving his number of connections into the thousands.

Hester started networking with everyone he could who was located in Raleigh. He tapped his existing network to put him in touch with like-minded individuals who lived in the area and kept searching for contacts. One of the contacts he made was the chief executive of iContact, an e-mail marketing company. Hester turned this contact into a job interview, and today he's the corporate communications manager for iContact. Even virtual persistence can pay off! Today, Hester continues to grow his LinkedIn network, for himself and for iContact, and he even encourages his local contacts in Raleigh to network "Live", or use LinkedIn Live, to be specific — a feature that I cover later this chapter.

✔ **Use LinkedIn Answers to ask the community.** Not every question on LinkedIn Answers is directly related to software development or venture capital. You can post your dilemma on LinkedIn Answers (see Chapter 7 for more information on how to do this), notify your network of your question, and see what the community says in response. Take a look at Figure 18-4, which shows how a young Australian looked for advice about moving to New York City by posting a detailed question. After he posted that question, he received 12 different responses filled with general and specific information to help him out.

When you post your question, be sure to select the My Question Is Focused around a Specific Geographic Location box and enter the ZIP code of your destination in the newly enabled text box next to the check box you just selected.

✔ **Start as early as possible.** Building a region-specific network will take time as you recruit new members, ask your existing contacts for referrals, and search for specific people who match the location and either an industry or job title. As soon as you sense that a move is necessary, or maybe when you're mulling over whether to move, start building your network so that you can tap those people for location-specific information before you actually move.

✔ **Look for contacts who used to live in your new city.** You might try entering the location of your new city in the Keyword search field rather than the Location field. By doing so, you might find first- or second-degree contacts who used to live in your target area but have since moved; they might reference their past location in their profile. Contact those people and see whether they can introduce you to any contacts they may still have in that target area, regardless of whether those contacts are on or off LinkedIn.

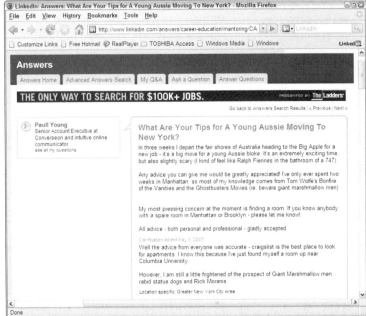

Figure 18-4:
Ask the
community
for advice
on your
move!

Arranging face-to-face meetings when traveling

LinkedIn can serve as a wonderful resource even when you're not moving to another city but are just traveling for business, a convention, or even personal reasons. Say that you know you have some extra time on your trip, or you want to make some local connections to reinforce your business trip. Why not tap your LinkedIn network and visit your contacts in person?

A growing practice of busy LinkedIn professionals who travel is to arrange face-to-face visits with other LinkedIn members on a business trip. This way, the traveler can meet with someone they are familiar with who could share similar interests and goals. Also, both people get a chance to expand their network by creating a stronger connection. To bring about in-person meetings, most people either post something to LinkedIn Answers or send a message to targeted members of their network.

If you're interested in making your next trip more of a LinkedIn adventure, keep these tips in mind:

✔ **Provide enough notice to attract people's attention.** If you're putting up a post on Monday night that you're available for Tuesday lunch, you probably won't get many responses in time to set up anything meaningful.

✔ **Give too much notice and your visit will be forgotten by the time you arrive.** Some notice is necessary to get on people's calendars, but too much notice will make people forget when your visit gets closer. More than two to four weeks in advance is probably too much notice.

✔ **Be specific with your availability.** It's great that you want to get together, but you probably have other plans when you're visiting. Therefore, when you contact other members, offer a few choices of when you can get together — and be specific. For example, you could say, "Hey, I'm going to be in San Jose for most of next week. Who's available either Monday night or Wednesday lunchtime to get together?"

✔ **Use your get-together to help prepare for business.** Your get-togethers with people in other cities don't have to be purely social. Say that you know you're traveling to that city for an interview. Perhaps you want to send a targeted message to a few contacts who used to work for your target company and ask to meet them in person before your interview so that they can help you prepare. Or maybe you want to practice your sales presentation on a knowledgeable person before you go into someone's office to do the real thing.

LinkedIn networking. . . in person!

Social networking is definitely a great way to stay connected, grow your personal and professional contact list, and learn about new opportunities. But after lots of e-mails, Instant Messages, and discussion boards, sometimes you just want the experience of meeting someone face to face. Lots of LinkedIn members have felt this way and have used the virtual power of LinkedIn to bring together people in the real world.

You can find all sorts of "chapters" of in-person networking groups inspired by people first meeting on LinkedIn and then connecting in-person with people from their network at a live event. Besides LinkedIn Live in Raleigh, I've discovered LinkedIn Live or LinkedIn Face-to-Face events in Phoenix, Chicago, and Philadephia, and there may well be more.

To find or organize a LinkedIn Live group from your network, here are some tips to keep in mind:

✔ **Search LinkedIn Answers to see whether anyone's tried to organize a group.** Do an Advanced Answers search and put in the word LinkedIn and a word such as Live, Face to Face, or In Person; also, include the city or region where you live. You might find a posting from someone like Chuck Hester, who started LinkedIn Live in Raleigh by posting something and alerting his network, as shown in Figure 18-5.

LinkedIn Live

If you use LinkedIn and you're in the Raleigh-Durham area of North Carolina, odds are you've heard of Chuck Hester. "I'm known as the Kevin Bacon of Raleigh," he smiles. "If I don't know a person, I probably know someone who does." He's the creator of LinkedIn Live Raleigh, an informal networking group formed in July 2007 and dedicated to having Hester's virtual connections meet up with each other in person so that they could increase their own networking. By that time, Hester had built up more than 700 connections in the Raleigh area alone, so he sent out an invitation and 50 people showed up to the event. The event was such a success that meetings are now held every other month, and attendance has grown exponentially, more than tripling in the first six months. In fact, Hester doesn't have to worry about the costs because he gets sponsors to donate the food, meeting space, and even door prizes!

Hester receives calls from more than a dozen other similar LinkedIn groups, each asking for advice on how to set up and maintain these live networking events. He's proud of the results from all this live networking, saying "At least 20–30 people have found new jobs from meeting someone at a LinkedIn Live." Of course, he has used the opportunity to build brand recognition for his company, iContact, which he found by networking on LinkedIn. (See the "Hello? Any opportunities out east?" sidebar, earlier this chapter) The LinkedIn Live Raleigh networking has also earned him mentions in the Fast Company blog, the *Wall Street Journal, Inc.* magazine, and *The New York Times*. You can find out more by reading Hester's blog at: `http://thepayitforwardchronicles.blogspot.com`. And if you're in Raleigh, check out a LinkedIn Live event!

✔ **Search LinkedIn Groups to see whether a group exists in your area.** Click Groups and then Groups Directory to see whether a Networking or Professional group of LinkedIn members shows up in your area. For example, when I looked at Networking Groups, I saw LinkedIn groups in places as diverse as New York City, Pasadena, and Silicon Valley, as shown in Figure 18-6.

✔ **Use the Internet to look for social networking meetings.** You may have to go outside LinkedIn to find an eager group of LinkedIn members. If you do a search with something like Google, you might find something like this posting, shown in Figure 18-7, that I found for a LinkedIn Live in Chicago. Another great site to find potential meetings is Meetup.com.

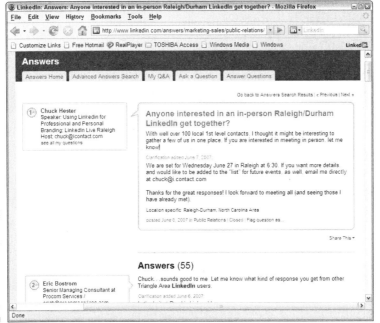

Figure 18-5:
Hester
started his
group using
LinkedIn
Answers.

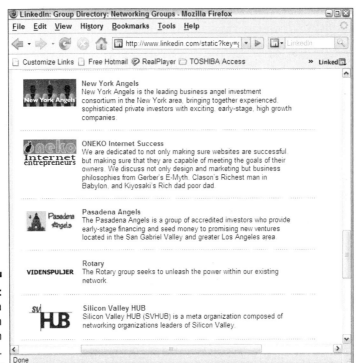

Figure 18-6:
Look for a
LinkedIn
group in
your area.

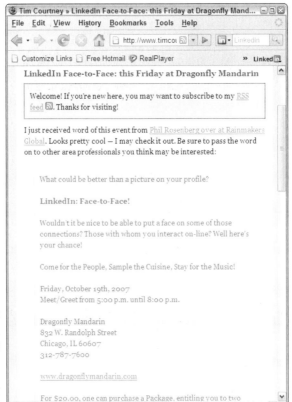

Figure 18-7:
Read about
LinkedIn in-
persons on
the Internet.

✔ **If nothing exists, start your own live group.** Post something on LinkedIn Answers and try to build a core group to start the first event. Send an update or message to your network members who live in the area and encourage them to pass along the message to their local friends who are LinkedIn members.

Andrew Warner turned to LinkedIn to help find interest for a regular get-together of technology folks known as Lunch 2.0, for which companies involved in Web 2.0 technologies open their doors to hungry technology workers who then learn about their host company over lunch. He posted a question on LinkedIn Answers to find a host company (see Figure 18-8) and got several responses, which led to some great meetings!

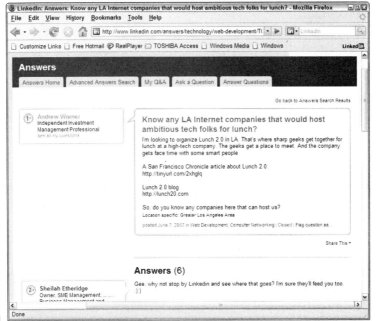

Figure 18-8:
Lunch 2.0
was looking
for a home
in LA!

Part VI
The Part of Tens

The 5th Wave   By Rich Tennant

"Oh wait. There's a Gracefully Decline option.
Whew. That's a much nicer way of saying NO."

In this part . . .

You've made it! In this final part of the book, I present
a beloved tradition in the *For Dummies* world: the
Part of Tens. I've created a great list of ten do's and
don'ts, as well as a list of ten useful resources you can
find on the Internet to make your LinkedIn experience that
much richer. Use them wisely, for while the right tips will
bring you lots of success, the wrong tips will . . . eh, probably just slow you down a bit.

Chapter 19

Ten LinkedIn Do's and Don'ts

I cover a lot of ground in this book — so much that it might be hard to remember it all as you're going about your daily use of LinkedIn. So here are ten essential do's and don'ts to help you build relationships and get the most value out of LinkedIn.

Keep Your Profile Complete and Current

Even though LinkedIn has many features, your profile is still one of the most compelling reasons to use the Web site, which is why LinkedIn is one of the best searchable databases of businesspeople available. And if you want to be found by others, you need to make sure that your data is complete and current. Here are a couple of ways to do that:

✔ **List all your former employers and schools.** Several features help users find and connect with former colleagues and classmates (see Chapter 6). Including your complete work and educational background in your profile can help you reconnect.

If you've had a lengthy career, you don't necessarily need to include details about positions early in your career — just the companies and titles will suffice. A good guideline is to include details on just the last 7–10 years. Additionally, you may only include positions that are relevant to your current work. I seriously doubt my first job at a McDonald's is relevant to my current work as an author, except if I want to write the sequel to Fast Food Nation.

✔ **Update your profile (and headline) any time you achieve a new position or complete a major side project.** Your direct connections will be notified (assuming they haven't turned off the feature) of the change. This is a subtle, unobtrusive way to notify your network of your career changes. And you never know when someone is going to be looking for what you have to offer. Make sure that, if you have a new position, you update your e-mail address with your new corporate e-mail address so people can still reach and invite you.

Don't Use Canned Invitations

There is never ever a good situation in which to use one of the default Invitation text messages LinkedIn provides when you send someone an Invitation to join your network on LinkedIn. Nothing says, "You're not really worth a few extra seconds of my time," quite like the all-too-familiar "I'd like to add you to my professional network" message.

That doesn't mean every Invitation has to be a lengthy personal epistle. Here are a few tips for keeping Invitations efficient but personal.

✔ **Keep it short when you can.** With people you know well and have been in recent contact with, the canned messages are actually too long. The message can be as simple as this:

Great to see you last night, Jerry — let's connect.

✔ **Make sure you know whether the person is already a LinkedIn member.** Someone who's already a member doesn't need to be convinced of LinkedIn's benefits. Maybe it shouldn't be annoying to them that you're explaining something they already know, but it's just an indication that you didn't really put any thought into making the connection.

✔ **If the contact is not already a member, offer to help with the registration process.** You can try to explain the benefits of joining LinkedIn in an e-mail, but almost no matter what you do, it's going to come across as a sales pitch, or at least a bit evangelistic. The best way to persuade people is to offer to spend a few minutes on the phone explaining it and how you're using it. That also turns the Invitation into an opportunity to strengthen your relationship with that person by offering your time to bring them something of value.

✔ **You can still personalize a batch of Invitations.** You can give the Invitation a personal touch even if you're sending it to multiple people. For example, you can send the same Invitation to all the people you met or ran into at an event. Or you can write out one Invitation to everyone in your chamber of commerce. Just remember to write it as if it were going to one person, not the whole group.

For more on Invitations, see Chapter 2.

Don't Expect Everyone to Network Like You Do

Setting rigid networking expectations can be a source of needless frustration and can actually prevent you from building relationships with some pretty great people. Here are some of the common issues that arise:

- **Different people have different standards for connecting.** Some people use LinkedIn to connect only with people they know very well. Some connect only with people with whom they share some common points of interest. Others connect with anybody. None of these approaches are wrong. If some people don't have the same standard for a connection that you do, don't take it personally, and don't judge them — they're doing what's right for them.

- **People might have perfectly good reasons not to allow other people to browse their LinkedIn connections list.** Don't hold anything against people who don't enable it. People may be concerned about client confidentiality, and thus be required to keep their connections secret. Or they may be connected to a competitor and not want their bosses and co-workers to know about it. Or they may just be concerned about their time commitments and not want to handle a growing number of Introduction requests if all their friends see their long list of connections. However, even if a person has disabled connections browsing, you can still get Introductions to people they know. Frankly, if you're just browsing other people's networks, maybe you should think about a more focused approach.

- **Not everyone responds in a timely manner.** If your request doesn't get forwarded or your InMail hasn't been replied to after a couple of weeks, don't take it personally. It doesn't mean that you're unimportant — it means the people you're trying to contact are busy. If it's really urgent, pick up the phone.

- **Some people are bad with names.** Just because you remember somebody's name doesn't mean she remembers yours. Unless you are 100 percent certain she will recognize your Invitation, contact her via e-mail or phone or a LinkedIn Introduction request before sending a connection request. Otherwise, don't be surprised when she declines your Invitation or hits the I Don't Know button.

- **Relationships aren't always symmetrical.** For example, if you were someone's client, you might be able to provide a great recommendation for him. That doesn't mean that he can do the same for you, so don't expect it.

- **Not everyone networks just to network.** Some people are extremely busy and not receptive to "I'd just like to meet you" requests. It's nothing personal, and it doesn't mean they're bad networkers. It just means that the demands on their time exceed the supply.

Do Your Homework

People provide you all kinds of guidance, both direct and implicit, regarding what to contact them about and how. If you're the one initiating the communication, it's your responsibility to communicate on their terms. And showing that you've taken the time to do your homework about them demonstrates a certain level of commitment to the relationship right from the outset.

The most basic rule of good conversation is to listen. In the context of LinkedIn, that rule means simply this: Pay attention to what's on a person's profile. Any time you contact somebody, review her profile first, as well as her contact settings. Respect what you see in her profile and contact settings.

So for example, suppose you have a business deal or a job inquiry that you want to contact John Smith about, but his profile says he's not accepting such inquiries right now. Don't think that you know better than John does about whether he might be interested, and definitely don't try to pass off your deal or job inquiry as a mere "expertise request" or a "request to reconnect" and then tell him why you're really contacting him.

When you send an Introduction request or an Invitation to someone you don't know very well, don't put the burden on her to figure out what the common areas of interest or potential opportunities are. You took the time to read her profile and determine that it's a worthwhile connection. Save her the trouble of figuring out what you already know and put your common areas of interest in your Introduction request or Invitation.

Give LinkedIn Messages Equal Importance

Many people have a tendency to treat LinkedIn communications as less important or less time-sensitive than an official e-mail or phone call.

Nothing could be further from the truth. People get jobs, hire employees, gain clients, and make deals as a result of LinkedIn-based communications. They are every bit as much a part of your essential business correspondence as the rest of your e-mail. (If they're not, you're connecting with the wrong people!)

Here are some tips for managing your LinkedIn communications:

✔ **Don't turn off e-mail notifications.** Missing time-sensitive communications is one of the worst things you can do. If the volume of e-mail seems overwhelming, you can use e-mail rules to move LinkedIn requests into a separate folder, but as a general productivity practice, you want as few different inboxes as possible.

To make sure you have e-mail notifications set up correctly, go to this URL:

`www.linkedin.com/secure/settings?msgdelivprefs`

You see the Receiving Messages screen, as shown in Figure 19-1. Here, you can set up what will come to you as an individual e-mail, a digest e-mail, or no e-mail (by setting Web Only) so you can decide what is most important.

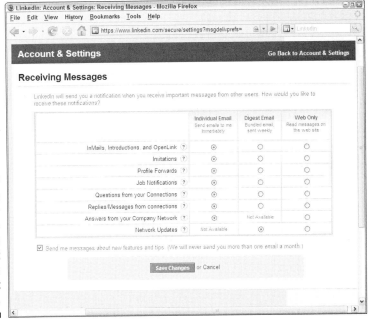

Figure 19-1:
Set your
e-mail noti-
fications so
you don't
miss an
important
message.

✔ **Handle your LinkedIn inbox every day.** Or at least every couple of days. You wouldn't go a week without checking your e-mail at work— don't treat LinkedIn messages any differently. (See Chapter 9 on how to manage your LinkedIn inbox.)

✔ **Do it, delegate it, defer it, or delete it.** This technique from David Allen's book *Getting Things Done: The Art of Stress-Free Productivity* (Penguin) will help you keep your inbox organized. As you're going through your inbox, if you can handle a request in under two minutes, go ahead and do it. Or you can delegate it by passing on the Introduction request or recommend one of your contacts as an expert to answer the person's question. If it will take a little more time, you can defer it by putting it into your work queue to handle later.

For additional tips on e-mail organization and productivity, check out David Allen's book *Getting Things Done,* and also take a look at 43 Folders' Inbox Zero collection at `www.inboxzero.com.`

Don't Spam

One person's networking is another person's spam. Better to err on the side of caution. There are plenty of ways to use LinkedIn productively without getting a bad rep as a spammer. Some basic rules of etiquette are

- ✔ **Don't post marketing messages, job listings, job search queries, or connection-seeking messages on Answers.** All of these will get your message flagged and fairly quickly removed. Don't waste your effort. There's a fine line between an advertisement and market or product research that calls attention to your company, which I cover in Chapter 7.

- ✔ **Don't automatically subscribe your connections to your newsletter.** This is admittedly a gray area. Connecting with someone indicates a certain level of receptivity to receiving communication from them, and it's reasonable to assume that should include something more than just LinkedIn Introduction requests. After all, they're supposed to be someone you know and trust, right? Well, that's not necessarily the same thing as signing up for a regular bulk newsletter.

    I think it's better to be safe than sorry, so I don't recommend auto-subscribing folks to your newsletter. People can get ticked off if they suddenly start getting some newsletter they didn't subscribe to.

    The best approach is simply to ask permission to subscribe your individual contacts to your newsletter. If you get their permission, even if they do complain later, you can politely point out that you asked first.

- ✔ **Don't send connection requests to people you don't know.** Unless they've given some kind of explicit indication that they're open to receiving Invitations (for example, announcing it on a forum, stating it in their profiles, or being a member of an open networking group), you have to assume that most people don't want to receive LinkedIn connection Invitations from strangers. LinkedIn has taken measures to curb such rampant inviting behavior, and it will get you suspended soon enough. Again, there's a simple solution: *Ask permission first.* Send an Introduction request, or contact the person via e-mail or his Web site, and ask whether it would be okay for you to send him a connection Invitation.

Be Proactive about Making New Connections

If you just set up a profile, connect with a few of your contacts, and then expect business to come your way, you're setting yourself up for disappointment. That's not to say that it can't happen, but being a little bit proactive goes a long way.

✔ **Search for people who can help you with your goals.** If you want to meet people in a particular city, industry, or target market, search for them specifically and make Introduction requests. Some people will be receptive to corresponding or talking just for networking purposes, but you'll get a better response if you have a specific need or opportunity as the basis of your contact.

✔ **Introduce people to each other.** LinkedIn's basic Introduction paradigm is reactive. For example, an Introduction is made when person A wants to connect with person C via person B. But an essential practice of a good networker is identifying possible connections between people in your network and introducing them to each other. You can do this by forwarding one person's profile to the other and Cc'ing the first person (see Chapter 5). You can send a LinkedIn message to both connections introducing them and telling them why you think they should get to know each other. You can also recommend someone in your network as an expert resource when answering questions in LinkedIn Answers.

✔ **Seek out questions to answer.** Your direct connections can send you questions that they think you may have a good answer for, but that won't help you meet new people. However, answering a single question in the Answers section allows you to interact with dozens, hundreds, or even thousands of people. Find the Answers categories that are related to your business and either check them regularly, or better yet, sub-scribe to them via RSS (see Chapter 18).

✔ **Ask questions.** The Answers section is the main form of public group interaction on LinkedIn. You can ask questions for highly focused activi-ties like market research, or you can aim for more general relationship-building by posing thought-provoking questions on relevant topics. One question can make dozens of new contacts for you and initiate private conversations around a topic currently relevant to your business.

Cross-Promote

Your LinkedIn profile is just one Web page of your total Web presence. It should connect people to your other points of presence, and you probably want to direct people to your LinkedIn profile from other venues as well. Here are some good cross-promotion practices:

✔ **Customize your LinkedIn profile links.** As described in Chapter 3, you can create up to three links on your profile that you can use to lead people to your business site(s), personal site, blog, your book, an event, and so on.

✔ **Include a link to your LinkedIn profile in your signature.** You can use this both in your e-mail signature and also on discussion forums. If you don't have a centralized personal professional Web site, your LinkedIn profile is a good alternative. I even cover how LinkedIn can help you create your e-mail signature in Chapter 10.

> ✔ **Link to your LinkedIn profile in your blog's About page.** Why rehash your entire bio? Put a couple of paragraphs that are relevant to the blog and then refer people to your LinkedIn profile for more details.
>
> ✔ **Put your LinkedIn URL on your business card.** It's not commonplace yet, but more and more people are starting to do this.

Add Value to the Process

LinkedIn is based on the idea that existing relationships add value to the process of people meeting each other. If all you're doing is just passing the Introduction "bucket" down the virtual bucket brigade, you're actually getting in the way of communication, not adding value.

To add value, you have to give those Introduction requests some thought. Is it an appropriate fit for the recipient? Is the timing good?

Add your comments to the Introduction request. Do you know the sender? In the context of the request? Saying "I worked with Michael Bellomo for several years as a co-author and he was hard-working, trust-worthy, and ambitious" goes a lot further than saying, "Hey, Francine, here's this guy Michael to check out." For additional guidance on how to handle this tactfully, see Chapter 5.

Don't Confuse Quantity with Quality

Just because you're doing a lot of something doesn't mean you're doing something well. And when you think about it, is *more networking activity* what you really want? Or do you really want *more results with less activity?*

If you want to track your real progress using LinkedIn, don't measure it by meaningless metrics like number of connections, endorsements, or questions answered. Use metrics that you know directly tie to business results, such as

> ✔ Leads generated
>
> ✔ Joint venture/strategic partner prospects generated
>
> ✔ Qualified job candidates contacted
>
> ✔ Qualified employers successfully contacted
>
> ✔ Interviews scheduled
>
> ✔ Speaking opportunities
>
> ✔ Publicity opportunities

Any of these may be a key performance metric for you; the number of LinkedIn connections you have or questions you've answered isn't one of them.

Chapter 20

Ten Helpful LinkedIn Resources

In This Chapter

▶ Useful forums and networking sites

▶ Helpful wikis

▶ RSS feeds, blogs, and podcasts

▶ Customized search engine and profile manager

As you continue building your LinkedIn presence, you might want to take advantage of additional Web sites I've rounded up a list of ten Internet resources that can provide extra information or functionality regarding your LinkedIn activities. Whether you use one or use them all, I'm sure you can find the resources that best match up to the way you like to learn and grow online.

The Official LinkedIn Blog

http://blog.linkedin.com

Mario Sundar, previously a LinkedIn "evangelist" who promoted the company on his own blog, was hired by LinkedIn to run its official company blog. Every week, Mario and various LinkedIn employees put up fun, informative, and timely blog posts about new functions or changes to the site, as well as success stories, case studies, and practical information to make your LinkedIn experience that much more rewarding!

In addition, the blog posts live on forever, and you can search them to find out valuable information or post your own comments to give your own feedback!

My Virtual Power Forum

www.mylinkedinpowerforum.com

As LinkedIn users began to develop their profiles and grow their networks, some of them wanted a place to go to discuss plans and swap ideas with each other. Therefore, in 2005, several users started the My LinkedIn Power Forum as a Yahoo! group where members could post messages, share ideas, and ask questions of other members. Today, they bill themselves as My Virtual Power Forum, a "networking and discussion group about building professional social media networks at ultimate *networker speed.*"

Membership is open and free, but the forum members stress that you should consider their five recommendations for using LinkedIn to build your network:

1. Don't build in the dark. Be aware of the image and network you're creating.

2. Don't build without a vision. Think about the purpose of your LinkedIn profile and goals for your LinkedIn network.

3. Don't build too fast or too slow. You don't have to achieve one million connections in 24 hours, but one connection per year is too slow.

4. Don't build without a written plan. List out some goals and milestones for creating your LinkedIn identity.

5. Don't build without profiting. As you grow your LinkedIn identity, you should be benefiting from some new connections, a job lead, or some other profit, which may or may not involve money.

LinkedInLIONS Forum

http://finance.groups.yahoo.com/group/linkedinlions

Throughout this book, I comment on the presence of LinkedIn open networkers, or LIONs for short. These are LinkedIn users who hope to network with as many people as possible and accept Introductions and Invitations from anybody. Some LIONs have started their own Yahoo! group to swap ideas, grow their networks, and talk about their open networking experiences. Although not all of their information will apply to every visitor, they have still built up a lively discussion of all things LinkedIn.

Similar to My Virtual Power Forum, this is a Yahoo! group that you can join for free and participate in openly.

MyLinkWiki

http://linkedin.pbwiki.com

A *wiki* is a newer Internet technology that allows multiple people to collaborate on gathering and presenting information. On a wiki site, anybody can create, add, or edit information on the site, and those changes are then reviewed by other users, and ultimately those changes are approved or rejected. The best known example of this technology is Wikipedia, one of the fastest growing repositories of information on the Internet. This online encyclopedia has rapidly become an authoritative source of information because of the collaborative knowledge gathering.

One great LinkedIn wiki is MyLinkWiki, which has users commenting and updating on the width and breadth of LinkedIn's functionality and usefulness. As you become more familiar with LinkedIn, you can contribute to this growing community as well!

RSS Feeds with Google Reader

http://reader.google.com

A relatively new Web technology known as RSS (commonly referred to as Really Simple Syndication) works as follows: If you wanted to follow all the changes, additions, and updates of a Web site, blog, or profile page, the easiest way is to read a list of just the information that has changed or been added, rather than seeing the entire site over and over again. An RSS feed provides this list of new information,

Many active LinkedIn users maintain an RSS feed for their profile, so their friends and connections can get a list of the changes and updates. You can create an RSS feed of your Network Updates, so you can keep track of your first-degree connections on LinkedIn. In addition, LinkedIn Answers provides RSS feeds for the growing number of categories that contain questions and answers from the community. Therefore, if you want to stay informed on your friends changes and updates, you need something called an RSS feed reader. I cover LinkedIn RSS Feeds in more depth in Chapter 18.

Google makes a great tool called Google Reader, which you can use to handle all the RSS feeds you subscribe to, whether or not it's related to LinkedIn. It's a free tool that you can install on practically any system. There are also other feed readers you can install and use for your RSS feed needs.

LinkedIntelligence Blog

`www.linkedintelligence.com`

When LinkedIn was growing a few years ago, blogger Scott Allen put together a site called LinkedIntelligence to cover LinkedIn and its many uses. Over the years, he built up a healthy amount of blog posts, links, and valuable information from himself and other bloggers regarding LinkedIn and how to use it.

One of his more ambitious projects started in May 2007, simply dubbed 100+ Smart Ways to Use LinkedIn. Allen had bloggers compete to provide valuable information and tips across all of LinkedIn's functions, and he created a table of contents of the best entries on his blog site. You can still find this handy resource at:

`www.linkedintelligence.com/smart-ways-to-use-linkedin`

The large repository of links and information can be helpful to new, intermediate, or power users of the site. The blog posts are divided into dozens of helpful categories, from LinkedIn News to Training & Coaching.

Podcast Network Connections

`http://connections.thepodcastnetwork.com`

The staggering popularity of the Apple iPod gave rise to a new way of broadcasting audio information to eager listeners — the podcast. Think of the podcast as a recorded audio broadcast that you can download to your iPod, computer, MP3 player, or other device. You can subscribe to engaging and unique podcasts, regardless of where in the world they are recorded and played.

If you go to The Podcast Network (`http://thepodcastnetwork.com`), you can find the Connections show, where show host Stan Relihan prepares a weekly audio podcast about the art of business networking. This 20-minute podcast features interviews that Relihan does with other members of his network of connections to discuss how different social networks (like LinkedIn and Facebook, as well as new Web applications) can be used to provide a benefit to any business. You can subscribe to this show and hear great interviews, tips, and stories of how other people and companies connect online.

MyLinkSearch Search Engine

www.mylinksearch.com

A couple of years ago, Marc Freedman wanted a better way to search through LinkedIn and related LinkedIn Web sites. Rather than going through different sites manually, he created the MyLinkSearch search engine, which is a part of Google Co-Op. This custom search engine digs through 21 different Web sites, including LinkedIn and their extensive database of users, and displays one list of relevant results.

This custom search engine can be very helpful, especially in these situations:

✔ You want to expand your LinkedIn search to include information, help, and support resources.

✔ You want to see Google-style searching and formatting compared to a direct LinkedIn search.

✔ You want to see public LinkedIn profiles of LinkedIn members who are not in your direct network.

✔ You want to find LinkedIn open networkers who publicize their e-mail addresses.

Marc is a part of the DallasBlue Business Network, dedicated to providing in-person and online events and programs for both their local Dallas–Ft. Worth area and throughout the world. This group appeals to networkers, all levels of executives, entrepreneurs, small business owners, and working professionals. The group has an impressive array of functions and information regarding LinkedIn. You can go to www.dallasblue.com to find out more.

Take Your Profile with You with LinkedInABox

www.linkedinabox.com

For many Internet users, their LinkedIn profile is simply one aspect of their overall online identities. However, some of these users have built up impressive LinkedIn profiles and, rather than duplicating the information on their other Web sites, would rather display their LinkedIn profiles dynamically across their online identities, so any changes to their LinkedIn profiles will ripple out automatically to these other sites without lots of work.

There is a solution — LinkedInABox! This is a special Web software application, or *widget,* that was written to be installed on your blog or Web page. This piece of code draws a box on your Web page and dynamically shows your public LinkedIn profile every time! You just have to cut and paste a few lines of code into the HTML source code for your Web page or the profile section of your blog software, and LinkedInABox does the rest!

LinkedInABox is just one of a growing number of widgets available that take advantage of LinkedIn. Do a Google search for "linkedin widget" to find new applications, or check out LinkedIn's new Widgets page at this URL:

```
www.linkedin.com/static?key=developers_widgets
```

One Update for Multiple Sites with Hello TXT

```
http://hellotxt.com
```

If you're active on LinkedIn and other social networking sites (like Facebook, MySpace, Twitter, and many others), you may find yourself going site to site to provide up-to-the-minute information about what you're doing and what you want others to know. Well, instead of site hopping, you can use one function to update your status across all your social networking pages and microblogs. It's called Hello TXT.

Hello TXT works like this: You log on to the site and enter your text message into the dashboard. You then select the sites you want to update with your new status message, and Hello TXT does the rest, reaching out to your various pages to add your new status message. It's a great centralized way to keep all your various profiles as up to date as possible and it is designed to update your LinkedIn status by answering the question "What are you working on?"

Index